Security for Business Professionals

Security for Business Professionals

How to Plan, Implement, and Manage Your Company's Security Program

Bradley A. Wayland

ELSEVIER

AMSTERDAM • BOSTON • HEIDELBERG • LONDON
NEW YORK • OXFORD • PARIS • SAN DIEGO
SAN FRANCISCO • SINGAPORE • SYDNEY • TOKYO
Butterworth-Heinemann is an imprint of Elsevier

Acquiring Editor: Brian Romer
Editorial Project Manager: Keira Bunn
Project Manager: Mohana Natarajan
Designer: Mark Rogers

Butterworth-Heinemann is an imprint of Elsevier
225 Wyman Street, Waltham, MA 02451, USA
The Boulevard, Langford Lane, Kidlington, Oxford, OX5 1GB, UK

Notices
Knowledge and best practice in this field are constantly changing. As new research and experience broaden our
understanding, changes in research methods or professional practices, may become necessary. Practitioners
and researchers must always rely on their own experience and knowledge in evaluating and using any
information or methods described here in. In using such information or methods they should be mindful of
their own safety and the safety of others, including parties for whom they have a professional responsibility.

To the fullest extent of the law, neither the Publisher nor the authors, contributors, or editors, assume any
liability for any injury and/or damage to persons or property as a matter of products liability, negligence or
otherwise, or from any use or operation of any methods, products, instructions, or ideas contained in the
material herein.

ISBN: 978-0-12-800565-1

Library of Congress Cataloging-in-Publication Data
Application Submitted

British Library Cataloguing-in-Publication Data
A catalogue record for this book is available from the British Library

For information on all Butterworth-Heinemann publications,
visit our website at store.elsevier.com

This book has been manufactured using Print On Demand technology. Each copy is produced to order and is
limited to black ink. The online version of this book will show color figures where appropriate.

Dedication

This book is dedicated to my daughter, Sarah, for her love and support.

Contents

About the Author

Brad Wayland is a safety and security management expert with over 28 years of experience in the field. As a graduate of the U.S. Air Force Academy, he entered the Air Force and served over 20 years in the Security Forces. He was selected on three occasions to command a Security Forces Squadron, where he acted as both the chief of police and director of security for installations ranging in size from 2,000 to over 20,000 personnel. Over the course of his military career, he was responsible for nuclear security programs and plans, law enforcement, and public safety management programs.

After his retirement from the military, he has continued to gain expertise and experience in the safety and security arena in both the public and private sectors. He has worked on security projects in the health care, education, banking, and manufacturing sectors and has provided expertise in security training and vulnerability assessments in a variety of functional areas. He has also worked overseas in the Middle East with the Department of Defense and Department of State in training host national police and providing executive protection to U.S. personnel assigned in hostile locations.

In addition to Brad's vast experience in the security and safety realms, he has also received training and experience in leading, supervising, and managing personnel and teams. Brad currently resides in Spokane, Washington where he is the president of Sentry Security Consultants, LLC.

1

Leadership and Management

Leadership and, to a lesser degree, management are the key factors necessary to make any type of organization efficient and effective—in fact, I believe that leadership in particular is going to be the ultimate factor in determining the success or failure of any organization and the business in which a group of individuals is. Unfortunately, leadership and management are not effectively put into practice in a majority of instances; I think that almost everyone has seen numerous examples of poor leadership and management in their business experience. This occurs in spite of the thousands of books that are written on the subject, the high-dollar seminars, the many courses on leadership and management that are offered, along with the dozens of degrees that are available on subjects relating to both leadership and management.

Due to the many less-than-stellar leadership and management techniques that are practiced, supervisors and managers are unable to achieve the main purpose of effective supervision—gaining the maximum efficiency and effectiveness of their employees to ensure that they meet their business goals and objectives. We will look at techniques for both leadership and management (which I believe are two very different concepts) while providing some helpful guidelines that can help you to improve your own leadership and management.

1.1 Relation Between Leadership and Management

President Harry S. Truman had one of the better definitions of leadership, saying "A leader is a man who has the ability to get other people to do what they do not want to do, and like it." [1] With this definition in the forefront, leadership is something that is exclusively people-centric. Leadership deals mostly with people's ability to communicate and interact with others to get them motivated and excited to accomplish tasks. Management differs from leadership. While it also concentrates on working with individuals, it is a process that is more focused on directing and controlling the affairs of a business, organization, or other body to ensure that it operates efficiently and effectively, to accomplish agreed-upon objectives [2]. In other words, leadership deals more with people, whereas management deals more with organizing the tasks that these people must accomplish to achieve business objectives. These two different aspects and definitions highlight the primary difference found between these two important functions. Although leadership and management both require skills to deal with people and to organize efforts and tasks, leadership is more directly linked to the ability to work and motivate people in order to get the most out of each individual, whereas management deals more with ensuring that the processes within an organization are understood, efficient, and measurable; stated otherwise, leadership is more focused on people and their wants and needs, and management is more focused on tasks.

Although there are differences between leadership and management, there is also a significant relationship between these two aspects. Good leaders must learn to practice good management techniques. Effective leadership requires the use of good management techniques, since good leaders must be able to efficiently delegate work and to ensure that all of their subordinates understand their roles and responsibilities. Unfortunately, the converse is not always the case, as many individuals who implement proper management techniques may not be good leaders. To better illustrate this relationship, let me tell you a story about a boss for whom I once worked. This individual had an extraordinary amount of leadership and management training and was very knowledgeable in both areas. This training equated with the fact that he was a very good manager—particularly in his ability to implement measurements that could identify problems within the organization. Unfortunately, this knowledge of good management techniques did not result in his being a good leader. Due to his strengths in management and measuring, he would typically sit in his office to review and analyze the reams of data that he had requested to work to identify issues within the organization. Although he was able to identify many issues early in his tenure in the leadership position, he could not implement most of these improvements, as he had failed to relate to the personnel under his supervision by insulating himself from them and their work. Furthermore, his ability to analyze management information would actually backfire when a decision was required. He would continue to ask for more and more information on the issue at hand instead of having the courage to make a choice when necessary, and, as a result, many of his decisions were either made too late to matter or were never made at all. This analytical ability and expertise in management techniques also affected his ability to lead, since he tried to make leadership a checklist process rather than focusing upon the people and their specific skills and needs. There were many instances in which my co-workers and I could actually see the boss's thought processes as he tried to use every one of his management analysis techniques and attempt to fit them into the problem at hand to come up with a decision. He would work hard to see the problem, obtain all of the facts, discuss all conceivable courses of action with subordinates (over and over again in many instances), and work to try to gain consensus prior to his decision. He would finally decide upon a solution and work to implement the decision. Although the process sounded good, it resulted instead in significant problems within the organization because most people saw through this "cookie-cutter" approach to leadership that the boss used. People within the organization saw the boss fail to reach a timely decision, which led to the organization believing that the boss was indecisive and not sure what to do when problems occurred, which ultimately resulted in a loss of confidence in the boss by the majority of people in the organization. This use of good management techniques, but poor leadership and people skills, resulted in the boss failing to gain the trust or respect of the subordinates and the organization. This illustration highlights the need for good leaders to be good managers; however, a supervisor that effectively uses good management tools does not guarantee that good leadership will result within the organization.

The last difference between leadership and management that we will discuss involves the practice and application necessary for each area. Management is primarily based on defining roles and responsibilities, implementing processes, and analyzing measurement information to identify improvements and produce a better organization. This dependence of management on relatively concrete principles and practices results in objective procedures and data that can be directly used to implement effective management practices through the application of scientific guidelines and organizational principles. This is not the case with leadership. Leadership is a much more subjective talent, and can be difficult to break down and define exactly what traits will guarantee success. Simply put, management is more of a science and leadership is more of an art, which makes leadership impossible to practice through a checklist or cookie-cutter approach.

Over the next sections, we will look at both leadership and management and discuss some techniques and traits to assist you in improving in both areas.

1.2 Leadership Techniques and Traits

My experience has shown that we learn more leadership lessons from poor leaders and supervisors then we ever learn from good ones. That is because it is easy to see the resulting problems that occur from a poor decision or from inaction than to see the results of good leadership that result in the right decisions. In many cases, good organizations with good leaders just seem to work well, and it can be difficult to identify exactly what makes these teams work so well.

As is the case with most people, I've worked for good bosses and bad ones (although it sometimes seems that the poor bosses and supervisors have vastly outnumbered the good). With the bad bosses and leaders, many of the poor decisions were immediately apparent, since they resulted in some type of negative result shortly after the decision; this result could have been a decrease in efficiency, failure to achieve an objective, loss of confidence by employees or supervisors, or a loss of morale within the workforce. Although bad leadership can be painful to experience and to live through firsthand, many of these poor decisions and bad leadership examples can provide lessons for those wishing to improve their own leadership techniques. It would be nice to be able to work from the good examples; however, it has been my experience that it is much more difficult to determine what a good boss is doing and learn from that individual, because in most of these instances the organization simply seems to run well and work in an efficient and effective manner. How to identify a smooth operation and how it is being accomplished will not be as readily apparent to most observers without a good deal of study and analysis, so unfortunately it can be easier to learn from the bad leaders and their mistakes, since most everyone can identify what went wrong.

Another reason to work at improving your leadership skills is that the effect of poor leadership on an organization can make an immediate impact but take a very long time to fix. An unfortunate truth is that a bad leader can have an impact on an organization almost immediately through poor decisions and loss of morale among subordinates. All this will bring down the team's effectiveness in a very short time, and it will take a much longer period of time to fix these issues than it took to create them. This makes it critical to provide the best leadership possible within an organization. Although leadership is an art that can be extremely difficult to accomplish well, we will look at some consistent traits that great leaders follow, so that all of us can keep them in mind in order to improve our own leadership skills.

1.2.1 Be Yourself

The first trait that all great leaders have is that they are true to themselves and do not put on an act in order to lead. This is critical for an effective leader, as one of the major problems with poor bosses is that they are often perceived as a "phonies."" People will quickly see through any kind of act, and it will become more and more difficult for leaders to "talk the talk" when it is evident that they do not "walk the walk"" and match the personas that they are trying to put forth. A good example of a leader who does not put on an act and continues to ensure that he is true to his own character is Pope Francis, the former Cardinal from Argentina and current leader of the Catholic Church. Prior to becoming Pope, the Cardinal drove his own vehicle to work and lived a very modest and frugal life. After his elevation to Pope, it would have been simple to get caught up in the trappings of the Papal office; however, since his selection, Pope Francis has continued to try to maintain a simple and modest lifestyle. Even as the head of all Catholics and one of the most powerful heads of state in the world; Pope Francis continues to keep his own calendar, he maintains a modest living area within the Vatican, and he continues to try to maintain contact with the poor and less fortunate. All of these acts are what he typically did while still a Cardinal, and his work to maintain these actions have resulted in near-universal acclaim for his work in leading the Catholic Church and have earned him the moniker of "the "people's pope."

1.2.2 Have Empathy

I have always been surprised that empathy is normally not included in many lists of leadership traits. I believe that this is an error, and it is my opinion that this trait is one of the most important for good leaders. Empathy not only enables leaders to relate to their subordinates and establish better ties with the people who are doing the real work, but it also provides a significant ability to develop understanding with subordinates, which will ultimately lead to better decision making.

The unfortunate fact is that many leaders do not practice this trait. How many people have seen peers be promoted to management positions and, once there, appear to have lost all memory of what the main issues or problems were while they were working at the lower levels? One of the biggest jobs that leaders have is to make their subordinates' jobs easier; by doing so, employees will see that their bosses care for them and their well-being, and will in turn work much harder and more effectively toward making the company's business goals and objectives much more achievable. When people have been promoted up through the ranks, they have unique perspectives from which to better understand the issues and concerns of their subordinates; unfortunately, in many cases, newly promoted supervisors do not focus on this advantage but instead try to distance themselves from the very people who accomplish the real work within the organization. The leaders forget about these issues and concerns of their employees and do not attempt to solve them. There may be several reasons for this; new leaders may feel that they should distance themselves from the lower level from which they came in order to attempt to show their bosses that they can now think like senior management (or what they believe senior management should think like), or perhaps they wish to show senior management that their promotion was not a mistake. Whatever the reason, these newly promoted supervisors should work hard to remember what it was like in the lower positions, since it gives them empathy, which in turn will show concern for and gain greater effort from their employees.

Although it may be easier for individuals who have moved up through the ranks to empathize with their subordinates, all supervisors can gain empathy and understanding with their employees by using the tried-and-true technique of "management by walking around" (MBWA). Although the term was made popular by both Hewlett–Packard management in the 1970s and by Tom Peters and Robert H. Waterman, Jr. in their book *In Search of Excellence: Lessons from America's Best-Run Companies* in 1982, the practice of checking on employees and operations on your own has been used by successful managers for a much longer period of time [3]. It is vital for all supervisors who want to be effective to get out from behind their desks and see with their own eyes what is actually going on. The advantages of moving out into the work areas and talking directly with the lowest-level employees are numerous. MBWA provides an actual hands-on perspective of the people and issues that are occurring in the supervisors' areas of responsibility, rather than hearing the filteredand, in many cases, biased versions from third parties who would likely have a stake in the boss's perspective.

It is vital for effective leaders to be able to place themselves in the shoes of their subordinates and to empathize with them. Not only will this help supervisors to make the employee's jobs a little easier, it will also improve their ability to better understand their personnel, which will ultimately result in a better team.

1.2.3 Communication and Understanding

Communication is closely linked with empathy, since the ability to understand your employees enhances your ability to communicate with him—particularly in listening and understanding these individuals and their concerns. Being able to fully empathize with subordinates enables not only an improved ability to listen but in turn improves anyone's ability to communicate. Eisenhower was an exceptional leader, both during his time as a military officer and also as President. This leadership was due in large part to his ability to listen and to be empathetic with the subordinates who were actually doing the real work. Whether he was training a small unit or commanding thousands, General Eisenhower never saw men as numbers or as push-pins to be moved across a battle map; rather, he always remembered that each man was an individual with hopes and dreams of his own, with a family back home who loved him more than anything else in the world. Eisenhower had a highly developed listening ability, and wherever he went he asked questions, welcomed complaints, and, if it was within his power, he worked to improve the situation. This effort not only endeared him to his troops but also enabled him to listen and to identify issues, which ultimately resulted in fixing problems within the entire organization. The ability to communicate and more importantly to listen and understand others is a critical aspect in people who are leaders.

Listening is a vital part of communication, as is the ability to directly talk with individuals. Technology has greatly assisted business, with the advent of different ways to communicate with others such as e-mail and social networking; and, although there are some advantages to these newer forms of communications, there are also drawbacks that have accompanied many of these advances. The biggest drawback that can negatively affect a person's leadership ability is the loss of personal interaction and direct communication with people, either on a one-to-one basis or in groups. Many people have worked their way up the business ladder using texting and e-mails as their primary means of communication; these methods are easy, but they come at the expense of simple face-to-face communication. Although many of these newer techniques can be effective to accomplish many tasks, ultimately managers and leaders must be able to effectively get their messages across by talking directly with their subordinates. This skill is becoming lost because of the ease of sending an e-mail or a text; however, messages can become lost through these technological means. Remember that communication involves two participants—a sender and receiver—and these newer forms of communication do not afford any opportunity to get feedback from the receiver to see if the message was received and understood. As a result, communication through these methods can become confused or lost. This is why leaders must ultimately be able to speak with their personnel—either one-on-one or with larger groups in order to ensure that their messages get across.

Communication by leaders can also be enhanced by MBWA, which was also discussed in the earlier section on empathy. MBWA not only improves an individual's ability to empathize with their subordinates, but it also provides opportunities for a supervisor to improve communication with the lowest-level employees. When I have been a supervisor and leader, it was always amazing how many times I would be walking around and talking with first-line employees only to hear them relate a rumor or version of company policy that was so far from the truth that it was hard to keep a straight face. Miscommunication happens all the time as items are passed from person to person; we have all played the telephone game as children, and can remember how simple phrases could be changed after only two or three repetitions. This miscommunication can be compounded within a large organization; but when employees can hear an issue directly from the boss, a lot of the miscommunication can be alleviated or prevented. Another advantage of MBWA is that it can provide greater face-to-face contact between bosses and their subordinates. With the ever-increasing amount of electronic communications, it has become easier and easier for supervisors to "manage by the ding." By that, I am describing supervisors who primarily manage and attempt to lead through e-mail and other electronic means. How many supervisors simply sit and stare at their computers, waiting for that next e-mail or text message that will spring them into action? There are several problems with this practice. First, many problems are not brought up to the boss until they are significant and unable to be easily resolved, so that by the time the leader is notified of the issue by e-mail or message, it is too late. Another problem is that the message may not accurately portray the issue due to misunderstanding of the message itself, the bias of the sender, or a desire to sugar-coat the problem in the message. Instead of waiting for these messages and walking around instead, it is much easier to identify minor issues before they become major problems, and a leader can also alleviate the miscommunication that occurs through many of these electronic means and the misunderstandings that they can cause. Supervisors who work hard to communicate with their employees through all means—especially in a more personal manner—will ensure a greater degree of understanding and will achieve greater buy-in among their subordinates.

Communication is a critical aspect of good leadership. The willingness to truly listen to your personnel and understand their issues and concerns, the ability to talk with your employees face-to-face, and the effort to get out from behind your desk and forgo the easy way to communicate—texts and e-mails—and interact with all of your employees provides some important methods to improve your ability to communicate.

1.2.4 Optimism

Optimism is another critical component of effective leadership. Many exceptional leaders have learned to put forth a persona of perpetual optimism—even though they may not feel like it at certain points in time. There are several benefits with leaders who can maintain their focus on the positive.

The first benefit is the boost that the leader gains from being optimistic. It can be easy for many leaders to become wearied by the continual decision making—particularly when these decisions can potentially affect their business and the livelihoods of their employees. Even when these choices can be relatively mundane, leaders are asked to make countless decisions on a daily basis, all of which can add to an inexorable and inescapable strain and tension that can continue to wear away at the leaders' endurance, judgment, and potentially even their own confidence. This pressure can become even more acute if the leader appropriately asks that their subordinates and staff present them with honest and, in many instances, the worst cases in many eventualities, since this results in hearing a lot of bad news and problems within the organization. All of this information can easily cause the leader to focus on issues and concerns, which places them in a position to continually deal with the negative aspects of the business. If leaders can maintain an optimistic viewpoint, however, their positive actions and sense of hope can tend to minimize potential problems that can wear any person down and perhaps even lead to demoralization.

Another benefit with an optimistic leader is that this attitude invariably filters throughout the organization and can produce many positive effects within the company. Leaders who can be positive even in the face of bad news will promote a culture of open and honest communication. We have all worked for people who frequently "shot the messenger"" when they were told of any problems or concerns. By doing this, bosses discourage anyone from providing them with bad news and ultimately make it impossible for anyone to give such leaders the true facts—especially if they do not agree with the boss's perspective. If, on the other hand, bosses maintains an optimistic attitude and take bad news well, it is much more likely that bosses who are good leaders will get open and honest feedback, which in turn will promote a situation in which all employees put their effort into finding solutions and opportunities rather than focusing on the problem.

Optimism from the leader produces several positive effects within the organization. Leaders can minimize the amount of stress that is inevitable with their positions. This positive attitude can permeate the organization and lead to improved efficiency and effectiveness. It can also promote better communication throughout the organization. Leaders who can maintain an optimistic attitude can definitely improve their organization, due not only to the positive effects produced on the employees and staff, but also the positive effects on others who come into contact with such leaders and their infectious attitudes.

1.2.5 Character and Courage

Character and courage go hand-in-hand, and both traits go together in great leaders. Character is a must in any great leader, as it is critical in developing trust throughout the organization and ensuring that people do the right thing. Courage ensures that the leader has the fortitude to do the right thing (because, in many cases, this entails more difficult choices).

Character is defined by Oklahoma Congressman J.C. Watts as "doing the right thing when nobody's looking." He goes on to say that "there are too many people who think that the only thing that's right is to get by, and the only thing that's wrong is to get caught." [4] Unfortunately, we see this rather frequently in today's society, as witnessed by the many people who lie, cheat, and steal in all walks of life and, when caught, attempt to blame this bad behavior on anything but themselves. True leaders maintain this definition of character, however, and understand that this is a vital trait and one that successful leaders cannot be without for several reasons. First, leaders must be able to establish trust with their subordinates and co-workers, and character is critical toward establishing this trust. If an individual acts with poor morals and ethics, it is impossible for others to trust that individual, which, in turn, leads to many people wondering if anything that they accomplish for such a boss is for the good of the organization or only good for the individual asking for the work. Second, a leader with good character will highlight superb performance and pass on praise to their subordinates, whereas an individual with poor character will take the credit and pass on blame (even when the outcome may have been due to their own action or inaction). Workers who are not praised for their hard work and who are blamed for their supervisor's mistakes will never put forth their best effort. Finally, leaders who demonstrate good character will filter these desirable traits to others across the organization and create a more desirable work environment, since the team will be focused on honesty and integrity.

Courage is another critical leadership trait and goes hand-in-hand with character. There are many ways to demonstrate courage: the willingness to take risks, making changes to the organization in order to improve efficiency and effectiveness, or identifying poor performance or behavior. This trait is necessary for a good leader. Courage can refer to either physical or moral courage. Physical courage is what we typically think of when we hear the term—it describes the ability to face situations that could cause someone physical harm or death. Although there may be times in any profession where physical courage is necessary (and in some professions, physical courage may be a somewhat frequent occurrence), it is much more prevalent in business that leadership requires moral courage. Moral courage is the willingness to maintain good moral convictions and to adhere to one's character, even when these actions may place an individual in a difficult position with superiors, subordinates, or peers. People are more inclined to follow individuals who are able to overcome the instinct to run away from a difficult problem and instead to think clearly and take action that they know is morally and ethically correct and that results in the correct decision.

Character and courage are critical to good leadership. The morals and need to ensure that you act correctly and do the right thing, along with the courage to take that action in the face of possible repercussions, will pay dividends with your immediate subordinates and across the organization.

1.2.6 Decision Making

Although it should be obvious, a good leader must be able to make decisions. This trait ties in with having the character and courage to be able to make difficult decisions when necessary. We have probably all seen supervisors who could not make decisions—either they felt that they did not have enough information, they hesitated due to the gravity of the decision, or they were simply scared to make the decision. What every supervisor must remember is that if their subordinates have come to them with a problem, they are looking for a decision—they are not looking for a way for the boss to "pass the buck" or mull over the problem. Remember the quote from Harry Truman: "the buck stops here." This should be a motto for many good leaders, since they must be able to have the courage and conviction to make a decision and stick with it.

1.2.7 Accountability

The last leadership trait I will cover is accountability. This trait is necessary in good leadership, as it should task the leader to ensure that people are meeting standards and that they properly adhere to the requirements within the organization. Many of the previous leadership traits that we have discussed are positive in nature; however, an unfortunate fact is that all leaders must occasionally deal with individuals who fail to perform or who refuse to act in an acceptable manner. This is where accountability becomes necessary.

In order to be effective, accountability must ensure that individuals who violate company policies and procedures are punished in order to discipline the perpetrator, correct the behavior, and deter further inappropriate action. This punishment should be fair based upon the specific violation and the individual's previous disciplinary history. The punishment should also be consistent throughout the organization and not overly punish one individual while letting another individual evade punishment, which could lead to a perception of favoritism. The disciplinary action should also take into account what is necessary to correct the behavior of the individual. Lastly, the punishment should be severe enough to deter others from considering the same violation. Ultimately, accountability will reap positive benefits across the organization, since all employees will come to understand that unacceptable behavior or poor performance will not be tolerated, and it has been my experience that few people want to put up with the few "bad apples" in the bunch.

A good example to show the need for accountability can be found in one particular organization. In this agency, the maintenance supervisor made several questionable and possibly illegal financial decisions. These included his hiring of companies to accomplish work for the organization that were owned by his relatives and to whom he paid fairly high fees for minor work. He also made excessive numbers of business trips over several years with no results or gains to the organization. These trips not only failed to show just cause for the expenditures, but they also appeared to pay higher than normal travel costs to the maintenance supervisor. These issues were brought up to the organization's senior leadership; however, no action was taken against the maintenance supervisor—in fact, he was not even counseled on these concerns. Due to this lack of accountability when the issues were initially raised, this same maintenance supervisor was eventually caught embezzling company funds several years later. The unfortunate truth is that if the organization had held the individual immediately accountable for the original questionable financial decisions, the embezzlement may not have occurred or at a minimum, and the individual would have been caught sooner, which would have lessened the losses to the organization.

Although accountability is one of the harder things that a leader must do, it is a necessary part of maintaining a well-run organization.

1.3 Management Techniques and Traits

Now that we have covered many of the traits necessary to good leadership, we will look at traits and techniques for good managers. As discussed earlier, good leadership will normally include good management techniques and traits, so it is important to identify these.

1.3.1 Well-Defined Organizational Structure and Appropriate Division of Labor

In my opinion, the most important aspect in effectively managing an organization is to establish an organizational structure in a manner such that all members clearly understand their own roles and responsibilities. In order to accomplish this, it is necessary to define these roles and responsibilities for every section and possibly even every team member within the organization. The ability to clearly define the organizational structure and to be able to easily explain this can pay great dividends in everyone's effectiveness and efficiency in accomplishing tasks. I can remember when I first entered the workforce after finishing college, and the confusion that I felt about accomplishing even simple tasks. One of the primary reasons that many of these tasks were so difficult was my ignorance of what other teams and offices were responsible for within the organization. Until I was able to learn how each section worked together within the organization and what each team's role and responsibilities were, it was almost impossible to determine who I needed to call for help or expertise to ensure that the work was done in the most effective manner possible. A goal of any organization should be to be able to draw their organizational chart in a simple diagram that is so easy to understand that anyone could identify what each section does. If you are unable to do this, it is very likely that you have failed to properly designate the roles and responsibilities within your organization. When team members can understand the role and responsibility of each section within the company, it makes things much easier not only to accomplish complex tasks but also to ensure that people do not waste time on tasks that other sections will accomplish.

In addition to developing and following a well-defined organizational structure, it is imperative that the roles and responsibilities of each individual match this organizational chart. Nothing can be more confusing than an organization that does not follow the organizational structure by the individual responsibilities. An example of one such organization would be the U.S. military headquarters within the Pentagon. I made my first trip to the Pentagon after I had already served in the military for several years. During this visit, I needed to conduct training and indoctrination prior to departing for a temporary assignment overseas in northern Africa. I spent one week in the Pentagon, working to accomplish some fairly simple tasks (or so I thought when I was first given the assignments). These tasks included getting some authorizations and equipment prior to my departure overseas; however, these assignments turned out to be anything but simple due to the uniqueness of the organization and responsibilities within the building that houses the U.S. military headquarters. When I first started to conduct these tasks, I went back to my experience and reviewed the organizational charts to determine what office I had to work with in order to get the assistance I required. After using this method for the first few offices I visited, I found that within the Pentagon this process did not work. In this labyrinth, I found instead that the people who were able to get things done for certain tasks bore little resemblance to the people or teams on the organization chart that I would have believed should have been responsible for accomplishing those roles. As a result, these tasks (which should have probably taken only half a day) ended up taking an entire week. I left the Pentagon in amazement at how this organization could function effectively and efficiently in the face of this organizational dysfunction that was due to the lack of fully established roles and responsibilities that adhered to the organizational chart.

1.3.2 Setting Clear Goals and Expectations

An effective organization must continually ensure that they can communicate goals that are simple for everyone to understand, that can be easily measured, and that are achievable. This is a standard mantra from most management books; however, it is amazing how many organizations fail to put forth goals and objectives that actually meet these criteria. There are many examples of organizations with poorly written goals and objectives. One school district's goal has so many different objectives and goals that they cover over two pages and the first goal states they wish to review "programs, curriculum/instructional strategies, and assessment tools in order to evaluate and improve the achievement of students with different ability levels as they work to achieve the learning standard." [5] I am unsure of what this goal means or how this can even be measured. Furthermore, this goal is not applicable throughout the entire school district since it does not apply to all employees—particularly the ones who may not directly deal with teaching and education, such as maintenance workers, bus drivers, or food service workers. Ultimately, a school district's primary function should be to teach children, so why doesn't the goal address this in a simple and measureable manner? Another example of a poor company objective is from Avon. Their mission statement begins with "Avon's mission is focused on six core aspirations the company continually strives to achieve," and then it goes on (and on, and on) [6]. It eventually ends at 249 words that cover topics ranging from surpassing competitors to increasing shareholder value to fighting breast cancer. While it may be great to try to do many important things all at once, an organization's mission statement should provide employees and the world at large with one or two key goals that define success in that company's specific universe—if the organization cannot encapsulate these thoughts into a sentence or two, they should go back to the drawing board and try again.

Good managers understand that their organization's goals and objectives must be simple enough for everyone to understand, and these goals must be measurable; and, with this in mind, these managers will ensure that their organization's goals actually accomplish this. If the organization's goals and objectives do not meet these characteristics, the managers and organization are in danger of confusing both employees and clients, and furthermore, their goals will sound like double-speak. Convoluted goals and objectives can not only confuse, they can potentially result in causing subordinates to wonder if the organization truly wants to better itself or if the senior leaders simply wish to sound good for a certain audience.

1.3.3 Know Your People and Their Specific Skills

The next management technique that we will discuss is ensuring that you know your people and their specific skills in order to tailor the organizational structure and individual roles and responsibilities to best utilize individual skills. Although it is important to have a well-defined organizational structure with established roles and responsibilities for each individual, as discussed earlier, this does not limit a good manager to tailor the organization to ensure the best fit with the specific skills of certain individuals. The first part of this technique is ensuring that managers know their personnel in order to be able to identify any special skills. This is accomplished by getting out from behind one's desk and seeing the work of individuals in their own office and environment; without knowing one's subordinates, it is impossible to determine what specific skills or experience they might have. A great example of knowing one's personnel and tailoring the organization around certain skills can be shown through a good football coach who will tailor his offense based on the observed skills of his quarterback and other players. If the coach has a tremendous passing quarterback and good wide receivers, he will likely modify his playbook to rely more heavily on passing plays; but if he has a very good running back and offensive lineman, he may weigh the playbook more upon the running game. Like a good football coach, a good manager will also tailor the organization and the individual roles and responsibilities based on key employees' skills and experience. A business example could be a financial team that contains one individual who has exceptional attention to detail (perhaps to the point of being obsessive-compulsive). A good manager will realize this individual's skills and provide that person with a job that best utilizes these traits, such as book-keeping or conducting financial audits within the organization. There are a variety of ways to achieve success when using the skills and experience of your personnel to their utmost abilities.

1.3.4 Delegating Work

Delegating work is another tried-and-true managerial technique; however, this is also a rare commodity in its actual occurrence throughout normal business situations. The main reason for this inability to delegate work is a lack of trust on the part of the manager to fully enable his employees with the necessary authority and responsibility. In order to trust the personnel to whom you will delegate work, you need to hire effective managers and leaders for the specific positions and tasks that they will perform. One of the key mistakes that many supervisors make in hiring individuals to lead teams under their supervision is to hire an individual that they would like to work for or that would fit into their own individual leadership style. This may work some of the time, but there are many instances in which the type of leadership and management for a subordinate section may be vastly different from the style that you may prefer. For example, an individual who is a terrific self-starter that can be given tasks in a broad sense so they can figure out exactly how to accomplish the effort may look to find other supervisors that fit that mold. This may work for sections that need little oversight and guidance; however, if the section has an extremely high turnover of personnel and accomplishes fairly simple and routine tasks over and over again, this type of leader may not be the right fit—instead, a micro-manager may need to be hired who has exceptional attention to detail and who can ensure that the details are correctly accomplished with that manager's new and rotating personnel.

The following are some principles that can help managers to delegate work more successfully.

- Clearly articulate the desired outcome and goal of the task to be accomplished. Once you can fully communicate the desired end state, it becomes much easier to break down the task into any other desired results.
- Clearly identify any constraints and boundaries with which individuals will need to contend. This should include the lines of authority, responsibility, and accountability. In addition, individuals should be provided with instructions on how to progress and periodically "check in," or report back, throughout the task. This should include telling them when they must wait to be told what to do, ask what to do, act and then immediately report results, or initiate action and report back only periodically.

- When possible, include people in the delegation process and empower them to decide what tasks are to be delegated to them and when.
- Match the amount of responsibility with the amount of authority; however, a manager must understand that although you can delegate some responsibility, it is impossible to delegate away ultimate accountability…remember, the buck stops with you!
- Delegate to the lowest possible organizational level, since the people who are closest to the work will always be best suited for the specific task—they are the individuals with the most intimate knowledge of the detail of everyday work. In addition, delegating to the lowest level also increases workplace efficiency and helps to develop people.
- Provide adequate support, and be available to answer questions. It is your job to ensure the project's success through ongoing communication and monitoring as well as provision of resources and credit.
- Focus on results and concern yourself with what is accomplished, rather than dictating how the work should be accomplished. Your way is not necessarily the only or even the best way—particularly since you are not the person actually conducting the task. Instead, allow the individual to control his or her own methods and processes, which will facilitate success and trust. General George S. Patton, Jr. said it best: "Never tell people how to do things. Tell them what to do and they will surprise you with their ingenuity." [7]
- Avoid "upward delegation," meaning the employee simply passing the task back to you in the event of any problems. If there is an issue, instead of allowing the person to shift responsibility for the task back to you; ask for recommended solutions and assist them in finding an answer.
- Build motivation and commitment when delegating the task. Discuss how success will have an impact on financial rewards, future opportunities, informal recognition, and other desirable consequences for either the organization or the employee. It is imperative that you provide recognition where it is deserved.
- Establish and maintain control over the task. Discuss timelines and deadlines with the employee and ensure that you both agree on a schedule of checkpoints at which you will review project progress. At these times, make adjustments as necessary and ensure that you take the time to review all submitted work.

In thoroughly considering these key points prior to and during the delegation process, you will find that you delegate work more successfully.

1.3.5 Know Your Place

The last managerial technique that we will discuss goes hand in hand with delegation: it is simply knowing your place and role within the organization. This means that each individual and, specifically, each senior manager, has a specific role that they must accomplish, and these executives should ensure they do not interfere with tasks that are the responsibilities of their employees. Instead, they must allow their subordinates to accomplish the tasks that they have been asked to accomplish. How many managers do we see that micro-manage work far below their level? This not only takes away from the organization's efficiency and effectiveness, it also breeds an extreme lack of trust throughout the team.

I worked for an organization in which the overall supervisor spent the vast majority of time redoing and making minor corrections to letters and presentations that had been accomplished by subordinates, rather than providing guidance and vision for the future. The problem was that there was not anything wrong with any of these products—they simply were not what the overall boss would have developed or composed. This focus created several problems. First, employees worried more about minor issues contained within documents rather than the real substance or purpose of these products, which ultimately caused communication and correspondence from the company to suffer. Second, without any clear guidance from the boss on major issues within the organization, individual employees were forced to guess what needed to be done for the future of the organization. Since several different individuals were forced to make decisions regarding the future, many of these initiatives conflicted with others due to the lack of clear guidance from the top. Lastly, the boss spent so much of his time making minor corrections that he rarely (if ever) had time to actually do his job. Although all these tasks can take up a great deal of time and keep people very busy, it will not help the organization to improve.

It is easy to see if another individual is micro-managing tasks below their level—the hard part is to determine if you are actually doing this. The following questions may help you to determine if this is the case.

- Do you find yourself accomplishing an inordinate number of corrections to documents?
- Do you repeatedly send out formats for various documents within the organization? Do these formats change frequently (more than once every two to three years)?
- Do you find yourself dictating exactly how to accomplish tasks for subordinates?

If the answer to any of these questions is yes, you may want to work to delegate more of your tasks and concentrate more on your own tasks.

1.4 Conclusions Regarding Leadership and Management

I cannot emphasize enough the importance of good leadership and management within an organization. Although an individual can be a good manager and lack some leadership skills, it is impossible to be a good leader without practicing good management skills. The differences between these two areas show the distinction between leadership and management. Leadership emphasizes the people side of business and is more of an art in its practice, whereas management deals more with business techniques and organizational structures to practice many of the scientific and objective methods necessary for good managers.

Although there are differences between both leadership and management, it is possible to improve one's ability to perform either area by emphasizing certain traits. Good leadership requires the following traits:

- Being yourself
- Having empathy

- Communication and understanding
- Optimism
- Character and courage
- Decision making
- Accountability

Like leadership, good management must also follow certain techniques and traits:

- Well-defined organizational structure and appropriate divisions of labor
- Setting clear goals and expectations
- Knowing your people and their specific skills
- Delegation
- Knowing the place and senior management's role in the organization

By keeping these traits in mind and adhering to them, it provides you with the tools to become a better leader and manager.

References

[1] Tsouras Peter G. Warriors' words: a dictionary of military quotations. London: Cassell Arms and Armour; 1994. p. 236.

[2] Oxford Online Reference. Definition of Management 2013.

[3] Peters Thomas J, Waterman Jr Robert H. In search of excellence: lessons from America's best-run companies. Harper Collins; 1982.

[4] Watts JC. Goodreads quotes. Web. January, 6 2014. www.Goodreads.com.

[5] Oceanside School District. Oceanside School District Goals and Objectives. Web. January 6, 2014. www.oceanside.k12.ny.us.

[6] Zetlin Minda. The 9 worst mission statements of all time. Inc Magazine; November 15, 2013. Web. 6 January 2014. www.inc.com.

[7] Patton Jr GS. The official General George S. Patton Jr. website. Web. January, 7 2014. http://www.generalpatton.com.

Recommended Reading on Leadership and Management

19 Stars: A Study in Military Character and Leadership by Edgar F. Puryear, Jr., Presidio Press.

In Search of Excellence: Lessons from America's Best-Run Companies by Thomas J. Peters and Robert H. Waterman, Harper Collins.

Lead On: A Practical Guide to Leadership by Dave Oliver, Ballantine Books.

Once an Eagle by Anton Myrer, Harper Torch.

Team of Rivals: The Political Genius of Abraham Lincoln by Doris Kearns Goodwin, Simon & Schuster.

The Mask of Command by John Keegan, Penguin Books.

Wooden on Leadership: How to Create a Winning Organization by John Wooden, McGraw-Hill Books.

Security Planning Considerations

There are several overarching concepts that should be taken into consideration with regard to safety and security planning. Over the next few chapters, we will look at these areas in order to provide you with the background necessary to implement a complete and viable safety and security program. The first area we will look is the safety and security principles that form the foundation to be used within your own organization's plans and procedures. The next area is planning, which encompasses the development of safety and security plans and procedures, risk assessment methods, and the identification of potential threats and vulnerabilities to your particular organization's critical resources. This chapter will also discuss the difficult process to quantify safety and security initiatives to justify certain improvements and match cost-effective solutions to mitigate these threats. The next chapter within the security planning area is safety and security administration that will look at regulatory requirements, considerations on having your own internal security guard force, and staffing methods for this function, along with security metrics and measurements your organization may consider. Finally, should your organization be looking to construct a new facility the last chapter within this section looks at considerations to build-in safety and security improvements during the initial planning and design phase of a construction or major renovation project.

2

Safety and Security Principles

The primary goal in developing an overall security program within your organization is to protect your critical resources—those people, items, information, and equipment that are vital to the operation of your business. This safety and security program should develop methods to ensure that employees consistently practice the outlined procedures and processes, and acquire the necessary equipment to improve your organization's security measures. In order to properly maintain your organization's security program, it is important to ensure that proper procedures and equipment are used and identify the best solutions to mitigate any possible threats. These procedures and equipment should work in concert with one another to ultimately meet the goal of deterring any potential intruder or terrorist from acting against you and your critical assets before they attempt any type of action.

The ability to deter against any potential criminal acts or attacks prior to their actual occurrence is accomplished through the implementation and practice of security plans and procedures, along with safety and security measures put into place to protect the critical resources within your organization. As a result, these safety and security initiatives should make it appear that any potential act or attack will be too difficult to accomplish, and thus the intruder will deem the risks are too great to even attempt any planned action against your organization and instead will decide to look elsewhere. It is important to note that no location can be absolutely impervious to any type of attack, and if an intruder or terrorist wants to attack a specific location; either due to personal grievances that they may have against the target or due to the symbolism or high-profile nature of the location; with this willingness and motivation, the attacker will work that much harder to identify ways around the existing security measures and still attempt the attack. Numerous examples have shown an attack against a specific location can be accomplished if the attackers are motivated and willing to throw their own safety away. Columbine High School, the site of the notorious school shootings in 1999, is one example, since this location was the only target for Dylan Klebold and Eric Harris based on their intention to harm their fellow students at the same school that they attended, and no amount of security at the school would have deterred the attackers from their attempt. Another example can be found in the infamous 9/11 attacks, as Al Qaeda was determined to attack several specific, high-profile buildings within the United States. They were successful in eventually destroying or damaging their primary targets: the World Trade Center and the Pentagon—and although the intended target of the fourth plane that crashed in Pennsylvania was never confirmed (possible targets included the White House, the U.S. Capitol, the Camp David presidential retreat in Maryland, or one of several nuclear power plants along the eastern seaboard) [1], these terrorists succeeded in attacking and destroying facilities that were thought to be extremely invulnerable based on the security measures in place, their sheer size, and their location. In these incidents and many others like them, the perpetrator's intention to attack a specific facility due to notoriety or personal issues resulted in the perpetrators finding ways around the security measures that were in place for these locations. Unfortunately, there is no perfect or impenetrable security system that can be established—no matter what the cost or inconvenience—to protect a location against a motivated intruder or terrorist. If they have decided upon an attack against a specific location, it is likely that they will be able to find a weakness to exploit in their planned attack. Fortunately, the likelihood of an attacker specifically targeting your particular business organization is small, and proper safety and security procedures and equipment can significantly mitigate the potential for any unwanted action. The bottom line is that, regardless of a motivated criminal intent on acting against a specific location, it is still good practice to provide significant deterrence against any security incident. This will not only stop most, if not all, of the potential actions against your location by many random perpetrators, but it can also minimize damage or injury in the event that your company is attacked.

In addition to helping deter any potential action against your facility, a strong safety and security program will help make your organization better. One of the primary considerations for employees is the need to feel safe and secure within their workplace. By having an active safety and security program in place within your organization, you not only increase the security of your business's critical resources but also alleviate concerns of your employees regarding their safety when they are at work.

2.1 Overview of Safety and Security Principles

In order to develop an effective and cost-efficient organizational safety and security program, the first and primary task is to consider and become familiar with the principles that are necessary to ensure that such a program is effective and efficient. This should be accomplished even before writing procedures or purchasing security equipment, since these principles will guide you in making the correct decisions when developing appropriate plans and procedures, purchasing security equipment, and integrating these areas into an overall safety and security program that has a positive impact on the protection of your organization's critical resources.

These principles, which we will look at over the course of this chapter, must serve as the foundation of your plans and procedures—the very documents that will form the most integral part of your safety and security program and provide the specific details necessary for your employees to follow. We will be covering the specific instructions on how to develop your safety and security plans and procedures in the next chapter, but prior to this discussion, we will look at these safety and security principles, since they compose the building blocks necessary to implement a good program. In addition to providing the background to safety and security plans, these principles will also provide the methodology to design an effective schematic of security equipment necessary to protect your critical resources, rather than purchasing and installing items without any good idea of how they will integrate around your overall safety and security program. This pre-planning will ensure that you spend money only on security equipment that directly ties into your overall plans and ultimately saves your organization a great deal of time and money over the long term.

The safety and security principles that we will look at include:

- Preparatory actions by perpetrators and terrorist prior to incidents or emergency situations
- Primary fundamentals of security
- Balancing the needs of safety and security with business efficiency and effectiveness

The first principle, preparatory actions prior to emergency situations, covers the typical warning signs that occur before any safety and security incident. These signs are inherent in a perpetrator's planning and are accomplished before any attack or incident. The knowledge of these preparatory actions can greatly assist you in the development of effective measures that mitigate many of these actions, since there are many different security measures that can make this preparation much more difficult. The next principle that we will cover looks at the primary fundamentals of security. These fundamentals include the following considerations necessary to any successful safety and security program:

- Identification of critical resources
- Defense in depth
- Notification
- Response
- Simplicity
- Securing the weakest links
- Use of choke points
- Unpredictability
- Redundancy or separation of duties

Within these fundamentals, we will cover each area in detail, as they should all be considered in order to establish effective and efficient plans and procedures. The third, and last, safety and security principle that we will discuss is the need to balance security measures with convenience and effective business operations that must occur in order to make your safety and security program realistic to meet the business environment that you and your employees need in order to accomplish your daily tasks. As we discussed in the introduction, security by its very nature is inconvenient. Thus, in order to continue to ensure that your employees and senior managers will support any security measures initiatives within your program, it is necessary to balance the inconvenience inherent in most security procedures with the operational needs of your organization, along with the tolerance of your employees to put up with certain inconveniences due to security measures. This balance is critical so that you can provide a safe and secure environment for your employees while ensuring that you do not squash personal initiative at the expense of security; this balance must be achieved so that your organization can continue to be innovative.

2.2 Preparatory Actions to Emergency Incidents

The first safety and security principle looks at specific actions that an attacker will take prior to an incident. Like any military unit, a terrorist or criminal will conduct some type of planning and preparation before the actual event. Knowing these actions can provide you with the awareness of what actions should constitute concern for your organization, and this knowledge will also assist you in planning and developing the security plans and measures that you should implement within your organization.

2.2.1 Reconnaissance

The first and foremost action that will be conducted by potential perpetrators prior to any attempted action is to accomplish some type of reconnaissance of the location that they plan on attacking. The purpose of this reconnaissance is to provide as much information as possible regarding the targeted facility and surrounding terrain, the weather (if this will affect the type of attack being considered by the perpetrator), security measures and personnel who are responsible for protecting the location and targeted assets, and the surrounding people and structures. All of this information is obtained so that perpetrators will better know the layout of the facility or targeted assets and can determine any obstacles that they must overcome, which in turn will allow them to further refine their plans so that they can provide a greater degree of success when they conduct the attack. Depending upon the size of the target facility and levels of security surrounding the resources targeted by the perpetrator, this reconnaissance can take a few minutes, a few months, or even years. Prior to the 9/11 attacks, Al Qaeda conducted reconnaissance for several years, beginning in 2009. This reconnaissance included in-depth studies on airport security, both outside and inside the United States, along with identification of specific flights that met the planned targets and objectives for their attack [2].

In the vast majority of instances of conducting reconnaissance, perpetrators can be identified due to certain suspicious actions. These actions can include taking pictures, making sketches, or taking notes in and around the location they are targeting. At this point in time, perpetrators can be very vulnerable and potentially caught or stopped, as long as this suspicious activity is noticed and reported. If perpetrators are aware that they have been seen and must avoid being caught at this early stage in their planning, it is very likely that they will forgo their attack against that particular location. In order to increase the chances that suspicious activity is noticed and reported, it is vital to involve all of your employees and promote a high level of security awareness throughout your organization. Throughout this book, we will discuss that one of the greatest (and also one of the cheapest and easiest) ways to augment your safety and security program is to develop your employees' security awareness. As the total number of employees will always outnumber the number of personnel directly tasked with security, if all of these personnel have a heightened awareness to identify suspicious activity—and, more importantly, to report it—your organization will make it very difficult for potential criminals or terrorists from conducting reconnaissance, which could ultimately cause such perpetrators to move to another target or abandon their plans altogether.

2.2.2 Assess the Effectiveness of Security

Another action conducted by potential perpetrators prior to any attack is to attempt to assess the effectiveness and response of the security measures in place. To accomplish this, criminals or terrorists will normally attempt to gain information on two specific areas: security personnel and security measures.

The assessment of the dedicated security personnel—the employees solely responsible for guarding and protecting the location or targeted asset—will normally include determining an accurate count of the number of guards, their methods and procedures, and the time that it takes to respond to an incident. Prior to any type of action against the location, perpetrators will need to identify the number of security personnel that they will have to contend with. Knowledgeable perpetrators will not only identify the number of personnel normally on duty but will also ensure they are aware of the number of any additional response elements for that area. These response elements may include contracted security guards or local law enforcement personnel, should the location not have their own dedicated response force. Depending upon the level of professionalism and the importance that they place on surviving the incident, potential criminals or terrorists may also need to identify the methods and procedures of the security personnel. This information will include the security personnel's normal duty locations, patrol areas, times for these patrols, and any standard issued equipment (e.g., radios, weapons, uniforms, etc.). Perpetrators will need to assess whether each assigned security guard spends most of the time sitting at a desk, monitoring cameras, or moving about the grounds; and perpetrators will need to determine what each guard's standard habits might be. For example, some considerations for perpetrator will be whether security guards take their breaks at the exact same time during every shift, whether the guards adhere to a specific schedule when moving about the grounds on a patrol, or whether additional response forces always respond from the same general location. This knowledge can greatly assist potential perpetrators to conduct and, particularly, survive a planned attack.

Perpetrators may also ensure that they know the response time of any additional security personnel who would assist the onsite guard force. This last item of information will typically provide potential criminals with a timeline to accomplish their desired objective, since their plans will normally be to attempt to leave the area rather than having to overcome any additional on-duty security personnel who are responding to the scene. If possible, potential perpetrators will also observe the effectiveness of the responding security personnel to see how quickly they can ascertain the situation and act to avert a potential threat. This information could be obtained by creating a false incident that requires security forces to respond and by observing the location well before the actual planned incident.

The last major piece of information that perpetrators will typically need to know prior to their attack is what security equipment and procedural measures are in place. This knowledge will enable them to know what obstacles will have to be negotiated in order to gain access to the target. If these individuals can obtain specific information on what type of alarm systems, security cameras, door locks, or entry systems are in place; they will be able to prepare exactly how to overcome these obstacles. This information will enable them to enter the location and reach their objective in less time, and, in turn, this quicker entry will make it more difficult for perpetrators to be stopped.

With all of this information that potential perpetrators may wish to gain prior to any type of incident or attack, it becomes possible that anyone familiar with these types of activities conducted prior to a criminal incident or attack—not just onsite security forces—can be aware of and report them. As we discussed in the previous section on reconnaissance, promoting security awareness among your employees can greatly deter criminals or terrorists from gaining this information without being detected, and this awareness can deter action against your organization.

2.3 Security Fundamentals

Now that we have looked at what actions potential perpetrators will normally take prior to conducting an action against a facility or business, we will discuss the primary fundamentals of security that should be considered when looking at either physical security measures, which describe aspects that protect people and resources within your organization; or information security resources, which. in many cases are synonymous with computer security and the measures taken to protect electronic data and other information. Keep in mind that the main objective of any safety and security program is to ensure that the resources that you are protecting provide the necessary deterrents and look difficult or impossible to damage, destroy, or gain access to by any potential intruder; taking these fundamentals into account while developing your safety and security program can greatly increase its effectiveness and efficiency.

2.3.1 Identification of Critical Resources

Not only is identification of critical resources the first security fundamental, it is also one of the initial tasks that you should undertake when beginning to develop your safety and security program. Before we explain this security fundamental, let us first define the term "critical resource" as we will use it within this book.

Critical resources are any essential resources, assets, equipment, or means and processes that are necessary to ensure that your business capability is fully operational and can meet your key organizational goals and objectives.

This means that the loss of a critical resource should result in failure of your business—either in the short term or in a more permanent loss of productivity. Many individuals will make the error of designating too many items as a critical resource, which will lead to spending far too much time and money protecting items that are not necessarily critical to your business, or spending too much time and money to overprotect an item that could be replaced without any appreciable loss to your business's activities. It needs to be noted that this definition differs from critical resources that refer to critical paths or bottlenecks in your organization's processes—these items deal more with operational efficiencies rather than an item's importance within the safety and security program and their ability to actually conduct operations rather than simply slowing them down. With this definition in mind, a critical resource will typically describe a specific piece of information, a required piece of equipment, or a key individual who cannot be easily replaced.

There are a variety of methods that can identify your organization's critical resources (we will look at a using a risk assessment matrix in the next chapter to accomplish this identification so we will not go into detail here). Whether you use the risk assessment matrix or another method, it is vital that you accomplish this identification and ensure that this list includes only your truly critical resources, rather than designating every asset or piece of information as critical. In this manner, you can ensure that you spend your limited resources only to protect these assets and not waste time or money on areas that may not be necessary.

Once you have identified your organization's critical resources, your safety and security program should be built around the protection of these items, followed by protection of other resources. One of the advantages in using a risk assessment matrix is that it not only helps to identify your critical resources but it also has the added benefit of further prioritizing all of your resources and assets. This resulting hierarchy of all of your organization's resources should be used to determine subsequent security measures once you have adequately accounted for the protection of your critical resources. By using this prioritized list, you can determine the level of effort and costs that you can incur in order to work down this list toward the eventual goal of providing adequate security for all of your resources.

2.3.2 Defense in Depth

Once you have identified your organization's critical resources, along with the other important resources and assets contained in your prioritized list, it is necessary that security measures are layered around these items in order to effectively protect these items; this is normally termed "defense in depth." To accomplish this, you should use several different security measures in order to form redundant security systems so as not to rely on one sole protection device to protect an individual resource. In order to provide the most effective security umbrella, it is also necessary that these security measures do not use the same detection capability; such as infrared detectors, motion, microwave, seismic, visual, etc. For example, if you have a room with a safe containing critical resources, having only cameras both inside and outside the room would not be the most effective solution. Instead, using fewer security cameras but augmenting the area with a magnetic alarm on the safe and an intrusion alarm at the door to the room would provide a better defense in depth and result in a much safer and more secure environment.

A good rule of thumb is to attempt to provide a minimum of three security layers when designing protection around your critical resources. Depending on the criticality of the resource and the potential costs due to loss or damage, it may be prudent to place even more layers of security around the asset; however, the number of layers will depend ultimately on the money that you are able to allocate to security, based on cost analyses weighing loss and damage versus costs of the security measures. Regardless of how many layers you are able to employ, providing redundant security measures around your critical resources will ensure defense in depth and will result in mitigating potential threats. Figure 2.1 highlights this process—protecting the asset in layers.

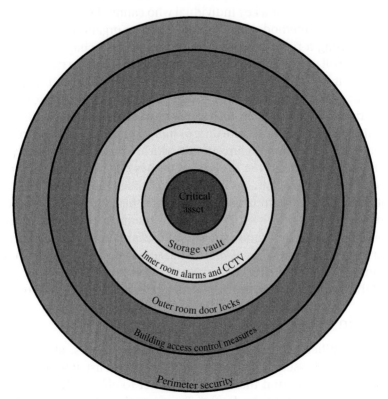

FIGURE 2.1 Layering protection of assets and critical resources.

2.3.3 Notification

The next security fundamental that should be considered within any safety and security program is the need for some type of notification method within your security system. Even if an organization has the best security system in the world—computerized access control, high-resolution security cameras, the most expensive high-security doors and windows, and all of the most technologically advanced and state-of-the-art security measures that can be purchased—without some method to notify appropriate individuals of any attempts to gain unauthorized access would render all of this amazing equipment useless. Although the most common type of notification within a security systems is some type of alarm, we will also look at other notification methods that can augment an alarm system and greatly improve notification.

As stated, alarm systems are the most common method for providing notification of unauthorized attempts to gain access to a building, room, or specific piece of equipment. An alarm system's notification is typically accomplished by detecting changes in the environment around the object or detecting breaks in some type of pathway (e.g., electrical, infrared, etc.) surrounding an area. We will cover specific intrusion alarm systems in great detail within Chapter 6, where we will look at the various considerations in determining when to use an alarm system and what type of alarm systems work best for certain uses. For our purposes now, these alarm systems provide an extremely reliable and the most common method to notify regarding attempts to access your organization's critical resources.

In addition to alarm systems, another notification method is to maintain up-to-date inventories and logs that track not only your critical resources but all of your high-dollar equipment. It is normally impractical and cost-prohibitive to install alarm systems throughout the entire facility, particularly in areas that do not contain any critical resources; thus, there will need to be other ways to determine whether unauthorized access has occurred and whether any equipment has been lost or stolen. In order to ensure that your organization has the means to identify any theft or loss, the use of inventories and logs that track your high-value equipment will greatly assist in this task. There are several reasons to maintain these inventories and logs. First, a significant amount of equipment theft and loss occurs from an organization's own employees. A 2013 study of U.S. retail businesses showed that apprehensions of employees for theft have increased by 5.5% from 2011 [3]. In many cases, the likelihood that these acts can occur will significantly increase when there is no notification method in place to deter employees or other perpetrators. Second, by maintaining up-to-date inventories, your organization can quickly identify exactly what items were stolen, and you can ensure that you are aware of any theft or access not only to critical resources but to other high-dollar assets. Lastly, the available information from an accurate inventory will assist law enforcement personnel in their investigation of any theft and will provide you with an accurate accounting of any missing items for insurance claims and replacement.

Another method to assist in notification is use of security personnel. If your organization uses on-site security guards, one of their primary functions is to identify and notify supervisors of any unauthorized attempts to access your critical resources. Although this can be a very effective method, it can also be costly depending upon the size of your company. Contracting or hiring your own security guard force will be an expensive proposition, especially for smaller businesses; and although a security guard force provides a much higher level of security to your facility and resources, you should look at the long-term costs and weigh these against the risks to determine whether this is the appropriate solution for your organization. We will discuss the various advantages and disadvantages of having your own internal security guard force in Chapter 4.

A last method to augment alarm systems and assist with notification is promoting awareness among all of your employees to report any unauthorized attempts to access your critical resources or to provide information on any loss or theft of company equipment.

We have already emphasized the need to gain a high level of security awareness among your employees, as it can help in so many different areas within your safety and security program. The best method to achieve this heightened security awareness is through initial and recurring training, which we will cover in Chapter 10. This high level of security awareness will greatly improve notification regarding any unauthorized attempts to access your critical resources. Employees are much more familiar with their own work areas—more so than any other individuals—and they will be much more likely to determine whether any unauthorized access has occurred. By achieving and maintain a high level of security awareness, you will be more likely to receive notification as quickly as possible, which will enable you to quickly determine necessary actions. Employees' security awareness can also assist in the event of internal employee theft, since it is much more probable that any notification, either at the time of the incident or prior to it actually occurring, will be more noticeable among co-workers and other employees. It is much more likely that a co-worker will not only notice theft but may even be in the immediate area when an employee attempts to steal company resources, rather than a supervisor or manager. For this reason, developing a high degree of security awareness for all company employees and ensuring that they take ownership of protecting company assets will greatly increase the chances that they will report any questionable actions by other co-workers.

Notification can be achieved not only by alarm systems but by inventories and logs, security guards, and your own employees who practice a high level of security awareness.

2.3.4 Response

The next security fundamental that we will discuss is response, which goes hand-in-hand with notification. This fundamental describes the need to have at least one individual, and, if possible a group of trained individuals or even security personnel, be able to respond to an incident once a notification of a security concern has been received. This is an important security fundamental—especially if the perpetrators have conducted reconnaissance of the location with the intent to assess the response of any security personnel. If potential perpetrators are aware that there is no response force once notification of any attempt to access the location has occurred, there will be no deterrent, and it is very likely that they will proceed with their planned action. Thus, it is important that some type of response occur.

There are various levels of response that your organization can provide in the event of an alarm. These responses range from one employee who goes to the location to assess the situation, all the way to armed security personnel storming the facility in the event of an alarm notification (although some responses later may seem a little extreme depending upon the situation). A first option, due to the lower inherent costs and ease of implementation, is to provide this response capability with a designated employee who receives notification of alarm activation. This individual will assess the situation, either based upon the location and type of alarms that went off, or by their own assessment of the area. If they decide that further action is necessary, they will then make a determination to request local law enforcement or security personnel to respond. Normally, an alarm system will provide initial notification of any situation to the system provider, so it is relatively easy to ensure that this designated employee be notified by the alarm system service provider. Again, the decision to have additional response can be accomplished either by going to the facility to assess the situation in person or through their knowledge of the facility and information on what the location and type of alarms that have been received. For example, if the employee is notified that only one interior alarm has gone off but that all other external alarms have not been triggered, it is likely that the interior alarm may be malfunctioning or providing a false alarm rather than detecting an actual intruder. Since the employee will normally have to make a judgment call on whether to request further response, it is advisable that the individual designated to receive alarm notifications have the appropriate responsibility and authority so as to be able to properly analyze the situation and determine the risks involved between a response by armed security personnel or a nonresponse. This option has the advantage that it is normally the lowest in cost, since many law enforcement agencies may charge for response to a false alarm.

The next option for response is to allow the alarm system service provider to directly notify local law enforcement of any alarm notification for their response. An advantage of this is the greater capability of any police who are going to respond and react to actual breaches to the facility. Another advantage can be the relatively low costs, although, as discussed earlier, many local police have policies and procedures that involve charging costs for response to false alarm notifications due to the loss of time and manpower in the event that law enforcement is continually forced to respond to false alarms. Initially, many local law enforcement agencies will respond to an alarm notification at no charge; however, many departments will begin to charge the business at some point in the event this response is due to false alarms or there is no evidence of any actual intrusion to the location. Should your organization consider this option, it will be necessary to ensure that you understand the local law enforcement department's policies regarding response so that you are not surprised if they begin to charge your business for false alarm responses.

At the other end of the response spectrum from having one employee receive the notification and determination the appropriate response, the last option is to contract or hire security personnel for full-time response to all of your organization's alarm notifications and incidents. This will obviously be the most expensive option; however, this option may work if your organization is large or if your critical resources are so expensive or dangerous that the risks of any loss or damage outweigh the costs of having your own dedicated security force.

No matter what option you choose, it is necessary there be some type of response by individuals once notification has occurred. Without any type of response, all you would likely have is an alarm sounding which may frighten away teenage vandals, but not a dedicated intruder who truly wants to gain access to your critical resources. This type of perpetrator will quickly discover the lack of any actual response and exploit this discrepancy.

2.3.5 Simplicity

Everyone has heard the saying "Keep it simple." This adage works well for almost everything, including safety and security programs, and applies to both the type of equipment you are using along with your organization's safety and security procedures.

2.3.5.1 Simplicity in Regard to Security Equipment

Keeping things simple is a significant determination in the complexity and technology of the security equipment that you are considering in your security system. When deciding what type of security equipment to incorporate, you should look at the following:

- Track record and reliability of the security equipment
- Dependence of the security equipment upon humans
- Ability to integrate newer and more advanced security equipment into an existing system
- Higher cost of more complex and more advanced security equipment technologies

In regard to security equipment, it is normally better to look at purchasing and using good equipment that has been used for a while with a reliable track record rather than using brand-new equipment that incorporates the latest technologies. Security equipment that has been in operation for a while will have a proven track record and the manufacturer will likely have worked out any problems, whereas, in the case of equipment that incorporates state-of-the-art technological advances, the manufacturer has probably not been able to work out many of the bugs that can occur with newer equipment. In addition, many newer technologies may have significant problems integrating with older equipment. This could create significant problems, since most security systems should work together in order to provide an easy-to-understand notification system.

An illustration of using simpler equipment rather than state-of-the-art items can be found in one job in which I was responsible for security within a nuclear storage site. As anyone can imagine, based on the sensitivity of the critical resources that we were charged with protecting, the security measures were designed to be as impenetrable as possible; however, many of these measures used several new technologies as part of the overall security system for the site. One such technology that was incorporated into the security system that at the time was truly state of the art was an early form of biometric identification. This system assisted in the identification and authorization of personnel who were attempting to gain access to the site. The specific type of biometric system that was utilized in this particular system was handprints of the individual. Although the technology for this system was available at this point in time, it was still relatively new, and, as a result, the system encountered a fairly high failure rate when attempting to identify individuals and their authorization. Of course, due to the critical nature of nuclear resources, the system was designed so that failures in the biometric identification would not allow access; but, due to these issues and problems resulting in a high failure rate, the system was almost useless at times, since a security guard had to recheck the authorization of the individual. Add to this the additional monies to fix the problems with the system, and the use of this relatively new (at the time) technology was probably not the best course of action. Over the last several years and with the many advances in technology, handprints and other biometric identification systems have become much more reliable, but at the time, use of this system illustrates the sorts of problems that can occur if you are trying to incorporate the latest technologies in your security system. Based upon the track record of the items' performance and reliability, it is normally better to use security equipment that is relatively simple to operate rather than brand-new, state-of-the-art equipment that may provide a better level of security but that will be more complex. Although newer and more complex equipment will typically be more sensitive and will utilize better technology, these items can lead to a higher rate of false alarms and downtime.

Another consideration with regard to the need to keep security equipment simple is that most security systems are ultimately dependent on the human factor—not the technology of the equipment. You can have the best security equipment money can buy, but if the individual tasked to observe the equipment or respond to alarms is not paying attention during an actual intrusion or emergency, the higher cost of these systems will not have justified their cost or resulted in any appreciable improvement to security of your critical resources or the facility. With this in mind, it is almost always better to provide more safety and security training to your employees or hire more security guards rather than paying the higher costs of the latest and greatest security equipment technology.

One issue that many organizations overlook when considering incorporating newer technologies is the ability to integrate this upgraded equipment into your organization's existing security system. An overall security system should integrate all areas and subsystems that compose its associated equipment, to include alarms, cameras, access control, and other items. These integration systems are typically computer operated and should easily show the user alarms across the entire system. If a new piece of hardware incorporates the newest technology, however, the overall integration system may not be able to process the data and other information from this one piece of equipment due to its more advanced technology. Another issue that can occur with higher technologies is a lack of compatibility in the operating system of this newer equipment. These issues could render the newer hardware incompatible with the current integration system, and cause you either to purchase a new integration system or to scrap the new piece of hardware.

The last consideration in regard to advanced technologies is that many security equipment items reach a point of diminishing returns due to the higher costs associated with more complex and newer security technologies. Even if the more complex security equipment has been thoroughly tested and works well, there may only be an incremental increase in its detection capability when compared with its less expensive alternative. One must determine whether the small increase in detection is useful or truly necessary based on any greater costs and complexity when determining what specific piece of security equipment to purchase.

2.3.5.2 Simplicity in Regard to Security Procedures

The other primary area in which to ensure that you keep things as simple as possible is in your security processes and procedures that must be followed by your employees. Let's face facts—most organizations are too busy working on their day-to-day business operations to allocate a significant amount of time to their safety and security programs. The time that is necessary to train your employees on each and every one of their security procedures and to conduct practice sessions in order to ensure that these procedures are understood to the degree necessary can be staggering if you allow it to be. Unfortunately, some time must be dedicated to your safety and security program, as shown by numerous after-action reports from actual security or terrorist incidents that have highlighted the unfamiliarity of many employees with their organization's emergency response procedures in the event of an actual emergency. These employees were simply not knowledgeable about the necessary actions or were not prepared to react to the actual incident; as a result, these employees did not know what to do when the actual incident started. For this reason, it is important to keep your safety and security procedures as simple and basic as possible.

Due to the myriad emergencies and incidents that could occur in any organization, keeping your organization's security procedures simple may seem difficult to accomplish, but let me promise you—it is not. Even with the many different types of incidents that could occur, there are basically only two different types of possible actions, and two actions only, that most of your employees would need to take in the event of an emergency. Although there are going to be more actions for senior leaders in order to manage and direct the response, the only two actions for employees are either evacuation or remaining in place (sometimes termed "lockdown"). We will cover both of these actions in detail in Chapter 9—Emergency and Contingency Planning, but by focusing your training efforts within your organization on these two simple procedures, rather than getting bogged down in the minutiae of the vast amount of security processes and procedures that are available, it will become much easier for your employees to understand what they need to accomplish in the event of an actual emergency.

2.3.6 Securing the Weakest Links

When evaluating your safety and security program, it is always a good idea to identify and strengthen the weakest links in your organization's overall security system, which is the next security fundamental that we will cover. This fundamental is particularly necessary if any of these weak links in your security system can lead directly to access of a critical resource within your organization.

The best method to determine what areas are the weakest links in your security system is to have an objective assessment of the equipment and procedures used within your safety and security program. This assessment can be accomplished either by hiring outside consultants or by asking an expert on security within your own organization to evaluate the overall system, identify the weak links, and provide solutions and areas for improvement. If you opt to use an internal expert to accomplish this assessment, it is best if that individual is not associated with security within your organization, in order to obtain an unbiased, more valid and true evaluation. It should be pointed out that the process of fully evaluating a security system can be lengthy; however, the dividends that will be gained by the identification of weak links that will lessen risks and result in cost savings from averted incidents will make it well worth the time.

Once the weak links within your security system have been identified, it is possible to ensure that these areas are strengthened through either equipment or procedures. Many organizations will first look at solving these issues with the purchase of additional security equipment in order to provide greater protection to these problem areas; however, it should be noted that many times there may be no-cost options that resolve these issues. These no-cost options can normally be accomplished by revising or augmenting existing procedures within a safety and security program. By identifying the weak links and providing corrective action, your safety and security program will be greatly enhanced.

2.3.7 Use of Choke Points

Choke points are another security fundamental that, once identified, will assist in the development of your organization's safety and security program. Choke points are areas that will narrow access into your facility for both personnel and packages that enter your business. The purpose in narrowing, or funneling, traffic through these locations has two purposes. First, it helps to better identify the locations where security measures are needed and should be focused. Second, by identifying the choke points, you may be able to limit the number of security equipment items required, since they will be implemented primarily at these funnels.

These purposes—the ability to minimize the number of entry points and the ability to funnel individuals (whether employees or visitors) through choke points onto your grounds and into the facility—are key factors in limiting possible vulnerabilities and deterring actions by criminals or terrorists. Quite simply, the fewer entry points into your business, the less money and time you will be required to spend on security measures. Fewer entry points also result in a much greater ability to identify people attempting to access your organization, as well as packages that may be suspect. In Chapter 6, in which we look at physical security measures, we will emphasize that the ability to control access to your facility is one of the most significant aspects that will have a positive impact on your organization's overall physical security system. In this chapter, we will go into the specifics of how to accomplish proper access control; however, this process ultimately utilizes the security fundamental of choke points to see that entry points are kept to a minimum, to better ensure the ability to monitor and secure these locations.

2.3.8 Unpredictability

Unpredictability can greatly enhance security. Most of us have seen movies in which intruders want to gain access into a restricted area and, in order to do so, they are able to time a security guard's patrol route down to the minute; although this level of predictability rarely happens in real life, any security guard that uses the exact same route movements and patrol zones day after day can make it very easy for potential perpetrators to time their entry when there is little chance of detection.

During my security training in the military, I was taught about the significant impact of unpredictability through an interview conducted with a Viet Cong general after the conclusion of the United States' participation in the Vietnam War. The general was part of a panel discussion with several senior American military officers from all the different U.S. uniformed services—the Army, Marines, Navy, and Air Force. When asked what forces had posed the greatest problems to the Viet Cong, most of the U.S. officers thought that it was obviously their service that had achieved this distinction and had been the most difficult to overcome for the enemy. The Army officer thought it might have been his normal soldiers, but more likely the Army Special Forces personnel, that would be singled out by the General. The Marine officer believed that his marines would be named due to their esprit de corps and training. Even the Naval officer expected that his sailors would be singled out, in significant part based upon the accomplishments of the SEALs. Surprisingly, though, the Viet Cong General stated that the most difficult troops that they had had to contend with were U.S. Air Force Security Forces personnel, who were primarily tasked to guard air bases in Vietnam. When asked why he had named this group, the General stated that it was due to their unpredictability. These forces never defended the base in the same way on any given day. One day, they would be posted in only a few locations with small numbers of defenders. On other days, they would have large numbers of personnel located at every security post along the perimeter of the base. Still other days, the Air Force Security Forces troops would be moving about the base perimeter in vehicles and foot patrols that were not fixed at any specific locations. Although this unpredictability may not have always been planned (it may have depended on the size of the party the night before or how many troops had a pass to go off base the day before), the Viet Cong General stated that these unpredictable actions made it extremely difficult for his forces to locate the exact number of defenders and to neutralize them.

Unfortunately, unpredictability can be difficult to achieve and can also become a double-edged sword. Although unpredictability makes it difficult for an adversary to anticipate your actions, being unpredictable can make security processes and procedures much more complex, which violates our earlier-discussed fundamental—that of simplicity. This complexity is created by multiple procedures for security personnel to accomplish, in order to allow for several different methods that will equate to more unpredictability. This paradox results in the need for your organization to create a balance between simplicity and unpredictability, while taking into account the level of knowledge and training of the employees who are the primary individuals who must implement and practice security procedures on a daily basis. A good rule of thumb is that any security procedures that apply to employees who are not primarily tasked to conduct security duties should emphasize simplicity; however, if your organization has employees who are tasked to conduct security duties on a full-time basis, such as an internal guard force or dedicated security department, it may be possible to place more emphasis on the unpredictability of security procedures with these individuals. By trying to implement many different options for any given security procedure in order to promote unpredictability, it will be likely that employees who are not directly tasked with security duties will begin to be confused. Since full-time security personnel will have additional time to train on a variety of different procedures that will result in more unpredictable security behaviors, it is possible to consider implementing various procedures.

Even without full-time security personnel, unpredictability can be achieved simply by emphasizing a certain aspect of your safety and security program throughout your organization over the course of any given year. Although there has been no change in any security procedure, this emphasis will result in your employees focusing on a variety of particular procedures over a period of time, which will be seen as unpredictable behavior within your safety and security program by an outsider.

2.3.9 Separation of Duties

The last security fundamental that we will look at is separation of duties. This concept is much like a check and balance system, since it avoids the possibility of one individual being fully responsible for different functions within an organization, which, when combined, may result in an undetected security violation. Separation of duties is all about validation…in fact, there is an old Russian proverb (which was also used by President Ronald Reagan) that sums up the concept: "Trust, but verify." [4] Understanding the meaning behind that saying is very important when it comes to understanding the principle of separation of duties.

When separation of duties is first introduced into organizations, there can be some significant discomfort—sometimes from trusted employees and other times from employees who have not had to undergo any type of check and balance process to review their actions; however, there are several reasons to implement this concept. First, any individual can make a simple error or accomplish a task incorrectly with the best of intentions, and it is unlikely that even the most conscientious of workers will catch their own errors. By implementing a check and balance system in order to separate these duties, a second individual who is verifying the task will provide the organization with assurance that the processes are being carried out accurately and correctly. The second reason is to ensure that employees are not taking advantage of their authority and responsibilities. An example would be having only one employee responsible for both maintenance and tracking of all funds within the organization. In this case, the one employee would easily be able to embezzle funds from the company, since there is no other individual who checks, or is even aware, of the status of the funds. By dividing tasks involved in obtaining, tracking, and spending money, it becomes more difficult for the organization to lose funds and makes it easier to identify concerns.

2.4 Balancing Security Measures with Business Operations

As we have discussed earlier, security is inconvenient, so it is necessary that your organization strike the correct balance between implementation of security measures and their effects upon business operations. This is the last security principle that we will cover: balancing these measures and procedures with your own business operational requirements. Within this principle, there are three areas that must be taken into account when

Security measure effectiveness

FIGURE 2.2 The security versus business operation triangle.

attempting to balance these specific security measures and the procedures for your organization and its business needs. These three areas—effectiveness of security measures, business environment, and employee willingness—form a triangle that should describe the balance between these areas in order to produce the right mix for your particular organization (Figure 2.2).

It is not necessary that the three sides of this triangle be equal, since each area's individual weight and importance can vary greatly from organization to organization based upon the specific needs of that company in its business and operating environment.

2.4.1 Factors that Affect the Security Measures versus Business Operations Triangle

In order to determine the importance of each of these three areas within your particular organization, it is useful to consider the following factors specific to your business:

- Senior management emphasis on safety and security
- Cost and importance of your organization's critical resources
- Organizational culture

The first factor to consider is what level of emphasis the organization's senior management places on safety and security. This is a critical factor, as the level of emphasis and involvement in safety and security from your organization's senior management will directly influence another factor—the overall culture of the organization. It is vital that senior management within your organization be honest and truthful in how much importance is placed upon safety and security, since it can have an impact on so many other areas within the company. For example, if a high level of security is desired or necessary within your organization, this will lead to more stringent security practices and, in turn, to a higher level of inconvenience. Thus, this factor not only shows the level of risk that senior management is willing to take, but it also affects the amount of inconvenience caused by these additional security measures that your employees must work around in order to carry out their normal duties. This higher level of inconvenience will lead to complaints and additional explanation of security procedures to employees, so if the high level of emphasis on safety and security by senior management is simply "lip service," it will become apparent, and many areas—in addition to your safety and security program—will suffer. It is important to note that most employees will go along with the implementation of more stringent security processes; however, senior management must truly believe in their decision regarding the level of importance of safety and security and be behind this decision.

The next factor to consider when determining the level of emphasis of each of the three areas contained within the triangle is the cost and importance of your organization's critical resources. If your critical resources are so vital that any attempt against them would be catastrophic (nuclear weapons or components would be a perfect example of this), then the level of security that you will need to implement will be much different from a business that manufactures low-cost items. The company that works with nuclear components will be required to place a huge emphasis on the effectiveness of the security measures that are put into place, based on the potentially catastrophic consequences of *any* action against the business and its critical resources. In this example, the other factors—business environment and employee willingness to work around inconvenience—become secondary due to the criticality of the business's critical resources.

The last factor that should be considered when determining the level of importance and how to balance each area within the triangle is the culture within your organization. As we discussed earlier, emphasis by senior management on safety and security can influence this factor; however, this emphasis can influence the organizational culture only in incremental degrees over time. Normally, an open corporate culture will not embrace strict security measures as much as an organization that is more autocratic. For example, if the current organizational culture is extremely open and easy-going (Google is a company that comes to mind to use as an example with this type of company culture), it will be very difficult to immediately initiate a large number of security measures that create a great deal of inconvenience to the employees. If it is determined that an open and easy-going organization needs to implement more controls and more stringent security measures, the culture of the company will need to be addressed; but it should be noted that these initiatives should be introduced over time in order to ease employees into the newer and more strict procedures.

Now that we have provided an overview of the three factors—senior management emphasis on safety and security, the organization's critical resources, and organizational culture—we will look at each of these factors in more detail in order to better enable you to determine how to balance the three areas within the Security versus Business Operation Triangle within your particular organization.

2.4.2 Effectiveness of Security Measures Portion of the Triangle

Effectiveness of the security measures describes the level of detection that the security system protecting a specific item should achieve. This level of detection will depend on the criticality of the resources that you are securing and what repercussions would occur to your business or reputation if any loss or damage were suffered with these items. For example, the repercussions based upon the loss of the weekly coffee fund are going to be dramatically different from the repercussions due to any security breach that would occur with any type of biological or chemical material. These repercussions lead to a very different level of detection necessary to protect either item. In the case of the coffee fund, it may be determined that you need to detect loss or theft only 50% of the time; however, with biological or chemical materials, the level of detection may need to exceed 99%.

Due to the significantly different repercussions and, conversely, the vastly different levels of detection necessary to protect the two items in our example, the other areas within the Security Measures versus Business Operations triangle will be affected. In cases in which a very high level of detection is necessary, there will be less consideration of the business environment or employee willingness areas that you should consider. For this reason, the effectiveness of security measures area forms the base of the triangle; and, as we discussed earlier, this triangle will likely not be equilateral, since this one area can dictate the impact and importance of the other areas.

2.4.3 Business Environment Portion of the Triangle

As in our earlier example, the type of business and the resulting company culture within your organization will have an impact on the level of security within your organization and, in turn, will affect the other areas within the triangle. For example, if your business depends upon customers who must visit and have access to your facility, the level of security that you will need to establish will be different from that of a manufacturing business that does not require any outsider access and sells only to suppliers located off-site. Another way to illustrate this point is to use retail business as an example. A retail store will not be able to implement significant security measures, since these could make it difficult for customers even to gain access into the facility and would likely result in the customers simply going elsewhere. This point should be obvious, but any security measures that are implemented should ensure that they do not take away from your primary business function. In the case of your particular business, you will need to look at what accommodations must be made in order to ensure the least amount of impact on your customers and implement appropriate security measures around these considerations.

2.4.4 Employee Willingness Portion of the Triangle

Employee willingness to work around inconvenience is the last side of the Security Measures versus Business Operations Triangle. It is necessary that employees be willing to work around the security measures that have been implemented, and your organization must work to ensure that your employees are satisfied with the working conditions. As we have discussed earlier, there are several factors that can have an impact on this willingness of employees. First, by placing a high level of emphasis on safety and security by senior management, it is likely this will lead to an increase in the amount of inconvenience that employees are willing to endure. Second, the culture of your organization will have a direct impact on the amount of inconvenience that employees are willing to work around—an open and free organization will have a different level of support in regard to safety and security initiatives, when compared to an organization that follows a strict hierarchy and is autocratic in nature.

One of the primary areas to consider when looking to implement changes in your organization's safety and security posture is to consider the impact upon your existing employees, as these are the personnel who will need to be sold on any modifications. There are several options that you can use to ensure success when discussing this with your employees. One option is providing several communications that notify employees of any upcoming changes in safety and security well before they are to occur. These communications should not only include the changes in security procedures that will be taking place but also why these changes are occurring (e.g., correcting current deficiencies in the organization's safety and security program, mitigating risks or vulnerabilities in the organization, saving money, etc.). Another option is to conduct group meetings with employees to discuss the changes and to answer any questions or concerns. A final option is walking around the various offices within your organization and talking with individuals or small groups to alleviate concerns and to answer questions. Any of these options will help employees to better understand these changes in your safety and security program and will result in greater success.

Fortunately, new employees who come on board after any modifications to your safety and security program will adapt to the existing procedures and the current environment; however, it will be necessary to spend time with the current employees as you implement any new safety and security initiatives. Ultimately, employees will learn to work under the new processes and procedures as long as senior management shows their support.

2.5 Summary

The primary goal in any security program is to protect your organization's critical resources by implementing security measures, which can include equipment, processes, and procedures. To accomplish this goal; we have looked at safety and security principles that included actions by potential perpetrators before an incident, the primary fundamentals of security, and balancing safety and security with business efficiency and effectiveness.

The first safety and security principle is to be familiar with certain actions that all potential perpetrators take prior to conducting any type of attack against a location. These actions include reconnaissance of the location prior to an attack, and assessing the security measures such as equipment, size, and capability of the on-site security force (if any), and what type of response occurs in the event of an attack. Knowing these actions can strengthen the security measures of your organization and assist in the ability of your employees to identify these actions through training.

The next safety and security principles that we covered were several security fundamentals that need to be taken into account when developing a safety and security program. These fundamentals include:

- Identification of critical resources
- Defense in depth
- Notification
- Response
- Simplicity (of both equipment and procedures)
- Securing the weakest links
- Use of choke points
- Unpredictability
- Separation of duties

The last safety and security principle that we covered in this chapter was the need to balance security measures and initiatives with your business operations. It is imperative that this balance be achieved, since security is going to create inconveniences with some processes and your employees. The main areas that affect this balance include:

- Effectiveness of security measures, or the level of detection necessary to protect your organization's critical resources
- Business environment, or type of business that your organization is in
- Employee willingness to work around the inconveniences created by the safety and security program

We introduced how these three areas form a triangle—although not necessarily an equilateral triangle—that should illustrate your organization's unique solution in balancing these three areas to ensure that you can maintain business efficiency while ensuring safety and security.

2.6 Safety and Security Principles Checklist

	Yes	No
Does your initial employee training include security awareness?		
Do you train your employees on potential actions by perpetrators and terrorists prior to an attack, to ensure that employees are aware of and can possibly identify such actions?		
Do your safety and security plans and procedures take into account the nine fundamentals of security?		
Have you sketched out your organization's Security Measures versus Business Operations Triangle?		

Note: All items are listed in priority order, so you should ensure that each answer is "Yes" prior to expending funds or effort on addressing the next question. This ensures that an executive with minimal security expertise can easily move down the list in order to implement an adequate security program.

References

[1] A&E Television Networks. 9/11 Attacks. November 27, 2013. http://www.history.com.

[2] The 9/11 Commission Report. Kean JM, editors. 9/11 Commission Chairman. http://www. 9-11commission.gov.

[3] Brooks, Chad. Employee theft on the rise and expected to get worse. www.BusinessNewsDaily.com. Business News Daily.

[4] Hoelzer David. Teach your boss to speak security: separation of duties. Forbes Magazine; 26 Apr 2010. Web. 10 Dec. 2013.

Recommended Reading on Safety and Security Principles

Surveillance and Threat Detection: Prevention versus Mitigation by Richard Kirchner. Butterworth-Heinemann.

3

Security Plan Development and Risk Assessment

Within this chapter, we will look at the overall process involved in safety and security planning. This includes the development of safety and security plans and procedures, risk assessment, identification of potential threats and vulnerabilities, how to quantify safety and security initiatives in terms of efficiencies and costs, how to match cost-effective solutions that work against these threats, and methods to justify safety and security processes to employees and shareholders. Each of the following sections will discuss these separate areas in detail.

3.1 Safety and Security Plans and Procedures

The primary method to implement any safety and security program is accomplished through a well-written organizational safety and security plan. Ideally, a security professional should be involved in the development of any detailed plan to ensure the document is complete and meets the specific needs of your organization; however, if this is not possible due to limited time or resources, there are several pieces of information that are useful for you to know that can assist you in the development of your own document, which can be used as a starting point until it can be further refined by an expert. These items should not only ensure that this process results in a safety and security plan that is properly accomplished and tailored to your organization, but that it can provide a consistent set of guidelines to your employees in the event of an emergency.

We will discuss these items that should be included in any safety and security plan by looking at the overall format of a typical document. This format should include the following sections to ensure coverage of all the necessary areas:

1. Executive Summary
2. Introduction to Security
3. Security Risk Assessment
4. Security Aspects, Requirements, and Mitigation Considerations
5. Physical Security
6. Information Security
7. Personnel Security
8. Emergency Response
9. Security Teams
10. Safety and Security Training and Exercises
11. Maintenance of the Plan and Audits
12. Appendices

Each of these sections will be looked at over the next several sections. In each of these sections, we will look at standard verbiage for many of the typical areas covered within that subject area, along with a discussion of what each section should cover.

3.1.1 Executive Summary

An executive summary of the organizational safety and security plan should be the first section of any good planning document. This section briefly covers some of the major points of the plan, along with summary information regarding your business and the local area.

The following paragraphs show a draft format of a typical executive summary, along with specific items that should be included in this section.

1. Executive Summary
    1.1. Introduction. Businesses are not immune to security incidents and crises, as has been seen over the past several years. These incidents can be as minor in nature, such as vandalism and petty theft; however, they can also include more serious events such as natural disasters, threats against the facility, visitors, and staff, or environmental hazards. These incidents may result in significant catastrophes such as destruction of the facility, or workplace violence incidents that could include active-shooter scenarios. This plan is designed to provide response actions for the organization's staff in order to mitigate these potential crises.
        1.1.1. Summary of the local area where your business operates. This brief description should include the geographic area, major population centers, and the types of typical criminal activity in the area such as minor burglary, vandalism, theft, break-in, or more violent crimes.
        1.1.2. Summary of the size of the business (e.g., number of buildings, number of staff, number and frequency of visitors, budget, etc.)
        1.1.3. Security Risk Assessment. The method to accomplish a detailed Security Risk Assessment will be covered later in this chapter. The executive summary should detail where this assessment is contained within this document, as the risk assessment will provide a listing of the business's risks with a high and moderate potential of occurrence.
            1.1.3.1. Include a list of specific risks within the organization that have a high potential of occurring that would result in critical consequences based upon the results of your risk assessment.
            1.1.3.2. Include a list of risks with moderate potential of occurring that would result in serious consequences based upon the results of your risk assessment.
    1.2. Plan Objectives
        1.2.1. Security Responsibilities. This section should delineate specific roles and responsibilities necessary to accomplish tasks required within the safety and security program. This should include:
            1.2.1.1. Designation of the overall position responsible for the organization's Safety and Security Program. This individual

should normally be the person who will be standing in front of the cameras in the event of a significant incident, so it may not necessarily be the individual who runs the program on a daily basis, but instead it may be the CEO or President.

1.2.1.2. Designation of the day-to-day management of the organization's Safety and Security Program (if different from the individual designated as the overall Safety and Security point of contact in 1.2.1.1).

1.2.1.3. Designation of various Security and Safety Teams. It is helpful to divide the effort within each of the major areas that comprise an organization's safety and security program amongst a group of individuals, in order to ensure the program can be properly maintained. It is useful to designate the following teams to assist in management and maintenance of the safety and security program. These sections should discuss what positions are included in each respective team and will also describe the functions listed within each team.

    1.2.1.3.1. Security Management Team should include the individual who is overall responsible for the organization's safety and security program; the individual responsible for day-to-day management of the safety and security program; the director of operations; the director of human resources (or personnel); the director of maintenance or facilities; the public relations director; the director of information technology, and a line manager.

    1.2.1.3.2. Plan Development Team should include the individual responsible for the day-to-day management of the safety and security program; the director of operations; the director of human resources (or personnel); the director of maintenance or facilities; the public relations director; and a director of information technology.

    1.2.1.3.3. Exercise Management Team should include the individual responsible for the day-to-day management of the safety and security program; the director of human resources (or personnel); the director of maintenance or facilities; the public relations director; the director of information technology; and a line manager.

    1.2.1.3.4. Physical Security Team should include the individual responsible for the day-to-day management of the safety and security program; the director of operations; and the director of maintenance or facilities.

1.2.1.3.5. Information Security Team should include the individual responsible for the day-to-day management of the safety and security program; the director of information technology; and the director of maintenance or facilities.

1.2.1.3.6. Security Incident Response Team should include the overall responsible individual for the organization's safety and security program, the individual responsible for the day-to-day management of the safety and security program, the director of operations, the director of human resources (or personnel), the director of maintenance or facilities, the public relations director, and the director of information technology.

1.2.2. Security Requirements and Mitigating Actions. This section provides a brief introduction and overview of the requirements and mitigating actions contained within the business's safety and security program. The following paragraphs are examples of what could be included in this section:

1.2.2.1. A robust Security Awareness Program is critical to maintaining an active and viable safety and security program.

1.2.2.2. Access requirements and procedures are provided to ensure facilities are able to maintain control and awareness over all visitors into the building. Adequate access control procedures can greatly reduce the potential of unauthorized or hostile personnel from entering the facility and gaining access to employees and restricted areas within the organization.

1.2.2.3. Physical Security requirements detail physical measures designed to safeguard staff, visitors, and resources.

1.2.2.4. Information Security requirements discuss techniques to safeguard computers and information systems within the organization.

1.2.2.5. Personnel Security requirements provide processes to provide proper employee screening and ensure protection of sensitive information.

1.3. Things to Know. This section discusses some basic considerations within a typical safety and security plan and may include the following paragraphs:

1.3.1. Some requirements contained in the safety and security plan may not be able to be accomplished at the present time because of budgetary constraints. It should be noted that requirements currently not met shall be the objective to achieve within the organization's safety and security program.

1.3.2. A discussion of where emergency response checklists for significant safety and security incidents are located within the plan. Note: the development of emergency response checklists will be covered in detail within Chapter 9.

3.1.2 Introduction to Security

The next section within an organization's safety and security plan is entitled "Introduction to Security." When people read your plan, they need to understand what you are trying to do and why. This introductory section helps to accomplish this by ensuring that the reader is familiar with the concepts and terminology within the plan.

The following paragraphs show a draft format of an introductory section, along with some areas that should be included in this section.

2. Introduction to Security
  - **2.1.** Security is defined as the condition of being protected against hazards, threats, risks, or loss.
  - **2.2.** Protection. Overall protection requires defense-in-depth—the strategy of forming layers of protection around a critical resource. In the case of businesses, critical resources can include the staff, authorized visitors, customers, other assets such as valuable items and equipment, and stored funds.
  - **2.3.** Detection is the act of discovering an attempt (successful or unsuccessful) to breach a secured perimeter (such as scaling a fence, opening a locked window, breaking into a door or walls, or entering an area without authorization).
  - **2.4.** Prevention requires plans and processes that will allow an organization to avoid, preclude, or limit the impact of a crisis occurring. The tasks of prevention should include compliance with policy, mitigation strategies, and behavior and programs to support avoidance and deterrence and detection.
  - **2.5.** Reaction and Response.
    - **2.5.1.** Reaction describes how staff and visitors will initially act in the event of an emergency or crisis situation. To ensure proper reaction, increase survivability, and minimize injury to people and damage to resources, this plan provides for detailed actions and easy-to-understand response procedures that should be disseminated to the staff and exercised on a periodic basis.
    - **2.5.2.** Response requires personnel to execute the plan, the identified resources necessary to perform those duties, and services to preserve and protect life and property as well as provide services to the surviving population. Response steps include potential crisis recognition, notification, situation assessment, and crisis declaration, plan execution, communications, and resource management.
  - **2.6.** Documentation requires factual reporting of the events surrounding the incident, reaction and response by the affected student and staff, and an accurate after-action-report to analyze and improve current plans and procedures.

3.1.3 Security Risk Assessment

The Security Risk Assessment identifies potential risks and vulnerabilities to your organization and includes a fully developed Risk Assessment Matrix to rank orders and prioritize these risks. We will only look at the areas and verbiage that should be included within the plan here, as we will discuss how to accomplish a detailed Risk Assessment Matrix later in this chapter.

3. Security Risk Assessment

    3.1. A primary response step is to identify potential crises and take action to mitigate these incidents prior to their occurrence. This section analyzes the safety and security risks of the business and provides a Risk Assessment Matrix of the potential incidents and emergencies that could be experienced.

    3.2. Incidents that include sabotage and malicious destruction are as follows:

        3.2.1. Active shooter

        3.2.2. Hostage situation

        3.2.3. Violent/Uncooperative visitor

        3.2.4. Unauthorized visitor

        3.2.5. Bombs, bomb threat, suspicious packages

        3.2.6. Vehicle-borne explosives

        3.2.7. Vandalism

        3.2.8. Terrorist threats/Threats of violence

        3.2.9. Gang activity

        3.2.10. Protest activity

        3.2.11. Homicide

    3.3. Natural disasters (e.g., tornadoes, hurricanes, earthquakes, floods, wildfire, etc.) that could potentially occur in your organization's region should be listed. Note that if there is no threat of a specific type of natural disaster, your plan need not include this type of incident nor take time to address response actions.

    3.4. Biological/Chemical threats (mail handling, food-borne threats, MRSA, etc.) that could affect your company should be listed.

    3.5. Facility Disasters that could occur to your organization could include:

        3.5.1. Explosions

        3.5.2. Structural collapse

        3.5.3. Major accidents

        3.5.4. Fire

    3.6. Criminal Activity that could affect your company such as:

        3.6.1. Pilferage

        3.6.2. Fraud

        3.6.3. Records manipulation

    3.6.4. Forgery

    3.6.5. Car theft

    3.6.6. Embezzlement

    3.6.7. Computer crimes

    3.6.8. Theft and burglary

    3.6.9. Illegal drugs (selling or possession)

3.7. Personnel Problems that your organization and employees could experience. These issues would include:

    3.7.1. Gambling

    3.7.2. Disgruntled employees

    3.7.3. Workplace violence

    3.7.4. Malicious, willful, or negligent personal conduct

    3.7.5. Absenteeism

    3.7.6. Misrepresentation

    3.7.7. Sexual harassment

    3.7.8. Staff narcotics and drug use

    3.7.9. Alcoholism

3.8. Miscellaneous risks

    3.8.1. Medical emergencies

    3.8.2. Traffic and parking accidents

    3.8.3. Improper maintenance

3.9. The completed Organization Risk Assessment Matrix should be inserted in this paragraph. Again, we will specifically cover how to accomplish this matrix later in this chapter.

3.1.4 Security Aspects, Requirements, and Mitigation Considerations

This section covers some broad safety and security concepts and forms the major part of any organization's safety and security plan. Here is where the plan discusses over-arching initiatives that should be part of any organization's safety and security program. This section also forms the basis for the next several sections that will discuss the three primary areas that comprise safety and security—Physical Security, Information Security, and Personnel Security. This section should discuss specific threats that should be considered along with the responses to these threats that are designed to minimize any damage, loss, or personal injury to your business. We will cover all of these areas and how they should be organized within this section over the next several paragraphs:

4. Security Aspects, Requirements, and Mitigation Considerations

    4.1. Introduction. Security aspects, requirements, and mitigation considerations discuss the nature of the threats to be considered and common countermeasures that should be deployed.

4.2. Security Awareness Program. An extremely significant factor in the success of a business's safety and security program is ensuring an active security awareness program amongst all staff. Over time, a successful program permeates throughout the entire organization and staff, which ultimately results in a greater ability to deter and detect potential threats before they can cause significant damage.

    4.2.1. Background. Security and law enforcement personnel cannot be everywhere. As a result, the likelihood trained security professionals will be an exact location at the initiation of any incident is extremely unlikely—security awareness amongst all employees greatly increases the number of personnel who can identify potential problems before they even occur and ensure these individuals can appropriately respond and react to an event as it happens.

    4.2.2. Implementation. To produce a robust security awareness program, the organization must accomplish periodic training of its staff on safety and security. This training should include the importance of security within the organization, basic procedures to communicate the staff's vital role in mitigating safety and security incidents, and test and exercise emergency response and crisis plans.

    4.2.3. Security Awareness Program Actions

        4.2.3.1. Initial or indoctrination employee training must include safety and security training along with security awareness.

        4.2.3.2. Recurring training for organizational staff on subjects to include company safety and security procedures, crime prevention, and emergency response.

        4.2.3.3. Promote a heightened awareness to any suspicious activity and to emphasize the need for employees to report same.

        4.2.3.4. Senior company leadership must periodically cover safety and security awareness items during staff meetings and conferences to emphasize its importance in order to emphasize senior leadership involvement in the program.

        4.2.3.5. Provide special attention to perimeter security and access control issues and maintain a proactive effort to monitor visitor access and control to company facilities.

        4.2.3.6. Emphasize secure access in order to ensure staff maintains locked entryways to facilities, storage areas, and utility locations.

        4.2.3.7. Develop, review, refine, and test emergency response and crisis preparedness guidelines.

        4.2.3.8. Assess health and medical preparedness and ensure organization staff prepares necessary actions for potential medical issues and incidents.

4.3. Travel Security. This section covers safety and security tips for individuals within your organization that travel. This area may not be necessary for all organizations; however, if your company requires its employees to make frequent business trips—particularly to countries and regions outside the continental United States—this section should be included within your organizational safety and security plan.

4.3.1. General Travel Security Considerations.

    4.3.1.1. Dress. Do not wear clothing that will stand out or identify you as an American. If you are traveling to a foreign country, do some research and emulate how the locals dress.

    4.3.1.2. Valuables. Leave fancy jewelry at home and clean out your wallet or purse before traveling so that you only take the bare minimum amount of cash and credit cards necessary for the trip.

4.3.2. Airports and Airlines. This paragraph should discuss security tips for employees that must fly through airports in the course of their duties. The following are some basic security awareness tips for employees who must use air travel:

    4.3.2.1. Luggage. Attempt to pack as lightly as possible. If an individual has several bags, avoid public transportation and use a taxi instead.

    4.3.2.2. Unsolicited Car Service. Never accept transportation from a person who first approaches you at the airport, grabs your bags, and says they have a car waiting.

4.3.3. Hotels. Stay away from hotels that are in bad areas of the town you are traveling to. Try to get a room on floors 2–8. A room on the ground floor will be more accessible to criminals from the outside, and a high-level floor can make evacuation difficult in the event of a fire or other emergency.

4.4. Security Guard Force Requirements. Chapter 4 includes a detailed discussion on whether your organization should consider the use of security guards along with many of the specific issues and concerns regarding these employees. Should your organization utilize a dedicated security guard force, this section would include requirements and other considerations for these individuals.

4.4.1. Personnel Requirements. This section covers the number of security guards necessary for your organization, arming requirements, and supervision considerations.

    4.4.1.1. Manpower. This section should detail the exact number of security guard posts necessary to protect your company and its facility. As will be discussed in Chapter 4, the number of posts differs from the number of actual guards to be hired since each post may vary in the hours and days it must be manned.

    4.4.1.2. Armed Guards. This section discusses whether or not the security guard force will be permitted to carry firearms and should include any special considerations that go along with any use of firearms.

    4.4.1.3. Supervision. This section covers the supervision requirements of the security guard force. This section should include their duties, ratio of supervisors to actual guards, chain of command, and other supervisory considerations specific to your organization.

4.4.2. Security Guard Services Statement of Work. This section covers the contractual aspects relative to security guard force activities and may include the following sections:

4.4.2.1. Scope of Work discusses the particular duties of the security guard force along with their capabilities and limitations.

4.4.2.2. Authority and Jurisdiction. This section details the authority and jurisdiction of the security guard force. This will vary based upon state and federal law, agreements with local law enforcement, and your status regarding the facility and property (i.e., do you own, rent, lease, etc.).

4.4.2.3. Use of Force Policy. In the event that your organization has an armed security guard force, you will need to detail a use of force policy and ensure that individuals are appropriately trained.

4.4.2.4. Equipment, Uniforms, and Materials. If your security guard force is required to wear a uniform and maintain specific equipment, they should be detailed within this section.

4.4.2.5. Training. Security guard force personnel must periodically accomplish training to ensure they are aware of any appropriate rules, regulations, and procedures. This is critical if your security guards are armed or required to apprehend or detain individuals prior to arrival of local law enforcement.

4.5. Security Incident Reporting. This section discusses the specific process within your organization for employees to report any suspicious activities, safety concerns, and security incidents.

3.1.5 Physical Security

This section discusses the physical security requirements necessary to properly protect your organization. A physical security program should focus on equipment and documentation designed to protect your employees and organization's critical resources. Physical security will be discussed in detail within Chapter 6, but for the purposes of a safety and security plan, the areas that should be addressed within this section include:

5. Physical Security

5.1. Introduction. This section of the plan details that part of security concerned with physical measures designed to safeguard visitors and staff, equipment, facilities, material, and documents; and to safeguard them against a security incident. The following paragraphs briefly discuss what topics your plan should cover:

5.2. Security Threats. The physical security of a facility can help to mitigate, or even preclude, some security threats. Specific threats that can be reduced through more robust physical security measures includes the following:

5.2.1. Active shooter, hostage situations, and violent visitor scenarios.

5.2.2. Bombs, Bomb Threat, Suspicious Packages, and Vehicle-Borne Explosives.

5.2.3. Natural Disasters (e.g., tornadoes, hurricanes, earthquakes, floods, or wildfire).

5.2.4. Criminal Activity to include pilferage, records manipulation, theft and burglary.

5.2.5. Industrial Disasters to include explosions, structural collapse, and fire.

5.2.6. Prioritization of Potential Security Threats. The Risk Assessment Matrix of the plan should be utilized to determine prioritization of critical resources when addressing potential security threats and determining how to expend resources against what threats.

5.3. Security Design Considerations. This area covers various subcategories that comprise areas within physical security. This section looks at the necessary requirements within each of these areas, along with any design considerations to provide adequate physical security within your organization.

5.3.1. Lighting. One of the most basic (and most inexpensive) components of a security system. Carefully designed and coordinated interior and exterior lighting systems can exert a significant deterrent effect.

5.3.2. Perimeter Control. Includes elements such as fences, walls, and landscaped berms that protect a facility's potential access ways.

5.3.3. Access Control. This area includes both the use of limiting entry points, security personnel or receptionists, and automated access control systems that can include card-readers, chip-readers, and electronic locks that read information encoded on the cards, disks, or keys carried by employees.

5.3.4. Pedestrian and Vehicular Traffic Control. Closely related to access control, pedestrian traffic control covers systems such as electronic turnstiles equipped with card-readers. Vehicular traffic and parking control components also often play a role in physical security.

5.3.5. Intrusion Detection. This section includes the many types of sensors and alarm systems now available and what type of systems should be used within your facility.

5.3.6. Monitoring and Surveillance. Includes CCTV cameras and the monitors and security command centers they serve.

5.3.7. Exterior Protection includes perimeter security measures. These measures include fencing, natural barriers, gates, and exterior lighting. Exterior protection measures do not necessarily prevent all security incidents from occurring against your facility but instead they are designed to define boundaries and funnel pedestrian or vehicular traffic.

5.3.8. Exterior Doors should follow be reinforced and installed with appropriate locks.

5.3.9. Windows should be in good repair and capable of being locked. When possible or practical, windows should be installed with burglar-resistant glass.

5.3.10. Manholes, Grates, and Storm Drains can be overlooked in many safety and security plans; however, it is important they be included to ensure they are secured and do not allow unimpeded access into your organization's facility and grounds.

5.3.11. Roof Openings should be locked at all times and staff shall check for tampering and condition of locks on a weekly basis.

5.3.12. Mechanical Areas. Mechanical areas should be locked at all times and never be left unsecured.

5.3.13. Building HVAC Systems. To enhance security, Heating, Ventilation, and Air Conditioning (HVAC) systems should not be located outside the facility. If they are located outside, they should be enclosed and locked to preclude unauthorized access.

5.3.14. Fire Escapes and Building Walls should be in good repair and checked periodically by school staff for serviceability.

5.4. Access Control. That part of security concerned with preventing unauthorized access to facilities through identification of people entering facilities, admittance into the buildings, and interior movement control.

5.4.1. Building Entry. This area should cover all entrances into the organization's facilities, to include the main entrance and any alternate entrances.

5.4.1.1. Main Entrance. Each facility should attempt to use only one entrance in order to limit access and better control individuals entering and exiting the building. This entrance should be well-marked to ensure that personnel can readily identify the entry, and should be under continuous observation by staff in order to identify personnel entering and exiting the building and identify persons of concern before entry to workplaces or access to critical resources can occur.

5.4.1.2. Continuous Observation and Monitoring. The entrance should be under continuous observation by staff (either security personnel or a receptionist). Several methods can be used in order to allow for continuous observation such as direct observation by personnel, cameras, door locks with entry controlled by a staff member, alarms for any personnel wishing to enter the facility, or all of these. These items can be used in conjunction with one another to provide redundant capabilities and ensure that greater access control is provided for company facilities.

5.4.1.3. Traffic Flow for Entry. Personnel entering the facility should be directed into the reception area through either physical barriers or entry design in order to ensure that staff has visibility over all personnel entering the building.

5.4.1.4. Additional Exterior Entry. In order to limit access into the facility, staff should ensure that all other doors that allow entry into the facility are locked to prevent outside access. In the event that it is necessary to have multiple entries unlocked, there should be a method to monitor these access points (either in the form of staff or other physical security measure).

5.4.2. Employee Entry and Monitoring

   5.4.2.1. Personal Identification. All employees should have an identification badge and ensure that it is worn above the waist, in plain view. Identification badges will typically have, at a minimum, the individual's picture, name, and position title.

5.4.3. Visitor entry and monitoring system should be detailed. Some items to consider include:

   5.4.3.1. The authorization process for visitors should be specified. This process ensures that everyone entering the facility has the necessary authorization and can be validated by an employee.

   5.4.3.2. Visitor Badges. All visitors shall be provided with a distinctive visitor badge. This badge should be worn at all times, on the upper part of the body.

   5.4.3.3. Visitor ID Accountability System should typically include a sign-in/sign-out log and a system to ensure accountability over any visitors within the facility.

   5.4.3.4. Special Event Considerations should be specified to ensure that during any special event within your organization's facility, staff can continue to maintain control over all visitors and guests.

5.4.4. Vehicle Control and Parking should include considerations for both staff and visitors. Any specific parking plans, designated visitor parking slots, or other details specific to your organization should be included in this section.

5.4.5. Material Control covers any deliveries of items to your organization in order to safeguard against the delivery of contraband or dangerous items into your organization's facility.

   5.4.5.1. Any contractors with material deliveries should follow your organization's visitor access procedures, which were detailed earlier for initial building access.

   5.4.5.2. Deliveries should be monitored by a staff member at all times until the safety of the items can be ascertained.

   5.4.5.3. Material deliveries should be segregated from employees until the veracity and safety of the items or equipment is verified by a staff member.

5.4.6. Interior Protection covers physical security areas inside the actual building.

   5.4.6.1. Interior lighting provides for work, visibility to critical resources, and safety. There are several considerations that should be included into interior lighting systems, such as back-up power supplies, emergency lighting, and tamper-proof interior lighting systems.

   5.4.6.2. Interior doors should be reinforced and be constructed with hinges located on the interior of the room.

   5.4.6.3. Secure storage provides high-security storage of critical resources.

   5.4.6.4. A key control system within your organization should be developed and strictly adhered to for positive control of all facility keys. This system should ensure that all keys can be accounted for by either the individual it has been issued to or the location where each facility key is stored.

 5.5. Medical Response and Mental Health Considerations.

  5.5.1. Medical Response. Review training and staffing of any organizational medical personnel for emergency medical response to safety and security incidents.

  5.5.2. Mental Health Services. Review procedures for mobilizing mental health services for visitors and staff in the event of a crisis, and plan in advance.

 5.6. Communications

  5.6.1. Office and work areas shall have intercoms with direct connection to the reception area.

  5.6.2. The organization shall ensure that all members of the Emergency Response Team have emergency communications. Radios are highly recommended for this use, as cell phone usage may be extremely limited in the event of an actual emergency.

3.1.6 Information Security

This section discusses the requirements to provide for security of your organization's information systems. Information security deals with the protection of electronic and hard-copies of critical information within your organization. Chapter 7 covers the specific details necessary to implement an information security program; however, the safety and security plan should include the following information:

6. Information Security

 6.1. Introduction. This section of the plan discusses requirements necessary to protect your organization's information while providing for the three pillars of information security—confidentiality, integrity, and accountability.

 6.2. Server Security. This section discusses specific information security measures to protect information stored on servers within your organization.

  6.2.1. Physical Security of server areas should include necessary requirements for these areas. These requirements should include the level of security necessary such as reinforced doors, locks, alarms, and access control measures.

  6.2.2. Access to Servers. This section should discuss what job positions will typically be provided physical access to the server areas and the processes used to allow access to the information stored within the servers. This should include authentication procedures, password requirements, and other issues relating to the access of server information.

6.2.3. Software Maintenance and Updates. This section should designate the authorized individuals to maintain, update, and upload software to your servers.

6.3. Work Station Security.

6.3.1. Organizational Requirements for Employees. This section should discuss any specific requirements within your organization that employees should adhere to when using company work stations. This can include positioning monitors to minimize visual access, locking the system when not at their workspace or when not in use, securely storing portable equipment and storage devices, and other pertinent company procedures.

6.3.2. Username and Password Requirements. This section should detail your organization's specific username and password requirements, such as how many and what type of characters constitute legal passwords.

6.3.3. Hardware Requirements. If your organization desires computers to be of a specific design or capability, this section should address these requirements, along with the desired time frame to replace older systems and the maximum age of systems that should be in use within your organization, as necessary.

6.3.4. Software Requirements. This section should discuss your organization's requirements in regards to allowable software loaded on employee workstations. Areas that should be discussed include who can update and upload software applications on individual work stations, what are the minimum software applications for employee work stations, and your organization's process for employees to request new software applications necessary to accomplish their duties.

6.4. Network Security. This section discusses requirements to maintain the confidentiality, integrity, and accountability of your organization's information systems. This section should include encryption (although this area can also be discussed within the paragraph on communications security) and methods to ensure secure remote-user communications.

6.5. Firewalls. This section should designate the responsible individuals to maintain and check firewalls within your organization's information systems, along with the methodology and type of firewalls to be used, and actions in the event of a security incident.

6.6. Website/Internet Security. This section will discuss any aspects of security necessary to protect your own company's Website and access to the internet.

6.6.1. Website Security. This section should formally designate the individual (or individuals) responsible to maintain and monitor your organization's website. This section should also discuss methods to protect your website from internal and external hackers, along with processes to periodically check the integrity of the website.

6.6.2. Internet Security. This section differs from website security, in that it is focused more on employee's access to the internet and methods for individuals to securely download information without compromise to your own organization's information systems.

6.7. Communications Security

6.7.1. Encryption Requirements. This section should detail what type of encryption is to be used within your organization. Encryption affects security across many other areas, to include individual work stations, your company network, websites and the internet, and the transmission of information across email and other communications systems.

6.7.2. Remote User Communications should discuss the methods your organization secures the ability fore employees to work from home or other locations outside your company's facility.

6.8. Actions in the Event of Data Compromise. This section should not only detail actions after an event, but also include security measures to preclude such an event from occurring. These measures can include redundancies in your organization's information systems and back-up storage.

6.9. Securing Applications. This section should cover any additional information security measures not already discussed in previous sections.

6.10. Attacks. This section looks at specific attacks and actions to preclude or hinder these attacks from occurring. We look at many of these attacks in Chapter 7, so we will only list a few potential attacks and not go into detail on each method of protection.

6.10.1. Virus/Trojan Horses target a host system with applications designed to slow or stop operation of the affected computers.

6.10.2. Denial of Service is done when a hacker exploits flaws or vulnerabilities in a computer system in order to fool the location into thinking that they are the master system.

6.10.3. Theft of Information can either include physical theft (obtaining the information by using discs or portable drives) or by hacking into an organization's information system.

3.1.7 Personnel Security

This section discusses the personnel security requirements within your organization. Many organizations may choose to include these requirements within their human resources plans and procedures rather than within their safety and security plan. Regardless of where these requirements are dictated, the paragraphs listed below provide an overview of the minimum items that should be included. Chapter 8 covers the specific details of personnel security, which ensures that all hiring and retention actions across your organization takes into account employee traits and help to determine that these are aligned with your company's interests.

7. Personnel Security

 7.1. Introduction. This section of the plan discusses requirements that help to determine an individual's character traits and the process to ensure that they integrate with that of your organization. Personnel security involves three primary steps: conducting pre-employment screening, investigating current employees suspected of violating rules and regulations, and protecting employees from discriminatory hiring or termination.

 7.2. Pre-Employment Screening. This section discusses the processes necessary to accomplish a consistent pre-employment screening process for all potential employees.

  7.2.1. Desired Organizational Traits in Prospective Employees. Chapter 8 provides the process to help your organization identify these traits. This section within your plan should formally list the desired traits that your organization wishes to emphasize and look for in your employees.

  7.2.2. Methods to Measure Prospective Employee's Character Traits. This section identifies various methods within your organization used to determine how well a potential candidate matches the desired character traits listed in the previous paragraph.

   7.2.2.1. Employment Application Form. A copy of your organizational application form should be included in the plan.

   7.2.2.2. Candidate Interview. Any specific processes, questions, or techniques your organization wishes to consistently use during candidate interviews should be included within this section.

   7.2.2.3. Background Investigation. This section lists the responsible individual (or office) that conducts background investigations. Any specific information that supervisors should be on the lookout for as a result of this investigation should be discussed in this section.

  7.2.3. Compiling Information on Prospective Employees. This section should discuss any specific information that supervisors should pay particular attention to, and methods that the organization wishes to consolidate from a candidate's employment application, interview, and background investigation.

  7.2.4. Hiring Decision Methodology. This section should detail any specific instructions on how your organization wants to determine who it should hire. This methodology may include scoring processes to determine interviewees or the final selection, procedures for hiring individuals, individuals authorized to conduct hiring, or other specific processes within your organization.

 7.3. Employee Investigations. This section discusses the procedures in conducting employees suspected of violating your company's rules or regulations.

7.3.1. Designation of Authorized Investigators. Within Chapter 8, we discuss the need to establish a small group of individuals who will conduct investigations within your organization. This section should designate these individuals and the process for supervisors to contact them in order to initiate an investigation.

    7.3.1.1. Qualifications and Requirements of Authorized Investigators. If any specific qualifications or training is necessary for your organization's designated investigators, they should be listed within this section.

7.3.2. Requirements and Procedures to Initiate an Investigation. This section should detail any specific requirements within your organization for an individual to initiate an investigation. Some issues to consider can include:

- Who can initiate an investigation—can it be anyone, or does it have to be a certain level of supervisor or manager?
- Does your organization require a minimum burden of proof prior to the start of an investigation?
- If the complaint involves harassment or discrimination, federal and state laws require that an investigation be conducted.

7.3.3. Employee Rights. This section should detail the rights of employees who are either the subject of the investigation or in the role of an eyewitness. This section can vary from organization to organization, based upon your specific employee or union agreements.

7.3.4. Conduct of an Investigation. This section discusses the various aspects that should be considered over the course of an investigation and can include the following issues:

    7.3.4.1. Evidence Handling. Discussion of the methods to preserve the chain of custody and where evidence should be stored.

    7.3.4.2. Employee Interviews. Who can and should be present during the interview?

    7.3.4.3. Investigation Result and Report. Who receives copies of the investigation report and makes final determination?

3.1.8 Emergency Response

This section covers emergency response actions within your organization. This area is a vital part of your organization's safety and security plan, since preplanning and preparation to potential emergency incidents will increase your ability to respond and minimize their impact. Specific details regarding emergency response and crisis action are contained in Chapter 9; however, this section of your safety and security plan should include the following paragraphs:

8. Emergency Response

    8.1. Introduction. Directing your organization's response during an emergency situation is one of the most demanding actions any executive would need to take. This section of the plan provides tools and checklists that ensure your organization is fully prepared to appropriately respond to an incident. There are four primary areas that ensure this appropriate response: mitigations, preparedness, response, and recovery.

    8.2. Mitigations are efforts taken prior to an incident in order to lessen its impact. Many of these efforts include the implementation of physical, information, and personnel security measures based upon your organization's risk assessment and available resources.

    8.3. Preparedness provides your organization's staff with tools to prepare for response and recovery requirements.

        8.3.1. Command and Control. This section delineates the chain of command during an emergency incident. It should also detail the various roles and responsibilities of each individual necessary to accomplish tasks during an emergency. This team should mirror the Emergency Response Team that will be discussed in the next section of the plan.

        8.3.2. Communications. This section should specify the procedures to notify leadership of an actual situation, the equipment necessary to allow your staff to talk to one other during an emergency, and the limitations and capabilities of your organization's communications system.

        8.3.3. Collection and Distribution of Resources. This section identifies available resources and designates where they should be located.

    8.4. Response includes the activities necessary to address situations as they arise over the course of an actual emergency.

        8.4.1. Command and Management of Emergency Operations. This section should provide instructions and procedures that determine where the Emergency Response Team will operate during an incident and how this information will be communicated to members.

        8.4.2. Fire Management and Facility Evacuation Operations. This section should include information obtained from your local fire department, the designation of specific personnel who would assist with evacuation, evacuation procedures, and shelter-in-place procedures specific to your organization.

        8.4.3. Traffic Control Operations. This section should designate personnel responsible to maintain crowd and traffic control, both within your company's facility and on the grounds. Coordination with local law enforcement in the development of this paragraph is necessary.

        8.4.4. Emergency Medical Operations. This section should provide for the treatment of injured personnel and, if necessary, assistance to coroner operations.

8.4.5. Staff Care and Shelter Operations. The primary focus of this section is to specify your organization's process to accomplish accountability of all employees. This should include designation of the overall point of contact to consolidate the information, responsible individuals who must account for employees in individual sections or teams, and the process to filter this information up to the Emergency Response Team. In addition to the accountability of your personnel, this section should also discuss the process to provide for basic human needs of your organization's staff, such as lodging, food, and child care.

8.4.6. Facility Management and Plant Operations. This area covers any temporary purchase or construction necessary to relocate your organization, in order to maintain operations during the course of the emergency (should this be necessary).

8.4.7. Internal Rescue Operations. Should emergency response personnel be overwhelmed if the emergency extends beyond your organization, they may be unable to accomplish rescue operations in a timely manner. This section identifies teams and processes to accomplish the rescue, care, and safe removal of employees, should this be necessary.

8.4.8. Emergency Response Checklists. Your organization should develop checklists for some of the significant emergencies that could occur in your area. Checklists help people accomplish all the necessary tasks—even when they may not be thinking clearly—to ensure that damage and personal injury are minimized. It is advisable to limit the number of checklists and provide them as a separate booklet to responsible individuals. Some of the areas that should be covered by a checklist include:

8.4.8.1. Active Shooter

8.4.8.2. Hostage Situation

8.4.8.3. Bomb Threat

8.4.8.4. Bomb or Suspicious Package

8.4.8.5. Felony Criminal Activities

8.4.8.6. Biological/Chemical Threats

A draft checklist is included in Figure 3.1 to show a typical format and tasks that should be included.

8.5. Recovery occurs after an emergency has occurred and includes necessary actions to return your organization to full, pre-incident operations.

8.5.1. Damage Assessment. This area details how initial damage assessment estimates will be accomplished. It should include the responsible individuals to accomplish this task, along with the process to collect data and schedule items necessary to obtain information. This area should also include information on where to obtain detailed inventories and surveys of your company's facility so that they can baseline this effort.

BOMB THREAT CHECKLIST

Action	Responsible Agent
If Bomb Threat is received by phone:	
Remain calm and professional with individual. DO NOT HANG UP, even if the caller does.	Call Recipient
Note the date, time, caller's phone number (if Caller ID is available), time caller hung up, and phone number where call was received.	Call Recipient
Notify a co-worker to contact law enforcement and district administration	Call Recipient
Complete the Bomb Threat Checklist. Write down as much detail as possible and attempt to restate caller's exact words	Call Recipient
Immediately upon termination of the call, DO NOT HANG UP and await further instructions.	Call Recipient
If Bomb Threat is received by handwritten note:	
Notify district administrators and School Board (per district instructions)	Note Recipient
Handle note as minimally as possible	Note Recipient
If Bomb Threat is received by e-mail:	
Notify district administrators and School Board (per district instructions)	E-Mail Recipient
Handle note as minimally as possible	E-Mail Recipient
Determination to Evacuate:	
Senior Manager shall determine if evacuation is appropriate based upon receipt of a valid threat and if there is reasonable suspicion that a bomb is present. If so, notify students and staff via public address system	Senior Management
Notify Law Enforcement via 911 and request bomb squad/detector support if evacuation occurs	Secretary
Prior to leaving, staff should conduct a visual inspection—DO NOT MOVE ANYTHING IN THEIR AREA—and notify school officials of any suspicious items	All Staff
DO NOT USE two-way radios or cell phones within 500 feet of the building as radio signals have the potential to detonate a bomb	All Staff
At conclusion of incident, report total accountability to district administration. List shall include: • Total personnel • Separate list of injured personnel • Separate list of casualties	Human Resources or Employee Accountability Point of Contact

FIGURE 3.1 Draft emergency response checklist.

8.5.2. Clean-Up and Salvage Operations. This effort oversees cleanup and decontamination.

8.5.3. Business Restoration. This section covers the processes necessary to bring your business back online after an emergency situation has occurred.

    8.5.4. Customer and Client Information. This area focuses on the responsible individual or office that maintains all customer and client information. This section should also include procedures to provide the public and your customers with accurate information regarding any changes in service hours, location, or procedures.

    8.5.5. Mutual Aid and Agreement Activities. This section determines what outside agencies can provide assistance and attempts to obtain support from these agencies.

3.1.9 Security Teams

To effectively manage security, it is desirable to assign responsibilities to various groups of individuals. Some of the teams listed below can be merged with business continuity teams (if your organization has a business continuity plan) or, within smaller organizations, many of these teams may be combined with one another. In any case, each team should be aware of their roles and responsibilities, what they need to accomplish in order to prepare for a safety or security incident, know their specific objectives in the event of an incident, and what should be done at the conclusion of the incident.

9. Security Teams

    9.1. Introduction. The individual ultimately responsible for your organization's safety and security program is the overall leader within the company. To assist this individual in the implementation of various initiatives and projects, along with oversight and day-to-day management of the safety and security program, the following teams should be formed. Within each section, the following paragraphs should be included (they are not shown within each team section for brevity):

    9.1.1. Responsibilities of each respective team should be discussed.

    9.1.2. Membership should be specifically designated.

    9.1.3. Preparation Tasks should be included.

    9.2. Security Management Team. This team oversees all aspects of security within your organization, such as top-level guidance on security planning and response, communication to employees and local media (as appropriate), and direction regarding the level of response to individual incidents.

    9.3. Safety and Security Plan Development Team. This team reviews, maintains, and updates your organization's safety and security Plan. This section should include the frequency of formal reviews of the plan (normally conducted at a minimum of once each year).

    9.4. Exercise Management Team. This team conducts security-based exercises and reports identified areas for improvement to the Plan Development Team for their consideration in updating your organization's safety and security plan.

9.5. Safety and Security Team. This team identifies any discrepancies of your organization's physical, information, or personnel security measures against any requirements contained in the safety and security plan, or identified vulnerabilities to the Security Management Team.

9.6. Emergency Response Team. This team is responsible to prepare for and react to any actual emergency incidents.

3.1.10 Safety and Security Training and Exercises

To ensure that your organization's safety and security program is effective, the people who will execute the procedures must be trained and periodically exercised in order to ensure that the overall plan can be successfully put into action. A plan that only exists on the shelf in a binder, or on a hard drive on a server, is not one that will be successfully put into practice when the need arises. Chapter 10 provides specific details on how to conduct training and exercises within your organization. However, for the purposes of your plan, this section describes the various methods by which the plan will be implemented amongst your employees through training, along with testing and exercising that will ensure the plan improves over time and produces a living document.

10. Safety and Security Training and Exercises

    10.1. Introduction. Employees who will execute the organization's safety and security program must be trained for successful response actions. Furthermore, exercises and simulations must be conducted in order to ensure personnel understand their actions and that the current procedures minimize damage and injury within your organization.

    10.2. Security Awareness Training. Security Awareness is the knowledge and attitude employees possess regarding the protection of critical resources of the organization. This training should be conducted with all newly-hired employees and conducted on an annual basis for refresher training to all employees. Security Awareness Training Topics can include, but not be limited to:

        10.2.1. Sensitive or valuable material and resources that they may come in contact with.

        10.2.2. Employee responsibilities for handling sensitive information.

        10.2.3. Workplace security, including building access, wearing of security/visitor badges, reporting of incidents, forbidden articles, etc.

        10.2.4. Consequences of the failure to properly protect information, including potential loss of employment, economic consequences to the firm, damage to individuals whose private records are divulged, and possible civil and criminal penalties.

    10.3. Emergency Response Training. Employee actions to an emergency situation are critical in mitigating and minimizing damage and injury within the organization. This training can be conducted through review of emergency response checklists, conducting exercises, or formal classroom training. The following areas can be included in periodic emergency response training:

10.3.1. Specific emergency response procedures for any potential incident. This can include active shooter, bomb threat, locating a suspicious package, natural disasters, medical emergencies, or other incidents.

10.3.2. Evacuation and shelter-in-place procedures, along with training on when to use one or the other.

10.3.3. Notification procedures in the event of an actual emergency situation.

10.4. Types of Safety and Security Exercises. There are two primary types of exercises: simulations and full-scale exercises. This section will discuss processes to accomplish either type of exercise.

10.4.1. Simulation (or Table-Top) Exercises can be conducted through discussion with staff on a specific type of incident, along with the necessary response actions or through a table-top exercise, which is a more detailed simulation and covers every necessary step that must be accomplished by individual staff members. Development of these types of exercises include:

10.4.1.1. Scenario Development and Exercise Scope. The first step in the development of any exercise is to determine the scenario, along with the exercise goals and objectives. In the case of a simulated exercise, the scope will be limited so that the Exercise Management Team must decide upon the specific actions they wish to evaluate and tailor the exercise scenario accordingly.

10.4.1.2. Establish a time and meeting location for the simulation. All that is needed is an adequate conference room for all of the exercise participants and the exercise moderator.

10.4.1.3. Conduct the exercise simulation through the use of discussion and review of the applicable emergency response checklists.

10.4.1.4. Conduct an exercise hot-wash and note any identified areas for improvement within your organizational safety and security plan.

10.4.1.5. Report any areas for improvement to the Plan Development Team.

10.4.2. A full-scale exercise is much more involved, as it requires significant planning and coordination with employees and other affected agencies; however, it results in better education and training, greater clarity to identify areas for improvement, and a higher level of experience to be gained by your organization's staff. Development of a full-scale exercise should follow this process:

10.4.2.1. Scenario Development and Exercise Scope. Again, the first step in the development of any exercise is to determine the scenario and exercise goals and objectives.

10.4.2.2. Identify an Exercise Director.

10.4.2.3. Establish a time and location for the exercise (e.g., does the exercise affect only one school, several schools, or the entire district?).

10.4.2.4. Coordinate exercise details with district stakeholders. Agencies to consider in the notification include school staff, students, district staff, parents, and any affected agencies (e.g., local law enforcement, fire department, civil response agencies, local government, and School Board of Directors).

10.4.2.5. Develop an exercise timeline that includes exercise inputs and expected actions by participants.

10.4.2.6. Determine the number of evaluators and identify each individual. The exercise will require a sufficient number of evaluators to oversee all aspects of the exercise and ensure that they can control the scenario as necessary. During the course of the exercise, all evaluators will ensure that they take notes of all items they see within their evaluation area.

10.4.2.7. Determine the number of role–players and obtain volunteers to act in each specific role required.

10.4.2.8. Notify all affected district stakeholders prior to the exercise initiation.

10.4.2.9. Conduct the exercise.

10.4.2.10. Conduct an exercise hot-wash with all evaluators and participants immediately following the conclusion of the exercise.

10.4.2.11. Develop a formal exercise report and note any identified areas for improvement and superior performers.

10.4.2.12. Provide the formal exercise report to the Plan Development Team for incorporation of any identified areas for improvement into the Safety and Security Plan.

10.5. Frequency of Exercises. This section should discuss how often your organization should conduct safety and security exercises.

10.5.1. It is recommended that simulation exercises be conducted once every 6 months.

10.5.2. It is recommended that your organization conduct a full-scale exercise once every 2 years.

3.1.11 Safety and Security Plan Maintenance and Audits

To ensure that the safety and security plan continues to meet your organization's needs, it needs to be maintained and periodically audited. This section discusses these requirements.

11. Safety and Security Plan Maintenance and Audits
   11.1. Introduction. In order to continue to meet your organization's needs, the safety and security plan should be maintained and periodically audited. This process ensures that the actions detailed in the plan are being taken, and that the plan meets its intent and original requirements.
   11.2. Safety and Security Plan Maintenance. The Safety and Security Plan Development Team is the primary group that ensures the plan is maintained and kept up-to-date. The team should develop processes to identify areas of concern and shortfalls within the plan, along with methods to identify and implement corrective actions. Some of the methods to identify areas of concern may include:
      11.2.1. Findings and results from exercises.
      11.2.2. Issues and concerns brought about by employees.
      11.2.3. Emerging technologies that result in new threats and vulnerabilities to the organization.
   11.3. Audits. The Safety and Security Plan Development Team is also responsible for developing audit procedures for the plan. Some items that should be considered include methods to prioritize vulnerabilities and solutions, resourcing experts to assist in plan development, copies of the plan, and storage of documentation.

3.1.12 Appendices

There is a lot of information that is useful to the plan, but may not necessarily form a part of the document itself. This information should be included as part of any appendices and may include the following areas:

12. Appendices
   12.1. Security Terms. This section can include glossaries of physical-, information-, and personnel security terms specifically tailored to your organization.
   12.2. Passwords. This section can include specific instructions inherent to your organization in regard to username and password development.
   12.3. Other Policies not included elsewhere in the document but necessary to the safety and security program within your organization.
   12.4. Forms that are part of your organization's safety and security program.

3.1.13 Summary of Safety and Security Plan and Procedures

Formal documentation is necessary to ensure that your organization's safety and security program meets your needs. The preceding sections have described what items should be included and in many cases, provided verbiage to ensure you can get a head-start on your organization's plan. Again, it is necessary to emphasize that much of this verbiage will only get you started—it will be necessary to tailor much of the document to your specific needs and requirements, either through further research or with the assistance of a security expert. Nonetheless, this section should provide you with a foundation to begin establishing a viable and effective safety and security program.

3.2 Risk Assessment

Developing a risk assessment for your organization is probably the best starting point when you are looking to either start an organizational safety and security program or accomplish any revisions to your current plans. This is because a risk assessment helps to identify all the potential threats and vulnerabilities that could occur to your business and facility. It also provides you with a prioritization of which threats and vulnerabilities are most critical, which will ultimately enable you to determine what security measures to immediately focus on with your resources. Since no one ever has enough time to accomplish all that is necessary in a given business day—particularly if you are trying to develop a safety and security program in addition to working on your other duties—this priority can help you to identify what individual tasks should be accomplished immediately and what areas can be addressed later on. This will allow you a lot of great information in developing and initiating an organizational safety and security program, rather than overwhelming you and your employees by trying to develop an entire program all at once. Additionally, this priority will provide you with better information on who best to spend the limited money and resources you have allocated for the safety and security program.

There are several different methods to accomplish a risk assessment, to include a hazard and operability analysis (HAZOP), Fault Tree Analysis, or a Risk Assessment Matrix. The Hazard and Operability Analysis is a bottom-up method to identify potential hazards in a system and help to identify operability problems that can create the event [1]. Fault Tree Analysis examines the system from the top down and investigates potential faults in order to identify the possible causes [2]. A Risk Assessment Matrix is also a bottom-up method; however, it differs from a HAZOP in that it looks at potential threats and prioritizes these based upon their probability and impact to a specific organization or facility. With respect to safety and security concerns, the best method to use is the Risk Assessment Matrix, since many other risk assessment methods provide better information once an incident has occurred in order to ensure the event is not repeated—this is not acceptable in the case of many different catastrophic safety or security incident such as an active shooter emergency or significant loss of an organization's critical resources. With this in mind, we will show you a step-by-step process to develop a Risk Assessment Matrix over the next several sections.

3.2.1 Step 1—Determining the Probability of Threats and Vulnerabilities

There are a large number of potential threats and vulnerabilities that can occur to businesses operating within the United States. Table 3.1 shows a fairly comprehensive list of

Table 3.1 Potential Threats and Vulnerabilities to Businesses

Absenteeism	Explosions	Major Accidents	Structural Collapse
Active shooter	Fire	Malicious, willful, or negligent personal conduct	Terrorist threats/Threats of violence
Alcoholism	Forgery	Medical emergencies	Theft and burglary
Biological/Chemical threats	Fraud	Misrepresentation	Traffic accidents
Bombs, bomb threat, suspicious packages	Gambling	Natural disasters	Unauthorized visitor
Car theft	Gang activity	Pilferage	Vandalism
Computer crimes	Homicide	Protest activity	Vehicle-borne explosives
Disgruntled employees	Hostage situation	Records manipulation	Violent/Uncooperative visitor
Disruption or downtime to information systems	Illegal drugs (selling or possession)	Sexual harassment	Workplace violence
Embezzlement	Improper maintenance	Staff narcotics and drug use	

these possible threats, in order to provide you with a starting point to identify all the possible threats and vulnerabilities against your particular organization.

Once you have identified all the potential threats and vulnerabilities that could occur to your organization, the next step in developing your organization's Risk Assessment Matrix is to determine the probability of occurrence for each of these incidents. Much of the probability depends upon the location your business operates in. For example, if you operate in a large metropolitan area with high crime rates, the probability for theft, burglary, and other felony crime will be much greater than if your business is located in a rural area far from any major population center.

Although identifying an exact probability for each type of incident may sound daunting, it is not necessary to accomplish such an exhaustive research project to do this. Instead, determining the probability of each incident can be fairly subjective based on the crime rates and societal factors within your specific region of operations. Thus, identifying each probability can be simply a matter of designating a number between one and 10 (one being that the incident is improbable of occurring and 10 being that the incident could frequently occur). This identification of each individual probability can be accomplished by coordination with local law enforcement, having one individual within your organization develop the numbers, surveying several employees within your organization on their assessment of various probabilities, or a combination of these methods. Once you have determined the probability of occurrence for each potential threat and vulnerability, you have a completed list for your organization. To better illustrate the overall process of developing the Risk Assessment Matrix, we will use a make-believe business (XYZ Corporation) throughout this section. In Table 3.2, we have identified the probabilities of the various threats and vulnerabilities that could potential occur against XYZ Corporation.

Table 3.2   Example Worksheet of Designated Probabilities

Potential Threat/Vulnerability	Probability
Absenteeism	9
Active shooter	1
Alcoholism	6
Biological/Chemical threats	3
Bombs, bomb threat, suspicious packages	3
Car theft	4
Computer crimes	5
Disgruntled employees	2
Disruption or downtime to information systems	3
Embezzlement	2
Explosions	1
Fire	1
Forgery	3
Fraud	3
Gambling	6
Gang activity	3
Homicide	1
Hostage situation	1
Illegal drugs (selling or possession)	3
Improper maintenance	6
Major accidents	5
Malicious, willful, or negligent personal conduct	4
Medical emergencies	8
Misrepresentation	5
Natural disasters	5
Pilferage	4
Protest activity	2
Records manipulation	4
Sexual harassment	5
Staff narcotics and drug use	3

Table 3.2 Example Worksheet of Designated Probabilities—cont'd

Potential Threat/Vulnerability	Probability
Structural collapse	2
Terrorist threats/Threats of violence	2
Theft and burglary	4
Traffic accidents	7
Unauthorized visitor	8
Vandalism	4
Vehicle-borne explosives	2
Violent/Uncooperative visitor	5
Workplace violence	6

Now that we have determined the probability of the various threats and vulnerabilities, the next step is to determine the severity of that incident, should it occur.

3.2.2 Step 2—Determining the Severity of Threats and Vulnerabilities

This step is similar to the determination of the probability; however, in this case you will be designating a number between one and 10 based on the severity should that particular incident actually occur. One is the designation of an incident that would cause negligible results within your organization and 10 is for an incident that would create catastrophic repercussions on your business. It should be noted that although none of the potential threats and vulnerabilities are desired, their outcome on the health of your business and organization is what this severity should focus on. For example, the severity of chronic absenteeism from one employee is much less than the severity of a hostage situation that occurs within your facility. This determination should provide the severity to the health of your business and employees in relation to all the various threats and vulnerabilities possible, even though they may not be probable of occurring.

Again, to illustrate using an example we have included Table 3.3, which provides numbers for the severity of each of the potential threats and vulnerabilities that could occur within XYZ Corporation.

3.2.3 Step 3—Combining Probability and Severity of Threats and Vulnerabilities

The next step is to consolidate the information form the various probabilities and severities you have designated for your specific organization into one table. This process is very straight-forward in that you simply place all the values into one table and determine the product of for the probability and severity of each threat and vulnerability. Table 3.4 shows how this is accomplished for XYZ Corporation with our example numbers.

Table 3.3   Example Worksheet of Designated Severities

Potential Threat/Vulnerability	Severity
Absenteeism	6
Active shooter	10
Alcoholism	4
Biological/Chemical threats	8
Bombs, bomb threat, suspicious packages	8
Car theft	2
Computer crimes	6
Disgruntled employees	4
Disruption or downtime to information systems	7
Embezzlement	8
Explosions	9
Fire	10
Forgery	6
Fraud	6
Gambling	4
Gang activity	3
Homicide	10
Hostage situation	10
Illegal drugs (selling or possession)	6
Improper maintenance	4
Major accidents	5
Malicious, willful, or negligent personal conduct	2
Medical emergencies	2
Misrepresentation	2
Natural disasters	8
Pilferage	5
Protest activity	1
Records manipulation	4
Sexual harassment	6
Staff narcotics and drug use	6

Continued

Table 3.3   Example Worksheet of Designated Severities—cont'd

Potential Threat/Vulnerability	Severity
Structural collapse	8
Terrorist threats/threats of violence	7
Theft and burglary	6
Traffic accidents	2
Unauthorized visitor	2
Vandalism	2
Vehicle-borne explosives	10
Violent/uncooperative visitor	4
Workplace violence	6

Table 3.4   Example Worksheet of Combined Probabilities and Severities

Potential Threat/Vulnerability	Probability	Severity	Product
Absenteeism	9	6	54
Natural disasters	5	8	40
Workplace violence	6	6	36
Computer crimes	5	6	30
Sexual harassment	5	6	30
Major accidents	5	5	25
Alcoholism	6	4	24
Gambling	6	4	24
Improper maintenance	6	4	24
Theft and burglary	4	6	24
Active shooter	1	10	10
Biological/Chemical threats	3	8	24
Bombs, bomb threat, suspicious packages	3	8	24
Disruption or down-time to information systems	3	7	21
Violent/Uncooperative visitor	5	4	20
Pilferage	4	5	20
Vehicle-borne explosives	2	10	20
Forgery	3	6	18

Table 3.4   Example Worksheet of Combined Probabilities and Severities—cont'd

Potential Threat/Vulnerability	Probability	Severity	Product
Fraud	3	6	18
Illegal drugs (selling or possession)	3	6	18
Staff narcotics and drug use	3	6	18
Medical emergencies	8	2	16
Unauthorized visitor	8	2	16
Records manipulation	4	4	16
Embezzlement	2	8	16
Structural collapse	2	8	16
Traffic accidents	7	2	14
Terrorist threats/threats of violence	2	7	14
Misrepresentation	5	2	10
Fire	1	10	10
Homicide	1	10	10
Hostage situation	1	10	10
Gang activity	3	3	9
Explosions	1	9	9
Car theft	4	2	8
Malicious, willful, or negligent personal conduct	4	2	8
Vandalism	4	2	8
Disgruntled employees	2	4	8
Protest activity	2	1	2

The last column, entitled products, is obtained by multiplying each incident's probability and severity. This number is used to rank-order each threat and vulnerability for your particular organization. In our example numbers, the highest ranked incident is absenteeism and the lowest is protest activity. The products of the probability and severity are the primary data that are used to produce an organizational Risk Assessment Matrix.

3.2.4 Step 4—Development of the Risk Assessment Matrix

The final step is to consolidate all this information into an easy-to-understand format. Although the rank order within Table 3.4 is what will likely be used to determine your priorities within the safety and security program, it may be necessary to provide this information in a format more suitable to presentations that can better highlight the significant threats and vulnerabilities that pose the greatest risk to your organization. This can be done through the use of a Risk Assessment Matrix, which shows all the potential threats and vulnerabilities based upon their combined probabilities versus severities. A Risk Assessment Matrix is typically color-coded for easier identification and improved presentation, and identifies the highest risk incidents in red that are located in the upper left-hand corner of the matrix. As one moves toward the lower right-hand corner of the matrix, the incidents are lower based upon their risk and the color moves toward green, which identifies the incidents with the lowest risk for that particular organization. Figure 3.2 shows a generic Risk Assessment Matrix for illustration of this explanation.

In order to accomplish the actual Risk Assessment Matrix with our example data for XYZ Corporation, it is best to start with the highest and lowest values and then fill in the matrix as you work between both extremes. In our example, the highest risk is absentee-ism and the lowest is protest activity, so these items will be placed into the upper left-hand and lower right-hand corner, respectively. We will then work back and forth between our remaining high and low risks trying to match their number values for product, probabil-ity, and severity until the matrix is complete. The final Risk Assessment Matrix using our example values is shown in Figure 3.3.

Please note that the placement of many of the potential threats and vulnerabilities within the matrix may not align perfectly with their respective probability and severity, as an item's placement in relation to the other potential risks is more important than try-ing to place each incident's probability and severity against their specific number. As a result, the placement of many risks will likely be somewhat subjective–particularly when comparing incidents with similar risk values; however, the important aspect to remember is how you and your senior leadership perceive each individual item's location within the matrix and against neighboring events. As you accomplish your own organization's Risk Assessment Matrix, you will likely find it may take several attempts until you are able to ensure the location of each incident matches your feelings when comparing the overall risks of all the incidents that were developed through the combination of both the prob-abilities and severities.

3.3 Quantifying Safety and Security Initiatives

Once you have finalized your organization's Risk Assessment Matrix, you can begin to con-sider what specific safety and security initiatives to implement; whether these initiatives may include the purchase of security equipment, more employee training, or the develop-ment of more stringent procedures. Unfortunately, most of these initiatives require fund-ing, so it is necessary to determine the effectiveness of these expenditures through some type of cost-benefit analysis. This can be difficult to accomplish with many safety and security initiatives, so we will look at how to quantify these possible expenditures over the course of this section.

	Probability				
Severity		Frequent	Probable	Possible	Remote	Improbable
	Catastrophic	Potential threat / Vulnerability	Potential threat / Vulnerability	Potential threat / Vulnerability	Potential threat / Vulnerability	Potential threat / Vulnerability
	Serious	Potential threat / Vulnerability	Potential threat / Vulnerability	Potential threat / Vulnerability	Potential threat / Vulnerability	Potential threat / Vulnerability
	Moderate	Potential threat / Vulnerability	Potential threat / Vulnerability	Potential threat / Vulnerability	Potential threat / Vulnerability	Potential threat / Vulnerability
	Marginal	Potential threat / Vulnerability	Potential threat / Vulnerability	Potential threat / Vulnerability	Potential threat / Vulnerability	Potential threat / Vulnerability
	Negligible	Potential threat / Vulnerability	Potential threat / Vulnerability	Potential threat / Vulnerability	Potential threat / Vulnerability	Potential threat / Vulnerability

Extreme risk incidents

High risk incidents

Moderate risk incidents

Low risk incidents

FIGURE 3.2 Risk assessment matrix.

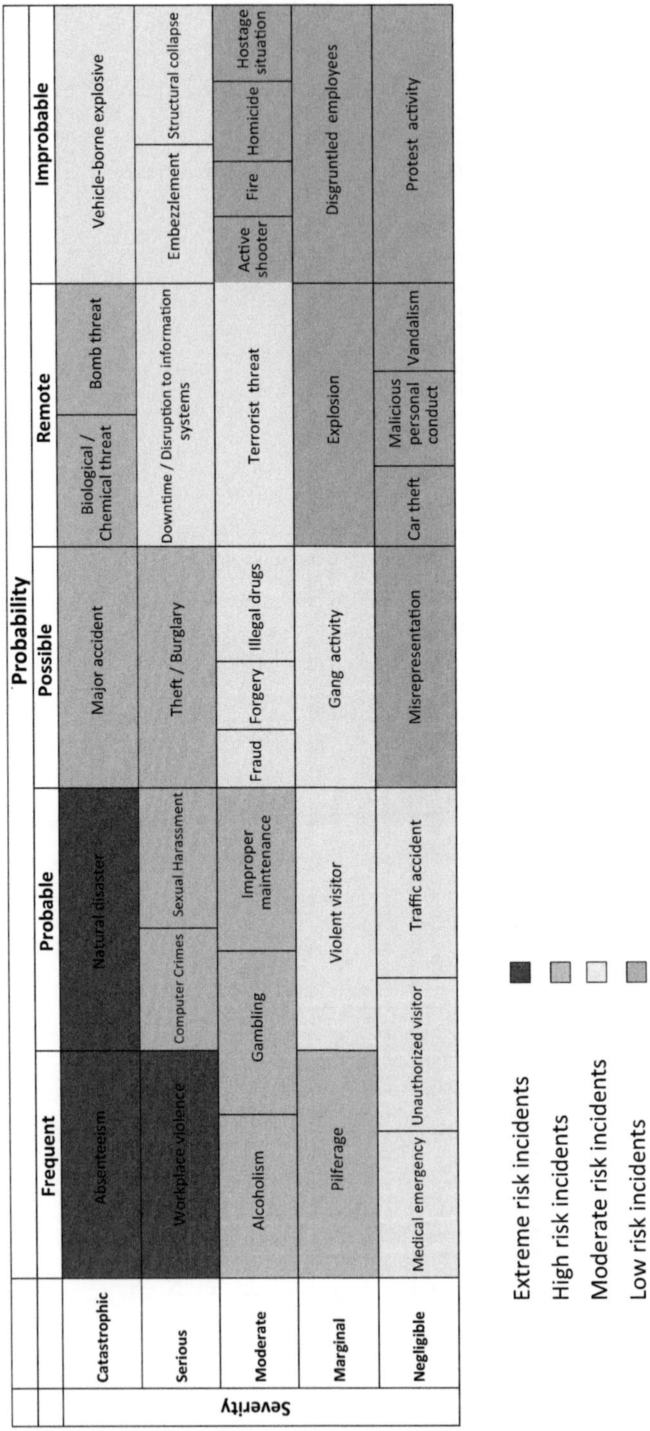

FIGURE 3.3 XYZ Corporation's risk assessment matrix.

Investments in safety and security have two kinds of resultant payoffs: an improved security posture and improved financial picture. While determining exact cost savings for improvements to the financial picture of an organization, it is much more difficult to determine cost savings based upon improvements to the security posture. This can make it difficult to justify any cost expenditures within the safety and security arena, even though it is necessary that all companies maintain a robust safety and security program in order to stay in business. This is because of the fact that if these security initiatives are properly doing their job, then nothing has happened—no security incident occurred, no mishap ensued, and no emergency arose. This makes it difficult to quantify any potential safety and security improvements in order to justify any associated costs with the purchase of these security initiatives. This difficulty must be overcome in order to ensure that your organization's safety and security program keeps pace with the continually evolving threats and vulnerabilities to business. Using the rationale that "nothing has happened, and thus no security initiatives are needed" is a trap. Having adequate security measures in-place and working to constantly improve your organization's security posture are the only real methods to minimize risk and adequately mitigate potential incidents from occurring. How, then, can you determine if your organization should expend money and resources on a particular security measure? Over this section, we will cover the methods necessary to conduct a thorough cost analyses for safety and security initiatives you may be considering so that you can better decide between security initiatives that should be implemented against potential threats and concerns, and which issues your organization should assume the risk due to the lack of any return on investment.

In order to accomplish this cost analysis, we will work through the following processes:

- Describe the project and determine the value and priority of the potential security initiative
- Calculate the costs associated with that initiative
- Determine the direct and indirect benefits of the security initiative
- Analyze the costs and benefits for that initiative

Once we have discussed each of these processes, you should be able to accomplish a cost analysis for any considered security measure and make a more informed decision on what areas to focus on within your organization's safety and security program.

3.3.1 Fully Describe the Project and Determine its Value and Priority

The first step in being able to quantify any security initiative is to ensure that you can fully describe the project. Although the necessity to provide a project description should be obvious, it is left out of the process many times because of time constraints and the other necessary tasks. Without a full understanding and comprehension of what the project entails and what purpose it should fulfill, it is extremely difficult to accomplish a thorough cost analysis. The description of the project's purpose should include a clear statement of the threats and vulnerabilities to be addressed, as well as the recommended solution or various options if a decision by higher management or external stakeholders is required.

A complete and easy-to-understand description of the issue will set the stage to capture costs, which will be accomplished within the next step in the process.

Once you can fully describe the proposed security project, it is necessary to determine the need for the security initiative. In order to accomplish this, it's important to address two aspects: value and priority. The value of any considered security project must consider the proposed initiative's time, effort, and cost to decide if the project is worthwhile. Obviously, answering this question requires a general understanding of what the initiative will accomplish and why it is important to your organization; hopefully, we have been able to do this when we described the project in the initial step of this process. It is important to remember that the real value of any project's return on investment is not determined solely by the numbers; it's also determined by the relevance, accuracy, and completeness of the cost and benefit data captured within the analysis. Next, assuming that your organization has determined that the project is worthwhile, the priority of the project should then be decided upon. This priority is determined through the use of your organization's Risk Assessment Matrix and rank-ordered priority listing of potential threats and vulnerabilities; development of which was discussed in the previous section.

It should be noted that although risk is a key factor in prioritizing any type of security expenditure, financial factors must also come into play. For example, there may be a planned IT project to upgrade your organization's entire network scheduled for the near future. If it has been determined that upgrading the security of your network is a necessary project from the safety and security program perspective, it may be more beneficial to put off the network's security upgrade and either assume some of the risks or implement some inexpensive and short-term counter-measures so that the security upgrades to the network can be included as an incremental addition to the overall IT network project. By taking into account other factors, you can achieve better cost efficiencies although still maintaining safety and security for the organization.

3.3.2 Calculate the Costs

Once the security project has been defined with a determination of its value and priority, we are now ready to calculate the costs associated with the project. When looking at costs associated with any type of security project, it is necessary to think about costs in a broader way than one may have typically done in the past, and consider costs not only through the life cycle of the project, but also include the effects upon organizational safety and security of various options that can be considered for a potential project. One option to be considered for any security initiative should include the cost of doing nothing—or the costs associated with maintaining the status quo—in order to compare the costs of the proposed project against a baseline. This choice may seem simple since it appears to be between "spending something" and "spending nothing" (although there will normally be ongoing costs related even in maintaining the status quo). These expenditures can include indirect costs based upon the associated risks your organization must assume without the security upgrade, operational costs such as higher maintenance fees, or the cost of performing a process manually (compared to automating the process) due to the use of older equipment. Additionally, if several alternative approaches are being considered, the costs and benefits associated with each of these options should be calculated and compared. Measuring all of the project's potential costs requires first identifying all these options and determining the financial outcomes associated with each.

Once you have identified all the various options, you will need to calculate the total cost of ownership of each potential project for the specific security initiative. This could be relatively straightforward, such as simply obtaining the purchase cost of a new item (if you are buying some minor equipment that requires little to no upkeep), or it could be very complex, such as calculating the life-cycle costs of a multilayered system (if you are looking at purchasing a system that is composed of multiple components and includes upgrade costs, maintenance, and other periodic fees). Regardless of how simple or complex the solution may be, it is important to capture all the relevant costs of the project in order to properly allocate the necessary budget and funds, assess project management over the course of the project, validate vendor claims, and ultimately measure the project's worth. To calculate the total cost of ownership, you should use the following formula to ensure that all the possible costs are considered and included:

Total Cost of Ownership = Cost to Buy + Cost to Install + Cost to Operate + Cost to Maintain [3].

As we discussed, this calculation can be a complex process even though this formula looks straightforward—it is not always easy to collect and organize all of the cost data associated with the various portions of the total cost of ownership for a project. Some issues and considerations to be aware of when you are trying to determine the various components of this calculation could include the following: the lack of in-place accounting processes that track overall system costs, the system in question may not be under the control of a single or centralized manager, or there is no process to track maintenance costs for the proposed initiative. Regardless of these challenges, the more complete and well-conceived your cost calculations will be, the more likely your decision on the security project will be the right one.

3.3.3 Determine the Direct and Indirect Benefits

Once we have calculated the total cost of ownership, we next must determine both the direct and indirect benefits of the security project in question. As with any costs, benefits must also be considered in a broader way—especially when looking at safety and security initiatives. It is best to start with the direct benefits, which are verifiable and easy to understand. Indirect benefits can be included later on, based on their contribution to the project's return on investment; however, it is not uncommon for indirect benefits to be 30% or more of the total financial benefit.

3.3.3.1 Direct Benefits
A return on investment calculation should justify a project based on the direct benefits attributable to that project. Many times, managers will try to justify a favored project

based on a number of intangibles that they will then try to tie into the project's direct benefits; however, these are not only difficult to measure or prove, but intangible benefits also do not materialize in many cases. The following list contains potential areas for cost reduction that may produce direct benefits from an IP-based physical security technology:

- Planning and design
- Fewer personnel
- Added space to the information systems infrastructure
- Improvements to servers, applications, or systems
- Additional storage
- Integration of systems
- Fewer calls for system maintenance and improved upgrades
- Decrease in power usage
- Less training

To use an example to better illustrate the determination of direct benefits, consider a security project that automates and consolidates an organization's alarm system. Prior to completion of the project, the alarm system had to be monitored at four separate locations; however, this consolidation project will now allow the alarm system to annunciate at only one workstation within the corporate headquarters. The result of this project will allow the organization to reduce the number of personnel monitoring the alarm system from four 24-hour a day posts to only one, which in turn will lower the direct payroll and training costs. These costs can be easily calculated to determine this particular direct benefit is caused by consolidating the alarm system.

3.3.3.2 Indirect Benefits

Indirect benefits are defined as benefits that cannot be directly observed but are nonetheless realized [4], and as such they are not so easily measured as direct benefits. Furthermore, the value of some indirect benefits may be difficult to quantify, even though it is easy to acknowledge their usefulness. For example, the indirect benefits due to the installation of security cameras include the deterrent effect toward potential wrongdoers, along with the reassurance to employees who see the in-place security measures. These benefits may be difficult to quantify; however, they are easy to understand without firm cost numbers and should still be included as additional factors.

Based upon the difficulty in quantifying some indirect benefits, they will normally require a degree of subjectivity. In these cases, often a rough "lowest-benefit" estimate will serve to provide an acceptable minimum value to your return on investment calculations. To better illustrate this, let's use an example of a project to upgrade an organization's credentialing system. This project should reduce the average wait time for personnel to receive temporary identification cards or access badges from 35 to 5 min. Although this results in a savings of 30 min to the employees who accomplish this task, most people would agree that the entire 30 min saved will not necessarily be used productively. In order to determine a more realistic benefit, management may determine that these employees are, on average, 70% productive in their normal duties, and to ensure an accurate estimate, determine that only 50% of the recovered time (or 15 min) should be used as an indirect benefit based upon the savings in time from the upgrade. This estimate would likely provide a more reasonable cost for this benefit and not overvalue this security initiative. Another method to quantify indirect benefits is to look at other proposals your company or other businesses have accomplished when considering a similar type of security project, and see what cost savings were achieved by these projects. Such proposals may provide clues as to the type of indirect benefits that are considered valid and usable for your cost-benefit analysis.

Many security projects can be used to increase efficiency or reduce labor by improving or automating various aspects of security operations. The following table shows some standard indirect benefits as a result of corresponding safety and security projects (Table 3.5):

This is just a small list of some of the possible indirect benefits that could be gained from some of the safety and security projects your organization may consider, and should help to begin to identify any other indirect benefits from a particular project.

Indirect benefits can come in the form of productivity improvements for individuals or teams, and should also be considered. These benefits may be incremental or represent a small improvement per employee, but, when multiplied across your entire organization's population or a large number of transactions, they may represent significant values in overall productivity, improved efficiency, or cost avoidance. In particular, indirect benefits that are related to corporate governance and regulatory compliance should be considered, as they can have a broad financial impact on organizations. For these reasons, it is

Table 3.5   Security Projects and Examples of Some Corresponding Indirect Benefits

Safety and Security Project	Indirect Benefits
Automated access control system	• Improved efficiency in credentialing employees • Record and identification of access to entryways • Provide uniform employee identification card (since all employees would be required to have a card to gain access) • Reduction of security personnel or receptionists
Installation or upgrade of security cameras	• Observation over areas of concern outside and inside the facility • Deterrence against unauthorized activities or entry • Capability to conduct video analytics applications (e.g., people counting, behavior tracking, etc.)
Installation of clearly marked perimeter boundaries (e.g., perimeter fencing or walls)	• Clearly defined legal boundary to facility or property • Deterrent against unauthorized entry • Limited protection against certain types of attacks (depending upon the type of perimeter boundary)
Procurement of emergency communications (e.g., facility loudspeaker system or portable radios)	• Improved communications capability in the event of an emergency • Facility or property-wide notification capability

important to take the necessary time to determine all the indirect benefits that may result from a security project.

3.3.4 Accomplish a Cost-Benefit Analysis

Once the cost and benefit data are collected for a proposed project, they can be consolidated into a cost-benefit analysis to determine the project's return on investment. Again, I must emphasize that because of the intangible benefits that result from the majority of safety and security projects, this cost-benefit analysis should not use the typical methods of comparing simple project costs or the total cost of ownership—these methods may not take life-cycle costs into account and they could ignore many of the indirect benefits from the initiative. Additionally, the value of the project's actual return should be able to show the timing of both negative and positive cash flows over the time period in question to graphically display the information, and ultimately the project's return on investment.

Over the next several paragraphs, we will work through an example to better illustrate this process. Throughout this example, we will work through the various processes to conduct our cost-benefit analysis of the proposed project that we covered: identification and description of the project, calculation of project costs, identification of direct and indirect benefits, and determination of the project's return on investment.

3.3.4.1 Example Project Description

XYZ Corporation is a large company with several different operating locations throughout the United States (the total number of employees is 4000 working at 20 different operating locations). Our example project will consolidate multiple access control systems operating at these geographically separated locations into one single system that will allow access for all authorized personnel within the company to enter any of the 20 company locations. Additionally, the consolidated system will be managed at one main office rather than the current process, which has one individual at each location manage their own separate access control system.

3.3.4.2 Example Project Cost Calculation

To accomplish the cost calculation for the various options, we first must identify all the options and the time frame to evaluate these project options. In our example, we will compare two different options: maintaining the system in its current configuration (doing nothing) and moving forward with the project to consolidate the access control system. XYZ Corporation senior management has requested that the cost-benefit analysis be developed based upon a 5-year time frame. To calculate the costs for either option, we will use the total cost of ownership formula, which combines the costs to buy, install, operate, and maintain the project. Since the first option is keeping the current system with no changes, there are no purchase or installation costs associated with the total cost of ownership—only operational and maintenance costs. The second option—consolidating the access control systems—has costs associated with all four areas that compose the total cost of ownership. Table 3.6 shows the individual calculations for the total cost of ownership for both options, and Table 3.7 shows the overall total cost of ownership over the

Table 3.6   Total Cost of Ownership Considerations and Individual Costs

	Maintain Current Access Control System		Consolidate Access Control System	
Purchase costs			Total purchase costs	$230,500
			Engineering/design	$18,000
			Software	$29,000
			Hardware	$183,500
Installation costs			Total installation costs	$104,000
			Infrastructure upgrades	$31,500
			Application integration	$62,500
			Other installation	$10,000
Annual operational costs	Total annual operational costs	$72,000	Total annual operational costs	$9000
	ID card purchases (due to loss or damage)	$12,000	ID card purchases (due to loss or damage)	$4000
	Training	$60,000	Training	$5000
Annual maintenance costs	Total annual maintenance costs	$54,000	Total annual maintenance costs	$20,000
	Card reader maintenance	$34,000	Card reader maintenance	$16,000
	System maintenance	$20,000	System maintenance	$4000

Table 3.7   Total Cost of Ownership for Both Options Over 5 years

	Maintain Current Access Control System	Consolidate Access Control System
Year 1 costs	$126,000	$363,500
Year 2 costs	$126,000	$29,000
Year 3 costs	$126,000	$29,000
Year 4 costs	$126,000	$29,000
Year 5 costs	$126,000	$29,000
Total life-cycle costs	$630,000	$479,500

5-year time period. Please keep in mind that these costs are being kept as simple as possible for the sake of our example and do not take into account several factors that would normally need to be considered, such as degradation of equipment over time, depreciation, inflation, etc.

3.3.4.2.1 DIRECT AND INDIRECT BENEFITS

As can be seen in Table 3.7, consolidating the access control system already has a lower total cost of ownership due to the significant decrease in annual personnel, operational, and maintenance costs. Now by looking at some of the other benefits of this proposed project—specifically the indirect benefits—we should be able to further determine its value.

In addition to the direct benefits of lower operational and maintenance costs per year, our proposed project also has the following indirect benefits that we will need to quantify:

- Increased employee productivity (due to less time to process into and out of company locations)
- Enhanced security capabilities
- Improved ability to meet regulatory and compliance requirements

The cost savings based upon increased employee productivity can be determined using an average amount of time that was required to enter and depart the locations with the old system and comparing it to this time required by the new system. Since the company has not yet installed the consolidated access control system, an estimate could be determined from a company that recently installed a similar system. If the difference between the current and consolidated system saves each employee an average of 2 min per individual every workday to enter and exit the facility, you can calculate a rough cost savings estimate based upon the number of employees, the average wage, the number of workdays per year, and your organization's approximate level of productivity. In our example, XYZ Corporation has 4000 employees and their estimated productivity is 80%— in order to ensure that the estimate is conservative, we will cut this number in half to 40%. We will use an average wage of $20 per h and 200 workdays per year for our example. All of these figures result in an approximate cost savings of $53,300 per year due to increased employee productivity. To determine the cost savings due to enhanced security capabilities, we could compare previous losses due to theft and compare the reduction in these losses that other businesses have experienced when utilizing a similar access control system. In our example, we'll use a figure of $5000 per year. Finally, to quantify a cost based upon the proposed project's ability to meet regulatory and compliance requirements, you could determine the amount of money spent on fines and look at how these should be reduced with the newer access control system—for our example, we'll use a figure of $2500 per year.

Now that we have been able to quantify all our indirect benefits, we can put this information together into a chart that can better senior leadership and other stakeholders the overall cost-benefit analysis of the proposed project. To accomplish this analysis, we will only look at the return on investment so that any initial costs due to the design, purchase, or installation of the system should be negated based upon the cost savings from direct and indirect benefits. An easy-to-understand method to show this analysis is in a bar chart format as shown in Figure 3.4, which uses the numbers from our example.

As can be seen in the chart contained in Figure 3.4, XYZ Corporation will pay off the initial equipment purchase and installation costs in the third year. Overall, our cost-benefit analysis shows that the proposed project will result in a total cost savings of over $250,000 over the entire 5-year time period.

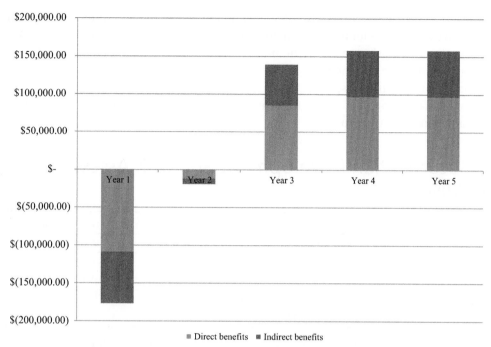

FIGURE 3.4 Return on investment of consolidated access control system.

3.4 Summary of Security Plan Development and Risk Assessment

Over the course of this chapter, we looked at how to develop safety and security plans and procedures, accomplishing an organizational risk assessment, and quantifying safety and security initiatives.

Safety and security plans and procedures are a critical part of any organization's program. In order to ensure that you can develop a working plan, we provided an overall format and verbiage for many sections in order to give you a head-start on this document. Although it is advisable to work with an expert in the safety and security field at some point to refine your plan and ensure that it fits with your particular organization and industry, this format should form a foundation of your overall safety and security plan.

Next, we worked through the development of a Risk Assessment Matrix. This product provides your organization with the basis to identify all potential threats and vulnerabilities that could occur to your business and facility. It also provides you with a prioritization of the most critical threats and vulnerabilities in order to provide you the information on what incidents you should address and mitigate through the use of safety and security initiatives, equipment, and procedures.

Finally, we provided a process to quantify the safety and security initiatives you may consider based upon your organizational risk assessment. Many safety and security initiatives can be difficult to justify solely through financial means, since the outcome of any effective initiative is for no incident, loss, damage, or emergency to occur; we looked at a process to accomplish a cost-benefit analysis while looking at all the direct and indirect benefits that could be obtained.

By developing your own specific safety and security plans and procedures and a comprehensive risk assessment, you can better identify and implement your own organization's safety and security program.

3.5 Security Plan Development and Risk Assessment Checklist

	Yes	No
Have you completed a risk assessment matrix for your company?		
Does your organization have a detailed safety and security plan that includes the various sections contained in this chapter?		
Does your organization have a process in-place to accomplish a cost-benefit analysis for proposed safety and security initiatives?		

Note: All items are listed in priority order so you should ensure each answer is "Yes" prior to expending funds or effort on the next question. This order ensures that an executive with minimal security expertise can easily move down the list in order to implement an adequate security program.

References

[1] Product Quality Research Institute. Hazard & operability analysis (HAZOP). n.d Manuf Technol Comm – Risk Management Working Group February 2014. www.oshrisk.org.

[2] Marshall Jane. An introduction to fault tree analysis (FTA), page 4. Presentation 2011. Retrieved from the web on 17 February 2014. www2.warwick.ac.uk.

[3] Connor James, Bernard Ray. Five steps to accurate and compelling physical security return on investment. CISCO; 2009. White Paper. www.cisco.com.

[4] Nucleus Research. Indirect benefits: the invisible return on investment drivers. N.d. MS Nucl Res Mar. 2004. Retrieved from web on 17 January 2014. www.NucleusResearch.com.

Recommended Reading for Security Plan Development and Risk Assessment

Broder JF, Tucker G. Risk analysis and the security survey. Butterworth-Heinemann.

4

Safety and Security Program Administration

In this chapter, we will look at various administrative areas that are necessary in order to implement an organizational safety and security program. These areas include regulatory requirements for employee safety, considerations and issues in using an internal guard force, staffing your own security guard force section, and some security metrics and measurements to evaluate your program.

4.1 OSHA Employer Safety Requirements

There are many responsibilities that employers must fulfill to meet the Occupational Safety and Health Administration (OSHA) standards and the various safety and health requirements that are in place. We will not attempt to cover each and every item (as this would require a separate book!); however, the following list provides a short summary of many of the key employer responsibilities that your organization must ensure are accomplished to meet the primary concerns within the regulations.

- Provide a workplace free of serious recognized hazards that complies with issued standards, rules, and regulations.
- Conduct examinations of workplace conditions to ensure compliance with applicable OSHA standards.
- Provide for or ensure that employees have and use safe tools and equipment. Employers must also ensure that this equipment is properly maintained.
- Warn employees of potential hazards through the use of color codes, posters, labels, or signs.
- Establish, maintain, and communicate appropriate operating procedures so that employees are aware and can follow safety and health requirements.
- Provide safety training for employees.
- Provide medical examinations and training when required by OSHA standards.
- Inform employees of their rights and responsibilities by posting the OSHA poster (or state equivalent) in a prominent location within the workplace.
- Report to OSHA any fatal accidents, or accidents involving hospitalization of three or more employees, within the required time frame.
- Keep records of work-related injuries and illnesses and provide access to this log by employees and their representatives.
- Dot discriminate against employees who exercise their rights in accordance with whistle-blower protection requirements.

- Correct violations by the OSHA deadline set in citations and submit the required abatement verification documentation. In addition, post OSHA citations at or near the applicable work area until the violation has been corrected, or for three working days, whichever is longer.

Again, this list is not comprehensive but provides a sense of the employer's responsibilities with regard to OSHA regulations and guidance. It is advisable that any safety and security procedures are reviewed against specific OSHA requirements on a frequent basis to ensure that your organization's processes meet appropriate guidelines.

4.2 Considerations and Staffing for Security Guard Forces

A major decision for any organization as it expands and grows is whether to employ internal security guards or continue to rely solely on the protection offered by local law enforcement. In order to determine your company's potential need to hire its own guards, you should consider the following factors:

- Size of the company
- Location that your company operates
- Requirements of the organization and facility

Normally, small companies need not worry about hiring an internal security guard force. This is due to the significant increase in payroll and overhead costs that will accompany an internal security guard force, especially when compared to a smaller current work force. An exception could occur, whereby a small organization may need to consider hiring their own guards; this situation may exist if your organization must protect extremely high-value resources that technology and procedures alone cannot adequately protect. If there is an exorbitant cost due to any loss or damage to these critical resources, a comparison may be useful to determine whether it is advisable to hire some security guards to provide the necessary degree of added protection. If you are unsure as to whether your organization should hire an internal security guard force, it is best to accomplish a detailed cost–benefit analysis to assist you in the decision.

Location also matters in determining the type of security force that needs to be employed. If your organization operates in a high-crime area or region that experiences relatively high threats, it may be advisable to consider security guards to provide either mobile patrols or fixed positions that are permanently located within your company's premises. The presence of these personnel not only reduces various risks against your facility and critical resources but can also provide a level of comfort to your employees in relation to a safe and secure working environment.

The last factor in helping to decide whether to staff your own internal security guards considers the specific requirements of your company, employees, and the facility in which you operate. What type of business you conduct (e.g., corporate, retail, manufacturing, storage, etc.) can affect your decision as to whether or not to use an internal security guard force. This is based on the value and criticality of the resources that you wish to protect, the willingness and ability of your employees to accomplish some additional safety and security tasks over and above their normal duties, and the amount of risk that your organization can assume based on any potential incident. We have already covered the need for some organizations, based on the critical nature of their resources, to use internal security guards. Again, this would be necessary if the value or sensitivity of an organization's resources is so great that no loss or damage could occur without significant repercussions to the overall business operations. If your organization has been able to promote security awareness among your employees, this can also have an effect on whether or not you may require an internal security guard force. In the case of an organization that has been able to promote an exceptional level of security awareness and all employees actively detect safety and security incidents, it is likely that these efforts either augment an internal security guard force so that you can lessen the number of security personnel or offset the need for internal guards entirely. The last area to consider when looking at hiring your own internal security guard force is the amount of risk that your organization can assume in the event of an incident. Some businesses cannot allow any type of safety or security incident to occur, no matter how insignificant, without some negative impact on their operations. Schools are a prime example of this, since even a minor incident such as an unauthorized visitor that poses no danger can create a newsworthy event and cast doubt on the school's ability to protect its staff and students. If your organization cannot allow any type of incident to occur, it is advisable to look at having your own internal guard force. By considering your own organization's needs based on the nature of your critical resources, the level of your own employees' security awareness, and the acceptability of some risk that could result in the occurrence of some minor safety and security incidents, you can better determine your own need to hire security guards.

There are also several advantages and disadvantages to consider, should your organization look at having your own security force. The major advantage of having internal security guards is the ability of these personnel to make decisions and immediately act to mitigate any potential emergency before the occur. A security guard can see things that cameras cannot detect, and, as such, they can immediately investigate concerns and secure an area if there is a questionable issue. Another advantage of security guards is the visual deterrent that they provide; it is difficult for any modern technology to match the impact to potential attackers and even your own employees of an on-duty security guard. Even with these advantages, the disadvantages to a security guard force are significant. A significant disadvantage is that they are costly; either by hiring the personnel yourself or by contracting the guards out to a security provider, you will incur additional costs, which can include specific equipment (such as uniforms, radios, hand-cuffs, and weapons), security guard training, maintaining the proper qualifications, and insurance. Another disadvantage is the increase in workload for other sections within your organization. In many cases; maintaining the necessary certifications, ensuring that all qualifications are met, and providing required training for a security guard force are normally going to be more detailed than that of the average employee. There are many requirements that security personnel must meet, and these items must be continually maintained and tracked—a task that can become overwhelming for smaller organizations. The last, and possibly the most significant, disadvantage of having your own internal guard force is the potential liability issues associated with these types of employees. In the course of their duties, it is likely that security guards will conduct searches of personnel, checks and searches of areas, or apprehension of individuals. In the event that these personnel are armed, they have the added potential to become involved in situations involving their firearms. All of these incidents can create significant liability concerns for your organization; as a result, it is imperative, should you decide to use internal security guards, that your organization insure itself against this liability, which will further result in additional costs along with possible legal concerns.

Now that we have looked at the various considerations, along with the advantages and disadvantages of having your own internal guard force, we will look at security guard force requirements, both for individuals who fulfill these specific duties and also for your organization as an employer of these personnel.

4.2.1 Individual Security Guard Requirements

Requirements for security guards differ from state to state; however, there are some standard items that must be accomplished within most states. An individual working as a security guard must do the following:

- Accomplish the proper security guard registration for that state or region
- Complete a minimum amount of training, which normally includes proper apprehension and arrest procedures, use-of-force training, and search and seizures
- Accomplish and pass a background check, including fingerprinting and a criminal record check

4.2.2 Requirements for Employers Who Hire Security Guards

As is the case with individual personnel working as security guards, the requirements for employers who hire and utilize security guards differs from state to state. Again, there are similarities across many of the states in that the following issues must be accomplished prior to a business being allowed to hire and use security guards:

- Accomplish the necessary application process; many states require renewals of this application every one to three years
- Develop and accomplish a training program that includes submission of a detailed training syllabus to the approving state agency (this training program should include initial and ongoing training for all individual security guards [specific number of hours differs from state to state]; in addition, the training program should provide to personnel certificates of successful completion)

In the event that your organization is considering the use of security guards who will use firearms, there are even more requirements that must be accomplished to meet your state's requirements.

- Develop a firearms qualification program and ensure that employees are properly trained in accordance with the program (this training should include periodic firearms qualification, use-of-force training, and firearms retention methods)
- Ensure that employees who pass the firearms qualification program are issued a qualification card (this card must be carried by the employee at all times while on duty)
- Possess liability insurance to protect the company in the event of injury, death, or damage to property

4.2.3 Determining Appropriate Security Guard Staffing

The last area that we will cover in regard to using an internal security guard force is the methodology used to determine how large the force should be for your organization. In order to determine the size of a security guard force, the mission and personnel duties must first be determined. The primary duty of typical security guard forces is to provide either static posts or mobile patrols (or a combination of these) within your company's facility and property. These posts and patrols are meant to prevent loss, enable response to emergencies, provide assistance to your visitors and employees, and enforce regulations. Static posts will normally be positioned at locations to enforce access control requirements, whereas mobile patrols may be conducted by numerous methods to include foot patrols and the use of vehicles. These vehicles can include automobiles, all-wheel drive vehicles, and bicycles, depending on the size of your facility, along with the terrain and weather within your region.

Once you have looked at the factors that affect the size of a security guard force, the next step is to determine the number of posts that should be manned, along with the hours that a security guard should be on duty. A security guard post is one location or area of responsibility that is occupied by one security guard individual. These posts can be manned for a few hours (in the case of an entry control position that may only be open during high-traffic periods such as morning and afternoon rush hours), or they can be manned on a continuous 24-h, 7-day-a-week basis. To ensure that you have adequate numbers of personnel needed to fill the necessary number of posts for the designated number of hours per day, you will need to ensure that you have a sufficient number of personnel to account for the hours in a work week, vacations, sick days, and other factors that may preclude an individual from working. Table 4.1 shows the standard number of employees required to properly man a variety of different hours for a given security post while taking into account standard absences.

Now that we have provided the basic information on manning considerations for a security guard force, we will illustrate this using an example. We want to determine the necessary number of security guards for our hypothetical organization, XYZ Corporation, at its corporate headquarters location. XYZ Corporation's main headquarters facility is a

Table 4.1   Number of Security Guards Required for Corresponding Security Post Hours

Security Post Hours	Required Number of Security Guards
24 h per day, 7 days per week	4.5
16 h per day, 7 days per week	3.0
8 h per day, 7 days per week	1.5
8 h per day, 5 days per week	1.1
4 h per day, 5 days per week	0.5

Muuss JP, Rabern D. The Complete Guide for CPP Examination Preparation. 2006.

large office building located in the suburb of a major metropolitan area. The facility itself is approximately 100,000 square feet with exterior dimensions of 250 by 200 ft. The building has four major entrances and is located on 40 acres of property. After a look at the main areas with which security personnel would be concerned, it has been determined that there are two primary duties for the internal security guard force. The first duty is to provide access control into the facility on a continual basis. As stated earlier, the building has four entrances, with each one located on one side of the building. Only one entrance is continually open, whereas the other three entry points are locked and secured during certain times. The second duty of the internal security guards is to conduct mobile patrols along the exterior of the facility. One mobile patrol will provide continuous patrolling on a 24-hour-a-day, 7-day-a-week basis. During normal working hours, this patrol not only helps to detect any attempts to access the grounds but also conducts checks of the employee parking lots. The second mobile patrol is only on duty during nighttime hours to augment the primary mobile patrol in detecting any unauthorized access attempts. Based on these duties, XYZ Corporation has determined that it will need the following number of security posts, along with the corresponding duty hours for each post:

Security Post Designation	Duty Hours
Main building entry control point	24 h per day 7 days per week
Secondary building entry control point	6 am–10 pm Monday–Friday
Alternate building entry control point	7 am–5 pm Monday–Friday
Rush hour building entry control point	7:30–8:30 am/3:30–4:30 pm Monday–Friday
Primary exterior patrol	24 h per day 7 days per week
Secondary exterior patrol	10 pm–6 am 7 days per week

By using the hours and days, along with the manning values contained in Table 4.1, it can be determined that 15.25 security personnel are necessary. Normally, this number is rounded up to the next whole number, so it can be determined that XYZ Corporation would require a total of 16 security guard personnel to properly man the posts listed above while taking into account illness, vacation, and other absences.

4.3 Security Measurements and Metrics

As with any area in business, safety and security should be measured and tracked—not only to assess the relevance and success of the current program, but also to identify areas for improvement. In order to accomplish this, it is important that any metric measured within your organization is able to meet the following characteristics of good metrics [1]:

- quantitative
- objective
- based on a formal model
- Has a time dimension
- universally acceptable
- Has ground truth
- inexpensive
- obtainable
- repeatable

It should be noted that one should exercise caution when collecting many safety and security metrics. This caution is that many measurements and metrics necessitate that you have an accurate method to correctly measure the metric and that the information obtained provides a valid assessment. In other words, if there are no methods to ensure that you can adequately measure the area that you are trying to evaluate, the metric may appear to be a good measurement, but the information will fail to accurately assess the safety and security effectiveness of that particular procedure or item of equipment. An example of this would be a metric that measures the number of unauthorized entries into a company's facility. Although the metric initially sounds good, the organization may have no method to accurately track this number (e.g., all entry ways are continuously unlocked; no access control is present at any entrance; and there is no method to identify an unauthorized individual, such as by use of employee identification badges). Thus, there is a danger in tracking such a metric, since it would likely result in very small numbers of unauthorized entries and provide a false sense of security that there is no issue within this area. Ultimately, this inability to accurately assess this security metric would likely result in taking no action to mitigate a significant risk until it is too late.

As we discussed in Chapter 3 in the section on quantifying safety and security initiatives, measuring an organization's program can be difficult, since security measures that are working well result in no successful incidents or attacks. This can make developing and generating safety and security metrics more difficult than in other business areas—particularly since many security experts will agree that the number of attacks, either unsuccessful or successful, experienced by a company is not necessarily an indication of how secure that organization is. Instead, an organization that is the victim of an attack can be based more upon the motivation and expertise of a potential attacker, their profile or politics, the organization being in a location that is convenient for the attacker, and so forth; or sometimes a successful attack can simply be a matter of luck. Obviously, you cannot measure luck when looking at your safety and security program; however, there are some methods that can assist in developing valid measurements when trying to evaluate your organization's program. The following steps can help to guide the process of establishing your organization's security metrics [2]:

1. Define the goal and objectives of the metrics program
2. Develop specific metrics to generate and measure
3. Establish benchmarks and targets for these metrics
4. Determine how the metrics will be reported
5. Create an action plan and ensure that it is acted upon
6. Establish a formal review process for the security metrics program

We will cover each of these steps over the next several sections.

4.3.1 Define the Goal of the Security Metrics

Since the development and maintenance of a security metrics program can take time and effort from other security activities, it is useful to define and agree upon the goals and objectives up front. This may sound overwhelming, but developing a single goal statement that clearly states the end toward which all measurements and metrics are directed can make the task easier. An example goal statement might look like this:

> *Provide metrics that clearly and simply measure how efficiently and effectively our organization is balancing security risks and preventive measures.*

Once an overarching goal statement has been developed, objectives within each area of your organization's safety and security program—physical, information, and personnel security areas—can be more easily developed.

4.3.2 Development of Specific Metrics

With formal goals and objectives formally established, a top-down approach to develop specific metrics can be used. This top-down approach should start with the objectives of each area within your organization's safety and security program, and work backward to identify specific metrics to determine whether the objectives are being met and what measurements are needed to track those metrics. For example, an information security objective might be "to reduce the number of virus infections by 30%." This would result in determining a specific metric that measures the number of virus alerts within the organization each month and comparing this metric against the previous year's baseline number.

Once the measurements and metrics are understood, a process to collect the necessary data will need to be developed.

4.3.3 Establish Benchmarks

This step identifies the appropriate benchmarks and sets realistic and achievable improvement targets. Benchmarking is the process of comparing an established performance measurement (either within your own organization, from peers within your industry, or from "best practice" organizations outside the industry). This process not only provides new ideas within your safety and security program but can also provide data to make your own metrics more meaningful. A key factor behind benchmarks is that they help to establish the achievable improvement targets for your specific safety and security metrics.

4.3.4 Determine Reporting

Obviously, no metrics are worthwhile if the results are not effectively communicated. The determination that you will need to make within your organization is who should receive this information and how widely the data should be disseminated. Some metrics may be meaningful only to the security manager or the responsible executive within that functional area, whereas other metrics may be beneficial to distribute across the entire organization. Each specific metric should be evaluated to determine who can benefit from the information and decide upon remedial actions as necessary. As the security metric program is developed; it is necessary to define the context, format, distribution, and responsibility for reporting each safety and security metric to ensure that the information is seen and acted upon by the appropriate decision makers.

4.3.5 Create an Action Plan

Once the preparation has occurred, it is necessary to create an action plan that includes all necessary tasks to be accomplished in order to start collecting your organization's security metrics. The action plan should include expected completion dates and assignments, along with the desired end date to report all of the security metrics.

4.3.6 Establish a Formal Review Process

The final step in the process is to ensure that there is a formal and periodic review process for the entire security metrics program. It is useful to look at several issues when conducting this review:

- Is there reason to doubt the accuracy of any metrics?
- Are the metrics useful, and do they meet the overall program goal?
- Is there too much effort required to measure any of the metrics, and is value derived from the effort?
- How do your organization's metrics compare with other standards and best practices?

These and other questions are important to answer during the review process in order to maintain the usefulness of collecting the information.

Table 4.2 Sample Safety and Security Metrics

Program Area	Sample Metrics
Physical security	• Equipment loss • Number of nuisance/false alarms
Information security	• Successful/unsuccessful logons • Number of computer viruses blocked • Number of virus infections
Personnel security	• Number of ongoing employee investigations • Percentage of employees with completed background investigations

4.3.7 Sample Safety and Security Metrics

We will next look at some examples of good safety and security metrics to provide you with some ideas of what can be measured. The list of sample metrics provided in Table 4.2 combined with the process for developing your own metrics, should give you a starting point with which to measure and track the effectiveness of your organization's safety and security program and assist in identifying some areas that may need change.

4.4 Summary of Safety and Security Program Administration Areas

Within this chapter, we first covered several of the OSHA employer safety requirements that must be met to ensure compliance with the safety and health regulations imposed by the federal government. Next, we covered the considerations, advantages and disadvantages, requirements, and methods to determine the staffing size of an internal security guard force, should your organization consider hiring your own security personnel. The last area that we covered was safety and security measurements and metrics. After reviewing this chapter, you should have a good background on the many issues concerning administration and tracking of your organization's safety and security program.

4.5 Safety and Security Program Administration Checklist

	Yes	No
Does your organization ensure that you meet all OSHA and other required safety and health regulations?		
Does your organization have safety and security measurements and metrics in place?		
Should your organization consider hiring internal security guard forces, does your company: • Meet all employer requirements? • Ensure that all security guards meet the individual requirements? • Have liability insurance?		

Note: All items are listed in priority order, so you should ensure that each answer is "Yes" prior to expending funds or effort on addressing the next question. This ensures that an executive with minimal security expertise can easily move down the list in order to implement an adequate security program.

References

[1] Abbadi, Zed. Security metrics: what can we measure? Presentation. Open Web Application Security Project. Retrieved from web on January 21, 2014.

[2] Payne SC. A guide to security metrics. SANS Security Essentials; June 19, 2006. Retrieved from web on January 22, 2014 www.sans.org.

Recommended Reading for Safety and Security Program Administration

Fundamentals of Protection and Safety for the Private Protection Officer by Robert J. Meadows. Prentice Hall.

Guard Force Management by Lucien G. Canton. Butterworth-Heinemann.

Measures and Metrics in Corporate Security by George Campbell. Elsevier Publishing.

Occupational Safety and Health Law Handbook by Alice H. Deakins, Barry Lopez, and Scott Nash. Government Institutes.

OSHA Laws and Regulations found at https://www.osha.gov/law-regs.html.

5 ▪▪▪ ▪▪▪ ▪▪▪

Facility Security Design

In the event that your organization is able to construct or renovate an existing facility for your business, there are many safety and security measures that should be considered as you move through the design and construction phases of the project. By including these measures during the initial planning and design, not only will you increase the ability of your organization to improve its safety and security program but you will also save a great many costs over those that would be incurred by implementing these measures once the building has been completed.

Many of the safety and security measures that result in the greatest cost savings when including these improvements during construction include most of the physical security measures discussed in Chapter 6. These security improvements include perimeter security measures such as walls, fencing, and landscaping features such as berms which are engineered earthen features designed to deny access to vehicles or personnel. Along with these physical security measures, which can be cost-effective when included during the design and construction of a facility, are some of the hardware-oriented information security measures, which were covered in Chapter 7. Although many information security measures can be incorporated at any phase in a building's construction with minimal impact on cost, there are some specific items that should be included in your design and planning for the facility. These include design considerations regarding the server room where you will store your information systems equipment, hardened and secure wiring for your information systems, and wireless networks. Of particular note, the design of a server room is critical, and, by looking at several considerations regarding the design and location of this space, you will save money and increase the reliability of your organization's information system in the long run. One consideration is the location and size of the area that will house your organization's servers and information systems. This area should be designed so that it is large enough to include all of the servers, wires, cables, and other necessary equipment—not only at the time of construction of the building, but in the future as your organization grows. One critical consideration in the design of any area designated to store your information systems is to provide adequate cooling capacity. A proper server room must stay cool and dry in order to keep all of the equipment from overheating, and in order to accomplish this there are several different options. One option is to install a raised floor to distribute cooling; another option is to use in-row cooling units. Yet another option, if possible within the layout of your building, would be to consider a higher ceiling than normal (12–18 ft) when designing the server room area to assist with cooling. Another consideration is to ensure the area will be large enough to accommodate any required maintenance of all equipment located in the room. This may include additional space for storage racks that could contain all of the hardware placed in the room and provide improved access. The final consideration in planning a server area and other information systems is to ensure the room has sufficient physical security measures, to include reinforced walls and doors, access control (e.g., card swipe or biometrics), alarms, and cameras. As discussed, the type of network that you are planning to use in your new facility can also be incorporated into the overall building design. For example, if you know that you will be using a wireless network, as opposed to using wires and cabling, this decision can be included in the planning and design of the facility. Since a wireless network is dependent upon the equipment but does not require wiring throughout the building, including this early in the planning and design phases of construction will save a great deal of money. Whatever security measures you consider during the planning and design of any facility should incorporate the principle of defense in depth (this principle, along with the other security principles, was covered in detail in Chapter 2). Defense in depth will help to ensure that you are including redundant security measures along each layer in your overall security design in order to better protect your organization's critical resources.

Although it may require some foresight in the planning and design phases of your company's facility construction, working through the physical and information security measures that should be included will save resources and provide a better building for you and your employees.

5.1 Crime Prevention through Environmental Design

To assist in determining what security measures should be incorporated into the building's design, there is an established method termed Crime Prevention through Environmental Design (CPTED) with which many architects and construction managers are familiar. The goal of CPTED is to reduce opportunities for crime to occur by using physical design features that discourage crime, while at the same time encouraging legitimate use of the environment. CPTED is a good concept for businesses, since the goal is to design facilities that offer necessary protection of the building and its occupants without resorting to the "prison camp" approach that can sometimes be seen in high-security buildings. The main idea behind CPTED is to integrate security into the overall design, reducing the negative visual impact that many security measures can provide; an example is readily apparent when one considers the different impacts of an attractive wooden fence vs the use of military-style concertina wire. As with the incorporation of any security measure early in the design and planning phase, CPTED is also cost-effective, since hardware applications are made during facility construction rather than added at a later date.

The following concepts comprise the main components of CPTED:

- Defensible space
- Territoriality
- Surveillance
- Lighting

- Landscaping
- Physical security [1]

We will look at each of these areas over the next few sections.

5.1.1 Defensible Space

To provide maximum security and control over an area, it should first be divided into smaller, clearly defined areas or zones, which describe the defensible space. These zones then become the focal points for the application of various CPTED elements. To differentiate between the level of security necessary in various areas, they are designated as public, semi-private, or private. Within CPTED, this designation defines the acceptable use of each zone and determines who is allowed authorized entry under certain circumstances.

- Public zones are generally open to anyone and are the least secure of the three zones.
- Semi-private zones are areas that are designed to create a buffer between public and private zones and may serve as common use spaces, such as interior courtyards. Although they are accessible to the public, they are typically set off from a public zone by some type of obstruction or barrier.
- Private zones are areas that require restricted entry. These areas have controlled access, and entry is limited to specific individuals or groups.

Physical or symbolic barriers divide the zones within CPTED. Physical barriers, as the name implies, are substantial in nature and physically prevent movement. Examples of physical barriers include fencing, some forms of landscaping, and locked doors. Symbolic barriers are less tangible in that they do not actually prevent physical movement. Instead, they are meant only to define a boundary between zones. Examples of symbolic barriers include low decorative fencing, flower beds, signs, or changes in sidewalk patterns or materials.

5.1.2 Territoriality

Territoriality describes an individual's perception of, and relationship with, that individual's environment. A strong sense of territoriality promotes security awareness among employees by encouraging them to take control of their environment and defend it against attack. This sense of territoriality greatly increases the security awareness among the employees in a given area, and can be fostered through architecture that allows easy identification of certain areas as the exclusive domain of a particular individual, team, or group.

Although it is easier to establish a sense of territoriality in the initial design of a facility, this concept can be promoted by using your organization's existing facility to group teams and sections within specifically designated rooms and areas. Through the use of your current building's layout, furniture, and partitions, you may be able to provide your employees with their own areas and begin to establish territoriality and ownership.

5.1.3 Surveillance

Surveillance is the principal weapon for protecting defensible space. Potential criminals are less likely to act when there is a high risk that their actions will be witnessed. Environments in which your own authorized employees can exercise a high degree of visual control increase the likelihood of criminal acts being observed and reported. There are two types of surveillance within CPTED: informal and formal.

Opportunities for informal or natural surveillance occur as a direct result of architectural design. Designs that incorporate open areas can minimize visual obstacles and eliminate concealment for potential assailants, which, in turn provides protection against crime. These open designs have the added benefit that employees will generally feel safer when they can easily see and be seen. Informal surveillance also utilizes the CPTED concept of defensible space, since the transition zones between areas provide both the occupant and intruder clear and definite points of reference to identify attempts for unauthorized entry. For your employees, these boundaries better highlight an intruder's entrance into restricted space, which in turn draws attention to the unauthorized individual and increases the ability for employees to raise the alarm. For intruders, entering restricted space that is clearly identified will spotlight their actions, elevate their anxiety levels, and greatly increase their risk of being discovered and apprehended.

Formal surveillance methods describe commonly used security measures, such as closed-circuit television, electronic monitoring, fixed guard posts, and organized security patrols. Within CPTED, these methods are normally used only when natural surveillance alone cannot sufficiently protect an area. Some areas that normally require formal surveillance methods include public and semi-private zones that are concealed from view, areas that experience regular periods of isolation or inactivity, elevators, interior corridors, parking lots, public areas of buildings accessible after business hours, and exterior pedestrian pathways.

5.1.4 Lighting

Good lighting is one of the most effective crime deterrents and, when properly used, can discourage criminal activity, enhance natural surveillance opportunities, and reduce apprehension and fear among employees. Many of the objectives of security lighting will be discussed in Chapter 6; however, with regard to CPTED, lighting can also play a part in creating a feeling of territoriality. Lighting can influence individuals' feelings about their environment from an aesthetic as well as a safety standpoint—a bright and cheerful environment is much more pleasing than one that appears dark and lifeless. Ultimately, positive aspects gained from proper lighting can generate a good feeling about your employees' environment, which then helps your employees to develop a sense of pride and ownership and leads to increased security awareness.

5.1.5 Landscaping

Landscaping design, like architectural design, plays a significant role in CPTED due to its versatility and ability to perform a variety of design functions. As a symbolic barrier, landscaping can mark the transition between zones. Landscaping can also provide a physical barrier through the use of some plants and trees. From a surveillance standpoint, landscaping can be critical when considering plant growth and the placement of plants in relation to potentially vulnerable areas. Visual corridors must be maintained in open, park-like areas as well as in densely planted areas—particularly when maintaining sight lines to critical resources or higher security zones. As a rule, visual surveillance corridors can be maintained by limiting shrubbery to a maximum height of three feet and trees to a minimum height of six feet at the lowest branches to ensure that visibility remains relatively unimpaired. A last function of landscaping in crime prevention is aesthetics, which in turn helps lead to territoriality, since an attractive environment generates a sense of pride and ownership.

5.1.6 Physical Security

As discussed earlier, physical security within CPTED is not intended to create an impenetrable fortress. Instead, the goal is merely to make penetration more difficult and time consuming for a potential intruder, which, in turn will lead to the criminal looking elsewhere due to the risks and trouble experienced; remember that degree of difficulty and length of delay are key factors in reducing the probability that crime will occur.

5.2 Conclusions Regarding Facility Security Design

Should your organization be in the process of constructing a new facility, it is extremely cost-effective to incorporate the vast majority of physical security measures, and to ensure that you take into account many of the information security aspects, early in the planning and design phase of the project. The physical security measures covered in Chapter 6 discuss what items you should consider in this early planning. Within the information security area, incorporating planning regarding your server room, information systems, and network can save you time and money.

An overall concept to consider when incorporating safety and security into your company's new facility is Crime Prevention through Environmental Design (CPTED). This method is used by many architects and looks at combining the concepts of defensible space, territoriality, surveillance, lighting, landscaping, and physical security into the planning and design of a facility to provide a safe and secure environment without compromising the building's aesthetics and approachability.

5.3 Facility Security Design Checklist

	Yes	No
Has your organization considered physical and information security measures during the planning and design phase of your facility's construction?		
Does your facility design incorporate any CPTED components into the building architecture?		

Note: All items are listed in priority order, so you should ensure that each answer is "Yes" prior to expending funds or effort on addressing the next question. This ensures that an executive with minimal security expertise can easily move down the list in order to implement an adequate security program.

Reference

[1] Gardner RA. Crime prevention through environmental design. Working paper. April 1981. Retrieved from web on January 19, 2014. www.crimewise.com.

Recommended Reading for Facility Security Design

Crime Prevention through Environmental Design by Timothy D. Crowe and Lawrence Fennelly. Butterworth-Heinemann.

Security Program Areas

When developing your organization's security program, there are three primary areas that compose any integrated program: physical security, information security, and personnel security. These areas look at the following issues:

- physical security safeguards people and prevent unauthorized access to equipment, facilities, material, and documents;
- information security assesses potential vulnerabilities and threats along with their impacts to critical information and resources; and
- personnel security ensures you hire people who will assist in meeting organizational goals and once hired, provide security to employees when carrying out their functions.

Although these three areas compose separate entities within a successful safety and security program, they must all work together in synergy with one another to provide the best possible environment for your organization. We will cover each of these areas over the next three chapters while providing the necessary details required for each of these critical areas within safety and security.

6
Physical Security

Physical security is one of the three primary areas within the overall safety and security arena, and arguably the most significant. This is particularly true if your business focuses on manufacturing or commodities, as the primary focus for physical security is on items and documentation that protect people and resources within your organization. Physical security will encompass and normally focus on equipment to include fencing and physical barriers around the perimeter of property or structures, door and window locks, lighting, access controls, alarm systems, closed-circuit television (CCTV), and safes and vaults. The other important item within physical security includes the necessary processes and procedures that provide safety and security guidance for your employees in relation to threats against your organization's critical resources—guidance that can help to ultimately heighten security awareness within the organization. We will cover both the equipment and processes that integrate into a physical security program over the next several sections; however, we will start with an overview of principles to help you in the development and implementation of various physical security safeguards.

6.1 Overview

In Chapters 2 and 3, we discussed the need to identify critical resources within your organization's infrastructure and provided you with the method to develop a Risk Assessment Matrix in order to accomplish this task. As we discussed, it is necessary to not only identify your organization's critical resources, but it is also necessary to develop a prioritized list. Again, this prioritization of critical resources is vital in developing your safety and security program, as this list will assist you in identifying what resources and areas within your company require more protection and focus—and normally indicate more money to be spent on security measures—than to protect other resources. In this manner, you will be better able to utilize your limited resources and be more efficient with the money you have allocated to safety and security. Once these critical areas are identified and placed into a priority order, the most effective implementation of any physical security safeguards is to provide defense in depth, or layering of security measures, around that asset with redundant systems to ensure better protection.

An example that should highlight the security fundamental of defense in depth, as discussed in Chapter 2, is the use of physical security measures in the protection of critical resources located on a military installation—we'll use military aircraft parked on a flight line.

As shown in Figure 6.1, there are several layers of physical security boundaries that provide security through the defense in depth fundamental. The exterior and initial layer of security, shown in blue, is a perimeter fence and entry control guards to verify

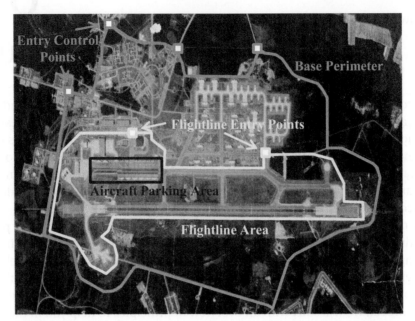

FIGURE 6.1 Example of security layers and defense in depth on a military installation.

that anyone entering the installation meets the necessary requirements. The perimeter fence, although fencing is not perfect security by any means, at least provides a clear delineation of the exterior boundary of the base and will normally be posted with warning signs to identify that the property belongs to the government. The number of access points into the installation is minimized along the perimeter where there are entry gates that allow people and vehicles to enter and exit the base. These entry gates are manned by security personnel who check identification and authorization of personnel prior to allowing access onto the installation itself. The second layer of security, shown in yellow, surrounds the flight line and runway areas in order to limit access to locations where the aircraft are parked. Access to these areas is limited and traffic is funneled through the use of barriers, fencing, and buildings—the buildings also have the added benefit to limit visibility of the flight line area from other portions within the installation. Similar to entry onto the base, entry to the flight line area has a minimum number of entry control points that are under the observation of aircraft maintenance personnel, and security patrols that are dedicated to the flight line. The final layer of security, shown in red, surrounds the aircraft parking area itself through the use of marked boundaries, where additional security patrols that are solely responsible to protect the aircraft are located.

Within this example, we moved from the perimeter of the protected area inward ultimately to the critical resources that are of primary concern. As we look at the various physical security measures over the next several sections, we will move through these layers in a similar fashion: working our way from the exterior of a facility's property, moving inwards toward the interior of the building, and ultimately reaching the areas with the highest security as they contain an organization's critical resources. With this in mind, we will begin with physical security measures placed at the perimeter of the property.

6.2 Perimeter Security Measures

As discussed in the example, perimeter security measures not only attempt to hinder access to the facility and its property, but also help to define your facility's physical limits. These limits can include areas that are necessary for the activity of the facility, such as warehouses, storage and loading areas, multiple facilities, parking structures, and any common areas within the compound. It is important to remember that any perimeter security measure cannot stop all access onto your property; however, it has several other uses and advantages that we will discuss.

In addition to providing a clear delineation of your facility's property, these security measures also ensure individuals and vehicles are funneled to areas where you can provide greater security and visibility, which meets one of the security fundamentals discussed in Chapter 2 —establishing and using choke points. These choke points are extremely useful in that they limit the number of areas that allow access to the facility, and thus minimize the costs to place observation devices along the exterior of the facility by only needing to concentrate on these primary entry points. There are also several types of perimeter barriers that can stop a vehicle from approaching the facility, which protects against a vehicle-borne explosive threat (as was used in the Oklahoma City bombing). Lastly, most perimeter security measures, such as fences and walls, provide the opportunity to clearly identify the property through the use of warning signs or notifications announcing that the enclosed area is private property. Although signage will probably not stop a motivated intruder from gaining access to your location, a clear delineation and notification along your property boundaries can deter some individuals and make it easier to stop others who may suddenly wish to create problems simply because they are passing through the area. These boundaries also clearly highlight individuals who attempt to access the facility without authorization—it is much more difficult for an alleged perpetrator to justify why they cut through a fence when attempting a break in than if there are no perimeter security measures to protect your property. Lastly, signage and the clear delineation of your facility boundary by some type of barrier can also help to cover your organization from liability issues.

There are several different types of perimeter security measures that can be used, and is a major factor to consider when you are looking at what type works for your property and what type of impression you wish to convey to the public and your potential customers. In other words, most facilities have some type of security measure to define its boundary, but what type of barrier should you use based upon your business and level of security you require? There are many options. Natural barriers such as berms, ditches, water features, and stone walls can be used, or there are many types of manmade barriers to include fencing and walls. Many of these perimeter security measures can provide a vastly different impression to the public although still meeting the need to provide some type of obstacle onto your property—an attractive pond provides the same result as a fence topped with razor wire—but these options portray a vastly different persona. It is up to each company and its unique personality to determine what solution works best for their business.

6.2.1 Natural Barriers

Natural barriers consist of topographical features that are normally an attractive feature that still deny access to your facility's boundary. These barriers include terrain, vegetation, obstacles (such as rocks, stones, walls, etc.), and water features. The obvious advantage to natural barriers is that they provide a striking and aesthetic appearance to your facility although still maintaining a significant deterrence against unauthorized entry. Unfortunately, natural barriers will typically be more expensive than manmade barriers, unless you are able to construct some of these natural barriers during the initial construction of your company's facility, or if the topography surrounding your building already has many of these features in place.

6.2.1.1 Terrain Barriers

Terrain barriers include berms and ditches that surround your facility. These types of barriers are primarily used to stop vehicle access, but will also assist in clearly identifying any people who may try to access the facility's perimeter. Figure 6.2 below shows typical dimensions of these barriers to ensure that they would stop most vehicles from accessing the area you wish to protect.

As stated earlier, costs for many of these terrain barriers will normally be more expensive than a simple chain-link fence; however, you should definitely consider their use if you can incorporate them during either new facility construction or if your facility is accomplishing major landscaping projects.

6.2.1.2 Vegetation

Certain types of plants or vegetation can provide a lower-cost alternative to terrain barriers that provide security to your property and facility, although still portraying a gentler persona to the public. Vegetation can be used to funnel people, and even vehicles depending upon the type of plant, toward primary entrances and areas that are under observation of either cameras or personnel. When using vegetation to prevent or hinder access onto your property or facility, you should consider thorny and hardy types of plants that will deter people from trying to move through these areas.

Of course, a major consideration in using vegetation is that it may take several years for these plants to form an effective barrier after they have been planted, so you will likely require another type of perimeter security measure in the interim. Another consideration is the upkeep required of many plants—it can take a significant amount of work in order to maintain plants as an attractive and useful feature. If you are considering using plants as a barrier, it would be recommended to work with a landscape designer or a local nursery in your area to get advice on what type of vegetation would work best in your environment

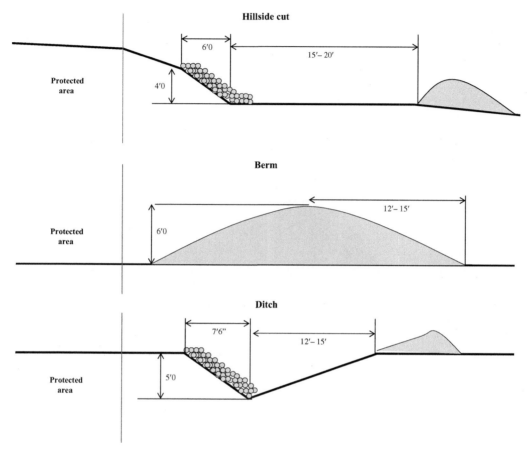

FIGURE 6.2 Dimensions of berms required to prevent vehicle access.

and region; however, there are some plants that work well in many environments and also provide a good natural barrier as shown in Table 6.1.

6.2.1.3 Natural Obstacles

Obstacles, such as rocks, stones, and walls, can provide exceptional barriers against both vehicles and personnel around the perimeter of your facility and at the entrances. They can be used in the same manner as berms and ditches, and they are an attractive landscape feature that can be used in the middle of pedestrian walkways to block vehicles from approaching building entrances. An example of natural obstacles in this manner is shown in Figure 6.3.

The last natural barrier we will look at are water features. These provide a superb barrier to either people or vehicles, and as with many of the other natural barriers, they will also funnel traffic to areas that are under observation by cameras or security personnel. Additionally, there are a variety of different water features that can be used to provide

Table 6.1 Plants to Deter Trespassing

Trees	Shrubs
Hawthorne is a dense hedge that grows 25 ft high and has sharp thorns, which can range from 1 to 5 in in length	Pyracantha, a thorny evergreen shrub, produces red, yellow, or orange berries in fall
Hardy orange is a fruit-bearing tree that grows up to 20 ft high and wide and is covered to the ground with lacerating thorns	Barberry are characterized by their distinctive three-spined thorns
Black locust produces creamy white flowers and short thorns at the base of each leaf	Some varieties of roses will grow into a dense thicket that is impenetrable to trespassers

Duffy D. Thorny solutions: bushes and other plants that deter trespassing. CSO Online; 2007

FIGURE 6.3 Rocks used as a natural obstacle at a building entrance.

FIGURE 6.4 Water features that act as natural barriers.

barriers or pathways such as waterfalls, ponds, and running streams. Two examples can be seen in Figure 6.4.

There are several disadvantages to these types of natural barriers: water features will have very high initial costs for installation; they will require a good deal of time and manpower to perform daily maintenance, cleaning, and upkeep; and there will be periodic

FIGURE 6.5 Examples of different fencing.

costs needed in order to properly maintain the water features and keep them in working order. Even with these disadvantages, many companies will still utilize these types of natural barriers because of their attractive features—particularly when compared with many of the other perimeter security measures.

Overall, natural barriers provide a much more subtle solution to the manmade barriers we will look at next, and depending upon the impression you wish to convey to the public, they can be an excellent investment to not only improve the security of your facility's perimeter security, but also to provide an attractive site for your business.

6.2.2 Manmade Barriers

Like natural barriers, manmade barriers also deny access to your facility's boundary; however, they do so with structural construction to the area. Although they are normally not as attractive, nor do they blend in with the environment to the extent of natural barriers, they are usually much less expensive and can be added to existing facilities much more easily.

6.2.2.1 Fencing

There are many types of fences that you can use should you decide upon this type of perimeter security measure, and these different types can provide very different impressions to the public. The types of fences can range from very attractive and relatively open, as is the case with wooden fencing, to the other end of the spectrum as shown by the forbidding nature of concertina wire fencing typically used by the military in hostile locations. Several different types of fencing that can provide viable perimeter security are shown in Figure 6.5.

There are several considerations for fencing to improve its ability to secure your building's perimeter. For chain-link, barbed wire, and concertina fencing, you should use the minimum gauge and other parameters that meet federal specifications. Fencing should also be securely attached to the ground; for example, chain-link fencing should ideally be placed in concrete footings and buried a minimum of 2 in into the ground. Table 6.2 contains specifications for chain-link, barbed wire, and concertina fencing.

It is important to note that fencing will not provide a serious deterrent to a motivated intruder—military security planners are advised that fencing will only delay an intruder for 10 s [1]—so your security plan should not depend solely on building a fence around your facility and thinking that your building is secure. As discussed earlier, using the security fundamental of defense in depth and having redundancies within your security system will be necessary. As with any security measure, fencing is not fool-proof; however, it does

Table 6.2 Fence Specifications

Chain-Link	Barbed Wire
9 gauge or heavier	12 gauge or heavier
Minimum height of 7 ft	Minimum height of 7 ft
No larger than 2 in mesh openings	4-pointed barbs no more than 6 in apart
Vinyl or galvanized coated	Twisted double strand
Fence must reach within 2 in of hard ground or pavement	Firmly affixed to metal posts no more than 6 ft apart

Military handbook 1013/10. Design guidelines for security fencing, gates, barriers, and guard facilities.

FIGURE 6.6 Constructed walls can provide an attractive perimeter security boundary.

accomplish several things that add to your physical security posture, to include providing a clear delineation of your facility's boundaries, controlling pedestrian and vehicle traffic, and providing a means to identify potential intruders when they climb or cut these obstacles.

6.2.2.2 Walls

Constructed walls provide another manmade barrier option and can be much more attractive than many types of fencing options. Walls will also limit visibility into your facility and grounds; however, this visibility will also limit the ability for security personnel and other employees inside the property to be able to see along much of the exterior of the perimeter. If it is necessary to ensure visibility outside your location due to the area your company is located, this problem can be resolved through CCTV cameras placed along the wall. However, this additional cost should be taken into account when considering walls as your perimeter security measure. Like many of the natural barriers we discussed earlier, these walls are typically going to be more expensive than fencing. An example of a security wall is shown in Figure 6.6.

6.2.3 Cost Considerations for Perimeter Security Measures

A primary focus of any security measure—whether you are looking at your perimeter or at other areas within your overall security system—will be cost. As we have now gone through the perimeter security measures you have to choose from, it is important to know

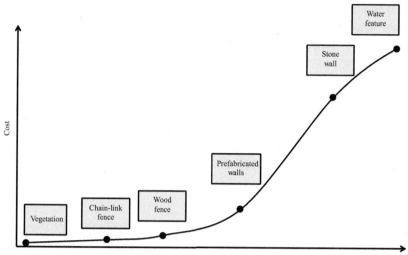

FIGURE 6.7 Relative costs of the various perimeter security measures.

the relative costs of these options. Figure 6.7 shows the costs of each of the perimeter security measures we have discussed in relation to one another.

Since actual costs can vary greatly based on several factors, such as year-to-year price increases, what region of the country you are located in, and the climate of the area you live in. The figure does not show actual costs but instead shows relative costs. For example, lower cost options such as planting vegetation and fencing are less than 1/10th the cost of the higher cost options. Still higher are options such as stone walls and water features, which are exponentially higher in terms of relative cost.

6.3 Doors and Windows

Doors and windows are part of the inner barriers of a building, and they are one of the weakest links in the security of the structure since they are much more fragile than the surrounding walls and foundation. In order to strengthen these weak links, aside from the obvious consideration that all doors and windows should normally be closed and locked, they must also be designed to resist attempts for forcible entry. This not only includes the doors and windows themselves, but also the surrounding frames.

6.3.1 Doors

Exterior doors to your facility, along with interior doors located at entrances in areas housing critical resources, should to be evaluated in regard to their structural strength and the type of locking mechanism. The doors themselves should be made of heavy and solid material, either solid wood or ideally steel. It is also a good practice that doors open toward the likely threat direction to preclude an intruder from being able to kick the door inward.

In addition to construction of the door itself; the frames, hinges, and locking mechanisms should also be reinforced. Ideally, door frames should be constructed using heavy and solid steel. Hinges on exterior doors and doors providing entry to your critical resources should never be located along the exterior of the structure (or the area from where a potential intruder would be approaching). If the hinges cannot be moved to the interior of the door structure, they should be either spot-welded or flanged (inserting a headless machine screw through the hinge leaf) in order to preclude an intruder from being able to dissemble the door and gain entry. The locking mechanism used on these doors should ideally be a dead bolt that meets a Grade 1 Specification as rated by the American National Standards Institute (ANSI).

6.3.2 Windows

Since windows are easy to break in order to gain access into a facility, they are typically viewed as the weakest point in the building's defenses. As such, potential intruders will typically look to these when attempting to gain entry to your facility. One option to combat this vulnerability is to consider placing bars, grills, or heavy screens across any windows that are less than 18 ft from ground level. Although this is one of the most secure options to protect windows, placing bars along all your exterior windows may not promote an open and inviting environment—particularly if you are in a customer-service business. If this option is undesirable, other options that still provide protection to these vulnerable windows are to reinforce them through the following methods:

- Burglar-resistant glass or safety glass that meets Underwriters Laboratories (UL) standards.
- Glazing, using either plastic or acrylic (Plexiglas), which will provide shatter resistance and in some cases bullet resistance.
- Wired glass, usually used in fire doors and windows.
- Tempered glass, which is four times stronger than annealed glass. When shattered, it will usually break into small fragments to protect against flying glass hazards, which may be a good option if a vehicle-borne explosive threat is a possibility.

Although doors and windows are some of the weaker points in any structure, there are a variety of options that can strengthen these areas and better protect your facility against unauthorized access.

6.4 Lighting

Lighting is an essential element of your physical security measures since security lighting will make detection of any potential intruders more likely. Furthermore, proper use of lighting can provide a significant psychological deterrent.

It is important to note that effective lighting is the single most cost-effective deterrent against crime since it is relatively inexpensive to maintain, and when used effectively can actually reduce the need for security personnel in some cases. Security lighting is one of the many physical security measures that should not be used as a stand-alone system, since the purpose is to provide observation to some type of response. As a result, lighting should be augmented with either security personnel or cameras to allow the detection of any unauthorized individuals and ensure an appropriate response to assess their intent. We will be examining lighting and how it improves security both outside and inside your facility.

6.4.1 Exterior Security Lighting

Exterior lighting allows observation in and around your facility in order to notify and provide detection for security personnel, cameras, or both. Adequate exterior security lighting consists of even light along areas bordering your facility's perimeter. Exterior lighting should ideally create glaring light into the eyes of potential intruders, although providing only low light in areas where security posts and patrols operate. There is a balance in the amount of lighting, however, since too much can actually become detrimental, making it difficult to see into surrounding areas. This results in standard exterior security lighting having less intensity than working lights.

When designing and planning an exterior security lighting system, the following considerations should be taken into account:

- Weather conditions that are common to your area that may affect the lighting system (e.g., fog, rain, clouds, etc.).
- Automatic lighting controls should normally be installed in order to regulate hours of operation. Since the majority of exterior lights are used in darkness, it is recommended that photoelectric cells be used since they turn off and on based on sunlight. This lighting control system is much easier to regulate than timers due to the ever-changing times for sunset and sunrise.
- Perimeter lighting should be under the control of security personnel and also be secured from attack or intentional disruption.

There are four standard types of exterior lighting typically used: Continuous Lighting, Standby Lighting, Movable Lighting, and Emergency Lighting. We will look at each of these separately.

6.4.1.1 Continuous Lighting

Continuous lighting is the most common form of exterior security lighting. This type of lighting consists of stationary fixtures and lights that are arranged to continuously flood a given area during hours of darkness. These types of exterior lights are most effective when illuminating boundaries around your facility and any entry points either into the facility or onto the grounds.

6.4.1.2 Standby Lighting

Standby lighting is also fixed in terms of its placement; however, these lighting fixtures will not be continuously lit. Instead, standby lighting is either automatically or manually turned on when suspicious activity is suspected or detected.

6.4.1.3 Movable Lighting

Movable or portable lighting employs manually operated searchlights that can be used as needed by security or maintenance personnel. These can be effective in the use of emergencies and contingencies that occur in darkness.

6.4.1.4 Emergency Lighting

Emergency lighting operates on an alternative power source, such as fixed or portable generators or batteries, and is used in the event of power failures or other emergencies.

6.4.2 Interior Security Lighting

Interior security lighting will normally serve two purposes: to provide additional lighting for critical resources and emergency lighting. Critical resources should be kept under continuous observation, by either security personnel or cameras. With the additional use of dedicated security lighting directed onto these resources, it enables improved observation and provides a level of deterrence to any unauthorized personnel who may be able to get near these assets. Emergency lighting, which again operates on an alternative power source, provides lighting to enhance safety for all employees during power outages and provides visibility to security personnel, should they need to respond to an incident during a power failure.

6.5 Access Control

In Chapter 2, we discussed the use of choke points, which is one of the nine security fundamentals. Access control is the security measure that directly ties into this fundamental by providing a process to identify the authorization of all individuals attempting to enter the facility through these choke points. It should be emphasized that access control is probably the single most important aspect of any physical security system. If you are able to account for and validate the authorization of all people entering and exiting your facility, it is extremely difficult for any individual to surreptitiously gain access not only to your critical resources but into your facility itself.

An access control system must be able to accomplish several objectives:

- Allow only authorized personnel to enter or exit the facility.
- Control access to sensitive areas inside the facility and ensure that this access is granted only to personnel with the appropriate clearance.
- Detect and prevent the entry or exit of contraband materials.
- Notify and provide information to security personnel for assessment and response as necessary.

An access control system can be as simple as checking an individual's identification against an approved list of authorized employees, or it can be an automated, computerized system that integrates employee identification cards with card readers and information databases to record each and every entry and exit for any employee. An area that is also included within the area of access control, but typically overlooked, is a process to maintain facility keys and locks—typically designated a key control system. We will look at these various areas within access control and provide you guidance on what you need to consider and what type of items you should include when designing your access control system.

6.5.1 Access Control Considerations

Before we look at specific access control systems, there are some simple and inexpensive improvements that any business can accomplish in order to provide better access control.

6.5.1.1 Limit Building Entry Points

Most facilities have more exterior doors and entryways than is necessary to conduct business and allow access into the facility for all your employees. Although all these doorways must allow for exit in the event of an emergency, the number of entry points should be minimized in order to funnel any people entering the facility through a central reception point. This area should normally have an individual (either a security guard or receptionist) who not only can verify the authorization of any individual attempting entry into the building, but can also provide a greater degree of customer service and professionalism to guests. Since a primary obstacle to minimizing the number of entry points is usually convenience among your employees, they can be better sold on the idea based upon the advantage to the company of having an individual with a professional demeanor greeting individuals who are entering the building.

6.5.1.2 Employee Identification

To better determine which personnel are authorized within the facility, and particularly in areas containing critical resources, your organization should provide employee identification cards to all your personnel and require everyone to wear these cards while at work. These cards should be designed so that they are highly visible and relatively simple; however, they should have some identifying markings to make duplication difficult. At a minimum, employee identification cards should include:

- Recent picture of the employee
- Employee name
- Organization or Corporate logo

By issuing and mandating wear of identification cards, it will become much easier to identify employees—particularly if your organization is large enough that all your personnel do not know each other. Additionally, these employee identification badges will cause many personnel to question an individual that is not wearing one, so that over time and with training, along with emphasis by management, employees will gain heightened security awareness and they will begin to assist in access control by identifying personnel within the building who are not wearing the proper identification.

6.5.2 Access Control and Individual Verification

We have alluded to some different methods to accomplish access control; however, a major decision you will need to make is how your business will actually provide access control into your facility. There are two primary methods to accomplish this: having personnel specifically designated to accomplish entry control, or the use of an automated access control system. We will look at each of these systems and discuss the advantages and disadvantages of each.

6.5.2.1 Entry Control Personnel

We have already discussed one advantage in having an individual that is dedicated to checking the authorization of personnel as they enter your facility. This advantage—adding a higher degree of customer service and professionalism to visitors when entering your facility—provides a significant reason to use some type of receptionist or entry controller; however, another significant advantage is in the improvement for security within your facility. Having an individual checking the identification of all personnel and validating their need to enter the facility is an extremely effective deterrent against unauthorized entry.

One of the business markets I have worked with is education, and within school districts, a significant safety and security issue they must face is the active shooter situation. Even though this threat continues to increase—and unfortunately occurs multiple times each month across the United States–many schools continue to allow access using multiple entries into their facilities, which violates the security fundamental of choke points. In addition to having these multiple entries, the problem is exasperated as very few entrances (if any) are normally under any direct observation from school administrators or teachers. This allows an individual to enter the school and gain access directly into classrooms and the students before anybody would even be aware the perpetrator is inside the facility. By limiting the number of entries into a school and posting individuals to stand at these entrances during high-traffic periods in order to validate the authorization of the personnel moving into and out of the building, this practice can greatly deter such a catastrophic incident from occurring.

In the case of your organization and the decision to utilize a receptionist, there are some disadvantages to having an individual posted to check authorization—the main issue being cost. If your facility is unable to limit the number of entrances, the costs of having entry control personnel or receptionists located at each area can quickly become cost-prohibitive. The costs can also be prohibitive if your business is small, since you may have to hire an additional employee to act as a receptionist, which could be a significant burden on an already tiny budget. If one of these reasons or another applies, the addition of a receptionist or entry controllers may not viable for your business, so another access control option to consider is the use of an automated access control system.

6.5.2.2 Automated Access Control System

The automated access control system is another option when looking to improve your entry control processes. Automated access control alleviates the need to hire a full-time receptionist or entry controller, and instead determines the authorization of an individual through the use of some type of credential, such as keys, tokens, or transmitters. The most effective credential in this type of system is photo identification card that can double as your employee ID. This photo identification card is encoded with each employee's personnel information. Each exterior entrance to your facility, along with any entry into restricted areas, will have some type of card reader and key-card entry. These card readers can work by a variety of methods such as a card swipe, card swipe plus a Personal Identification Number (PIN), or combined with the use of biometrics identification (e.g., voiceprint, fingerprint, retinal scan, etc.).

As with any process, there are advantages and disadvantages associated with an automated access control system. We will first look at the advantages. A significant advantage of the automated access control system is the visibility that it provides on your employees. These systems record not only every individual's entry and exit for any doorway with the installed card reader, but most systems will also record any door openings. This can provide an exceptional record of unauthorized entry, potential issues with employee theft, and employee attendance. Another advantage, as discussed earlier, is that the identification cards can (and should) double as your organization's employee identification card. This is a minor cost savings since your organization does not need to procure separate employee ID cards, although it should be noted that access control cards will normally be more expensive than a standard identification card. The last advantage we will discuss is that an automated access control system is usually going to be cheaper than having to hire additional employees as receptionists whose sole purpose is to check and validate identification at every entrance. With the advantages, however, there are several disadvantages to this type of system. The automated access system does not work well if your business has a lot of visitors, since the only access to the facility should be through the card readers and identification cards. If your business has a significant number of visitors, you would either need to have a telephone located at an entrance where they could contact the employee they wish to visit, or your business could provide one entrance that has a receptionist for any visitors. With the first option, a telephone may not portray a very personal touch. There will also be security issues since you would need to post some type of employee roster with telephone numbers. With the second option, you have just incurred the additional costs that you may have been hoping to save due to the need of this additional employee. Another disadvantage of the automated access control system is the accountability that must be required for the employee ID cards. If an employee loses their card or if they are leaving employment with your company, there must be several tasks that must now be accomplished. There needs to be a process to ensure the invalid cards are turned off in the system; cards must be turned in prior to an employee's departure from the company, and the information for that particular employee contained in the automated access control database must be deleted in order to ensure that access cannot be granted to any individual no longer working for the company. These tasks require additional work to establish and maintain a tracking system to ensure employees who have departed, particularly if they do so under less than desirable circumstances, do not have continued access to the company and its facilities. This accountability can definitely be a

	Security personnel / receptionist	Automated access control system
Does your facility have multiple entrances and exits that cannot be minimized?	Con	Pro
Is your business small (to where hiring an additional employee creates a severe problem)?	Con	Pro
Do you wish to provide a more personal touch to visitors entering your business facility?	Pro	Con
Do you have multiple areas that require different levels of authorization due to security clearance or other issues?	Con	Pro
Do you have a lot of visitors to your business facility?	Pro	Con

FIGURE 6.8 Pros and cons between personnel acting as entry controllers and automated access control systems.

challenging task if your company has a large turnover of employees or other authorized personnel who require access to your facilities (such as schools, universities, and public institutions).

The following matrix in Figure 6.8 provides a summary between the two options for access control: using security personnel or a receptionist and an automated access control system. This matrix lists the pros and cons of both options, based upon the advantages and disadvantages we have discussed.

6.6 Alarm Systems

Alarm systems are a standard item within any organization's security system and are the primary method to provide notification, another of the nine security fundamentals. The basic operation of any good alarm system is to provide this needed notification of any unauthorized attempt to gain access to a building, room, or specific piece of equipment. This is normally accomplished by detecting changes in the environment around the object or by detecting a break in some type of pathway (e.g., electrical, infrared, etc.). We will look at the various considerations you should look at when determining when to use an alarm system and what type of system will work best in a particular application.

Most people are familiar with alarm systems; however, there are several things to consider before you decide to utilize one in your overall security program.

- What risk or vulnerability you are protecting against
- Past history of any burglary, unauthorized entry, or vandalism
- Type of sensors needed based upon their location and the environment

- Are tamper resistance or tamper-indicating devices necessary in the particular application
- Who will be notified of an alarm and what is the response time to the location
- Cost-benefit analysis

Alarm systems are primarily used to protect critical resources or at least the areas surrounding these assets; however, like many other security measures, an alarm system is useless unless it is used in conjunction with other systems. For example, if an alarm sounds but does not provide any type of notification to a response force, the usefulness of the alarm is negated. This will typically make an alarm system more expensive than the initial installation cost due to ongoing costs to ensure notification, and these costs should be factored in as you consider whether alarm systems will be used.

One of the best alarm systems I saw during my career in the U.S. military was in the use of animals as part of an integrated security system. Most people are familiar with the use of sentry dogs in the military, and these are extremely effective. I participated in several exercises with U.S. Army Special Forces personnel who acted as aggressors in simulated war games. In these exercises, these highly-trained personnel attempted to attack and damage areas we were tasked to guard. At the conclusion of these exercises, these Special Forces professionals would state that the single greatest challenge to their ability to infiltrate and enter any secured areas were sentry dogs. Their sense of smell and ability to detect movement in all weather and at any time of day are a great deterrent to a potential intruder. In addition to sentry dogs, there are other animals that have been used as early warning alarm systems. One such animal that is not normally associated with security, but occasionally used, are geese. Brazil uses geese that act as their primary alarm system along prison boundaries, and several European nations also have geese to act as sentry alarms at military areas. The point here is that you may be able to utilize some unique solutions to provide an inexpensive but effective alarm system for your facility.

6.6.1 Alarm Sensors

The type of alarm sensor to be used can vary throughout your overall system, as each individual sensor depends upon the object it is meant to protect, the area or space, and the perimeter surrounding the object. Basic principles of the different types of alarm sensors include:

- Breaking an electrical current
- Interruption of a light beam
- Detection of sound or vibration
- Detecting a change in capacitance due to the penetration of an electrostatic field
- Detecting changes in imagery

With these principles in mind, you should make a quick analysis of the area that the alarm sensor will be operating in. For example, if there is a great deal of noise in the area, even during nonworking hours in places such as utility areas, where equipment or other machinery must be in continuous operation, an alarm system that detects noise would probably not be your best option. Another example is if the sensor will be operating outdoors and the area of the country your company is located in can experience severe weather on a fairly frequent basis, the use of an alarm system sensor that detects motion changes through the use of cameras would not be a good choice. Table 6.3 provides a list of some alarm sensors and where they are typically designed to operate.

Table 6.3 Alarm Sensors and Designed Operating Environment

Exterior Alarm Sensors	Interior Alarm Sensors
Buried line sensors are in the ground, usually along the facility's perimeter. Various types of buried line sensors are available • Pressure or seismic sensors respond to disturbances in the soil • Magnetic field sensors respond to changes in the local magnetic field caused by movement of nearby metallic objects • Ported coaxial cables respond to motion through a high conductivity near the cables • Fiber-optic cables are very sensitive and respond to movement above the wires through changes in their frequency response due to minute bending of the wires	Boundary protection sensors are used to protect openings into the facility such as windows, doors, vents, and skylights • Electromechanical switches use a magnet that breaks a circuit when the door or window is opened • Metallic foil, or window tape, is used on glass surfaces and alarms when broken
Fence sensors are mounted or attached to the fence to detect motion or shock caused by an intruder climbing or cutting the fence • Fence-disturbance sensors are attached to the fence and are sensitive to vibration • Taut-wire sensors use material to form the fence itself and detect separation or cutting of material	Area and space protection sensors provide invisible means of detection for interior spaces • Photoelectric sensor, or electric eye, transmit an electric beam and alarm when the beam circuit is broken • Motion detection devices detect motion through changes in either radio frequencies or infrared
Freestanding sensors are mounted on a support in a clear zone • Active infrared sensors transmit an infrared (IR) beam and the alarm is activated when the beam is broken • Passive infrared sensors detect thermal energy from intruders • Microwave sensors detect changes in the radio frequencies between the sensors • Video motion sensors detect changes in the pictures from CCTV	Object protection sensors detect the activity at a single location, such as a desk or safe • Capacitance alarm systems establish an electrical circuit between the protected metal object and control unit to detect changes in the circuit • Vibration detection systems detect any vibration or sound on the protected item
Dual technology sensors utilize different detection capabilities in order to reduce false alarms	Duress alarms may be fixed or portable for use by employees to signal a life-threatening emergency

Muuss JP, Rabern D. The complete guide for CPP examination preparation. 2006.

6.6.2 Fire Alarm Systems

Although the main emphasis of this book is primarily meant to provide information on security systems, your fire alarm system cannot be neglected. This system must meet minimum building and fire codes for your area; however, there are many additional options that can be included in your system above and beyond most minimum requirements. The system that you select, along with the variety of options you choose to include, depend upon the impact to your business that a fire could cause (for example, a brick-making company may not see as much damage as a paper manufacturing business), what critical resources you plan on protecting, and the overall cost of the system options. For example, if your company deals primarily with information that is kept on computer servers outside your primary facility, you may only require a system that meets the minimum requirements. On the other hand, if your company manufactures hardware and has all your tools, equipment, and material stock in the same building as your administrative offices, you may require some additional options included in your fire alarm system.

The primary purpose of a fire alarm system is to provide early warning in the event of a fire so that building occupants are able to reach safety. Fire alarm systems can also perform several other functions, to include sending alert notifications to the fire department, making an initial notification to building maintenance staff prior to sounding the general alarm, automatically engaging fire suppression systems, and the implementation of building safety measures to minimize the spread of the fire (e.g., recall elevators, activate smoke exhaust systems to ventilate a fire and reduce heat buildup, and activate equipment to pressurize stairwells and shut down recirculating air systems). Again, you will need to evaluate the potential loss to your company in the event of a fire and conduct a cost-benefit analysis against the price of many of these options to determine the system that best fits your company's needs.

6.6.3 Alarm Monitoring Systems

The purpose of an alarm is to provide notification of a possible intruder; however, without some type of response to check out the alarm, the overall system is useless. This is where an alarm monitoring system comes into place.

The alarm monitoring system alerts the proper authorities to stop a crime in progress or lead to the apprehension of the intruder. There are two general types of alarm monitoring systems: a Local Alarm System and a Central Alarm System. We will look at each of these in turn.

6.6.3.1 Local Alarm System

A local alarm system results in some type of visual alarm, such as a bell, horn, siren, or flashing light that only occurs at the facility experiencing the alarm. This notification provides security personnel within the area of an incident so that they can respond. Although this system provides deterrence to a possible intruder, it is useless if there are no personnel who can respond to the alarm. A good use of a local alarm is to provide warning of a fire or other type of safety incident, which requires action by the employees in the immediate area.

6.6.3.2 Central Alarm System

A Central Alarm System transmits the alarm signal to a central station, usually located outside the immediate business establishment. This central station should be monitored 24 h a day to supervise, record, and maintain any alarms. Upon receipt of an alarm, the central station notifies the proper authorities, such as fire or police, to respond to the incident.

6.7 Closed-Circuit Television

Closed-circuit television, more commonly known by its acronym CCTV, is another security measure that can augment any physical security system. Like many of the security measures we discuss, however, CCTV cannot be the only item or act as the only protection asset within your system. Additionally, if cameras cannot be kept under continuous observation—ideally by an individual or at a minimum by recording their output—other security measures should be considered instead of CCTV. I have come across many individuals throughout my career who believe that having a camera, even if it is not kept under observation, can provide a deterrent sufficient enough to alleviate all their other security needs. Although the deterrent value of a camera is valid, simply having a camera will not outweigh the actual cost of the installation and maintenance. For example, I have seen many organizations that have had cameras that are not under any observation, or in some cases, not even working. Although the deterrent effect may work for a short time, in the vast majority of these instances the personnel within the facility usually knew within a few days that the cameras were not working, and thus were not going to catch anyone. These cameras had a minimal deterrent value and as a result, these items did little to deter bad behavior or even criminal activity. If your organization plans to use security cameras solely as a deterrent, it is advisable to use fake cameras that provide the façade of CCTV but are not operational—these items are very inexpensive and you do not need to worry about observation; however, as we discussed earlier, the deterrent value will quickly go away as people realize these cameras are fake.

6.7.1 Types of Cameras

There are several types of CCTV cameras on the market. What type of security camera you choose should be based upon where the camera will be mounted, what you wish to observe in that particular location, and what conditions the camera will typically operate in (e.g., indoors, outdoors, low-light, long distances, etc.). We will look at the various types of cameras currently on the market.

- Bullet Camera. A bullet CCTV camera, shown in Figure 6.9, is a wall-mount or ceiling-mounted unit that is typically designed for indoor use, but can also be used to fulfill some outdoor applications. This type of camera does not possess any ability to change its viewpoint—typically called pan/tilt/zoom, or PTZ—but instead can only be fixed to observe one particular viewpoint.

FIGURE 6.9 Bullet camera.

FIGURE 6.10 Dome camera.

- Dome Camera. These cameras get their name from the dome-shaped housing in which they sit. These housings are designed to make the cameras unobtrusive; however, they are not completely covert or hidden. These types of cameras serve a dual purpose: potential perpetrators will know that the facility is under observation, and employees will feel at ease knowing that the facility is being protected. Some dome cameras allow the camera to spin quickly within the housing to rotate their observation area to another location, and are often referred to as "speed domes." A picture of a dome camera is in Figure 6.10.
- Covert/Desktop Cameras. These tiny cameras are well suited for desktop use when using Skype and other low-resolution teleconference applications. Many personnel use these types of cameras in conjunction with their computer in order to conduct video conferencing.
- Discreet Cameras. These types of cameras are disguised as other items, such as a clock, smoke detector, or motion sensor as shown in Figure 6.11. These cameras can be placed in locations that would not normally be available to standard cameras due to their size, and because they are not readily identifiable as an observation device.
- Infrared/Night Vision Cameras. These types of cameras have the ability to see images in pitch black conditions by using infrared light-emitting devices, or LEDs.

FIGURE 6.11 Discreet cameras.

FIGURE 6.12 Outdoor camera.

- Outdoor Cameras. These types of cameras are normally no different from many of the other cameras we discuss—the main key to outdoor cameras is the housing itself, which must be impenetrable to moisture, insects, dust, and other elements. A photo of an outdoor camera and its housing is shown in Figure 6.12.
- Day/Night Cameras. Day/night cameras compensate for varying light conditions to allow the camera to capture images. These are primarily used in outdoor applications where the security camera is positioned onto an outdoor parking lot, for example. In many cases, units are advertised to have a wide dynamic range so that they can function in a variety of conditions to include glare, direct sunlight, reflections, and strong backlight, which enable these types of cameras for 24-h-a-day use.
- Varifocal Cameras. Also known as a zoom camera, these items are equipped with a varifocal lens that allows the operator to zoom in or out, although still maintaining focus on the image.
- Network/IP Camera. These cameras, both hardwired and wireless, transmit images over the Internet, often compressing the bandwidth of the information so as not to overwhelm the system. IP cameras, shown in Figure 6.13, are easier to install than analog cameras because they do not require a separate cable run or power boost to send images over a longer distance.

FIGURE 6.13 Network/IP camera.

FIGURE 6.14 Pan-tile-zoom/speed dome camera.

- Wireless Camera. Not all wireless cameras are IP-based. Some wireless cameras can use alternative modes of wireless transmission, but no matter what transmission method is utilized, the primary benefit with these types of cameras is still the same: extreme flexibility in installation.
- PTZ/Speed Domes. Pan/tilt/zoom cameras give the surveillance operator the ability to move the camera left or right (pan), up and down (tilt), and to zoom the lens closer or farther from the area under observation. These types of cameras, shown in Figure 6.14, are normally used in surveillance situations where there is an actual security guard or surveillance specialist who can monitor and control the images; however, PTZ cameras can also be used in applications where the specific camera is automated so that the pan/tilt/zoom functionality allows the camera to be moved to observe specified locations on a timed basis. These types of cameras can also be used to cover a wide area with only one camera, or to avoid poor lighting conditions such as a setting sun.
- High-Definition Cameras. Ultra high-definition cameras are often relegated to niche markets, such as casinos, due to their expense. These cameras give operators the ability to zoom in with extreme clarity (to look at gamblers who may be suspected of cheating). In the past, these cameras were tube-based analog cameras, but today's digital technology has replaced these older units so that many of these types of cameras now transmit their images by using HD closed-circuit television.

6.7.2 Monitoring Options for Closed-Circuit Television Systems

There are three primary options you can choose to utilize when considering how your organization will monitor the installed security camera system:

- Monitoring by a dedicated security protection guard or agency

- Monitoring all cameras at one location by an individual
- Monitoring cameras through the internet

We will look at each of these options separately and discuss the advantages and disadvantages of each.

6.7.2.1 Monitoring by Dedicated Security Personnel

This option provides the most complete solution; however, it is also the most expensive method to monitor a CCTV system. Monitoring of the cameras is accomplished on a continual basis by either security guards working for your company or by outsourcing this service to a private security firm. Either solution provides the single most important advantage to this option—it ensures the most complete monitoring of the security camera system and is the most likely solution to observe any attempts of criminal activity at the moment they are occurring. The major disadvantage is the large price tag, due to several costs associated with this option. One cost is the initial installation fee that must be paid—even if your organization already has an operational CCTV system, the service provider will likely need to accomplish some type of equipment installation in order to monitor the cameras from their own monitoring location. Furthermore, if the service is to be outsourced to a security service provider, this cost could be very significant based upon the distance between your company and the security firm, depending upon the method that will be used to monitor the camera system. The second cost for this option is the ongoing periodic fees—typically paid on a monthly basis—for monitoring the system, either paid to an outside agency or for the salaries of any internal employee who will monitor the cameras.

Although there are several disadvantages to this solution, this option may work well if your organization is large. Within a large organization, there will be a need to hire personnel to exclusively work safety and security issues, if you do not already have a dedicated security department or guard force. Additionally, larger companies will likely have a significant number of areas under observation, and thus a large number of security cameras that will need monitoring—this task cannot be effectively accomplished if this task is given to an employee as an additional duty. Again, if your organization is large, having a dedicated section of security personnel will not only provide the most complete monitoring capability but will also ensure that other safety and security aspects are maintained.

6.7.2.2 Monitoring at Single Location

Many organizations choose this option since it is usually the least expensive option—particularly if your organization is not large enough to provide for a dedicated security section. In this option, all cameras are tied together so that they can be monitored at one single location within the facility (normally this location is in a central area such as reception, or at the primary administration focal point's desk within the organization). Again, the primary advantage of this solution is the relatively low costs due to the shorter distances between the cameras and monitoring station. The primary disadvantage of this option is that it is extremely unlikely that the cameras will capture an actual act or incident as it is occurring. This is because the monitoring station is either at the desk of an individual who has other primary duties, or the monitors are located in a central area and under no direct or continuous observation by any employee. Another disadvantage to this option is that since there is only one location where the monitoring equipment is located, it can be easy to sabotage the equipment if it is not under direct control or observation of one individual.

Based upon the lower costs, this option works well if your organization has limited funds or is not large enough to justify a dedicated security section. A key point that must be made regarding this option is that since it's extremely unlikely an act or incident would be observed as it occurs, the best result you can hope to achieve is to ensure the system captures and records the incident, which can be used in the investigation.

6.7.2.3 Internet Monitoring

This solution provides an alternative for smaller organizations, rather than having only one location with monitoring capability. In this option, security cameras are able to be monitored over the internet through the use of particular security cameras, which send their output to an IP address. This IP address will typically be password-protected so that any authorized individual within your organization can observe the cameras in real-time or previously recorded segments. The advantages for this monitoring option are the flexibility of the system and the difficulty to sabotage or delete the recordings. The disadvantage is that this option is more expensive than tying your cameras into one central monitoring station (but still considerably less than having a dedicated security section continuously monitor the CCTV system). The higher costs are due to the higher expense for cameras that have IP capability when compared with hardwired CCTV cameras, and the potential for periodic monthly costs required for the upkeep and maintenance of the website where the camera output is located.

This option provides a good alternative—especially for smaller organizations—to the central monitoring station option. As with the central monitoring station option, however, it is unlikely that an incident would be observed as it occurs. However, due to the greater flexibility of the system, the ability to have multiple employees with the capability to observe cameras will better help them to manage their areas and provide a greater deterrence against any unwanted activity.

6.8 Security Integration Systems

Depending upon the complexity of your organization's security system, you may consider using a security integration system. This type of system is not a necessity; but if an overall security systems includes several complex subsystems to include lighting, access control, alarms, and CCTV, your organization may wish to consider an overall security integration system.

A security integration system provides one overall computerized system to monitor and control several different portions of your physical security system. For example, such a system can control all exterior and interior lights, it can provide notification and information on alarms, provide information on an organization's automated access control system, and monitor all security cameras within a CCTV system. The advantages should be fairly obvious—consistency within all your various security systems that would result in ease of use of these varied systems, along with more flexibility and control of the overall security system. Unfortunately, there are also significant disadvantages—the primary one being cost. Integrating all these aspects of your physical security system into one overall system can be extremely difficult; particularly if these various systems were installed at different times, with different levels of technology, and by different manufacturers. This disadvantage, due to possible compatibility problems between these various pieces of hardware, can make the integration of all your security equipment into one easy-to-use computerized system very expensive, if possible at all.

A good rule of thumb is if you have a large amount of equipment from several different manufacturers and installers for your organization's security lighting, alarms, access control system, and CCTV cameras, it may not be possible or practical to attempt to integrate these into one integrated security system. If, however, you have little or no current security measures in place and are starting from scratch, it may be advisable to work with one vendor in order to obtain one integrated security system for all these various physical security measures.

6.9 Safes and Vaults

Valuable assets belonging to your company need to be placed in some type of high-security storage area, such as a safe or vault. The primary difference between the two is size—a vault is a larger storage area that is normally a separate room, and that is part of the building's structure but with significantly stronger with thicker walls, floors, ceilings, and doors. Vault doors should be made of a minimum of 6 in of steel, and the walls, floors, and ceiling should be reinforced concrete at least 12 in thick—normally twice the thickness of the door. Vaults must usually be located at or below ground level because of their structural strength and significant weight. A primary disadvantage of vaults is the expense in construction. If you have an existing facility that does not have a vault, the required construction may be cost prohibitive; however, if you are currently constructing your facility or accomplishing a major renovation, it may be advisable to consider the addition of a vault.

A key item of consideration for safes and vaults is what you wish to protect against—burglary or fire—since these compose the two separate categories of protection for safes and vaults. Although most secure safes and vaults provide protection against both to some degree, you should ensure any device you are considering meets Underwriters Laboratory, or UL, minimum ratings against your primary concern for your specific company assets. Many burglar-resistant containers may not provide against fire and conversely, many fire-resistant containers may only provide a minimal deterrent against theft. Typically, the higher the rating in either category, the more expensive and more secure the safe or vault.

6.10 Summary

Central to providing a viable physical security program is the need to employ security measures in layers around your critical resource, or to provide what is commonly termed by security professionals as defense in depth. In the manner of concentric circles moving inward, it is important to work from the perimeter of your property and facility and incrementally strengthen the security measures as you work your way in, until eventually the strongest security measures protect your organization's designated critical resources.

Perimeter security measures provide a barrier not only to distinguish the property boundary or facility, but also to attempt to limit access onto the property. These perimeter measures can employ natural or manmade barriers. Natural barriers include the use of terrain, vegetation, obstacles (such as rocks, stones, walls, etc.), and water features to delineate your company's perimeter boundaries. Although natural barriers are more pleasing to the eye and can provide a more subtle method for perimeter security, these security measures can be much more expensive. Manmade barriers typically include fences and walls, and although they are less expensive than natural perimeter security measures, they may look less welcoming to visitors and potential customers.

Security measures along the inner barrier to your facility must take the doors and windows into account, as these items are the most susceptible to damage and break in. In addition to ensuring that your organization always locks and secures these openings, it is also important to strengthen these areas with robust frames, solid construction doors, and strengthened windows.

Lighting is another important physical security measure. Exterior lighting is meant to assist with observation in and around your facility for security personnel, cameras, or both, whereas interior lighting should provide additional lighting to critical resources and meet any emergency lighting requirements.

Access control is a critical piece of your physical security system—probably the most critical piece. This aspect of the physical security program ensures that only authorized personnel enter or exit the facility. Access control also controls entry into sensitive areas, it detects and prevents contraband materials, and it alerts security personnel of any issues. Some easy methods to improve access control for any organization include limiting the number of entry points into the facility, providing a process that identifies employees, and providing personnel who are responsible to monitor entry and exit for the facility.

The next aspect within most physical security systems is an alarm system. This is meant to provide notification of unauthorized entry to the grounds, building, or your organization's critical resources. Alarm systems can also identify employees; however, it is more acceptable to have the alarm system make notifications directly to security personnel or law enforcement.

Another aspect that was discussed was the use of closed-circuit televisions and their use within a physical security system. As part of this discussion, we looked at different types of cameras and options to monitor the video output of these cameras.

We also looked at the security integration system, which is the overall system that ties many of the various physical security measures, such as access control, alarms, and CCTV, into one coherent system that can be easily accessed and analyzed.

The last area within the physical security area that we reviewed was safes and vaults. These items are typically used to store items that your organization has determined as critical.

In order to ensure an adequate number of layers within your organization's physical security program, it is important that you employ equipment and procedures that cover most—if not all—of these areas. This not only provides multiple problems for a potential intruder, but it also offers some redundant systems to increase your organization's security posture.

6.11 Physical Security Checklist

	Yes	No
If size allows, do you store and lock your critical resources in a safe or vault?		
Does your company limit the number of access points into your facility?		
Does your company utilize identification cards and do you require continuous wear while in the facility?		
Does your company have a program to monitor entry by all employees and visitors (e.g., entry guards, sign-in/sign-out logs, automated access control system, etc.)?		
Do all door and window locks on your facility meet minimum acceptable UL ratings?		
Do all windows on your facility have additional security protection (e.g., glazing, wire-mesh, burglar-resistant, etc.)?		
Are all exterior doors and frames of sufficient strength and reinforced as necessary?		
Does your facility have an intrusion alarm system? Does this system notify local police and fire (as applicable)?		
Does your company's facility have perimeter security measures (e.g., fencing or natural barriers) located along the property limits?		
Does your facility have exterior lights located along the perimeter and at primary access points?		
Does your company have signage to identify your property boundaries?		
Does your facility have emergency lighting?		
Does your facility utilize CCTV cameras to observe critical resources, primary access points, and areas vulnerable to potential criminal activity?		

Note: All items are listed in priority order, so you should ensure that each answer is "Yes" prior to expending funds or effort on the next question. This ensures that an executive with minimal security expertise can easily move down the list in order to implement an adequate security program.

Reference

[1] Military handbook 1013/10. 3. Design guidelines for security fencing, gates, barriers, and guard facilities. [chapter 2].

Recommended Reading for Physical Security

Effective Physical Security by Lawrence Fennelly. Butterworth-Heinemann.

Physical Security Systems Handbook: The Design and Implementation of Electronic Security Systems by Michael Khairallah. Butterworth-Heinemann.

7

Information Security

Information security has become an increasingly prominent aspect of any organization's security program as computers and information systems have become more and more predominant. Before the age of computers, information security was limited to ensuring files and hard copies of your sensitive information—normally your employees' personal information—was properly secured. However, now with the vast amount of critical information contained in media other than the older (and in many cases antiquated) filing cabinets and hard copies, these electronic means demand that all organizations have an information security program to ensure they have adequate procedures and processes in place to protect information contained within computers, servers, and wireless networks. Add to this change from paper to computers the explosion in the amount of information that must be protected due to the significant increase in these electronic information storage means. All of this information, along with the interconnectivity among various business environments, has resulted in an ever-growing number of threats and vulnerabilities to information. All of these factors have resulted in the success of an organization to be tied in part to its information security program.

During our discussion on the information security program, we will briefly touch on hard copy information because these older and more traditional means can still be important to many businesses, particularly within the human resources arena because many companies still retain a portion of their employees' personal information on file; however, the main thrust of this chapter will look at information security measures as they relate to electronic information and media, such as computers and other more modern devices.

7.1 Overview

Information security has three main pillars to maintain an effective program: confidentiality, integrity, and availability. Many information security professionals will use the more familiar term, Central Intelligence Agency, when discussing these main areas. It is important to ensure these information security pillars apply to the protection of any type of information and data and to include electronic information, paperwork, and documentation, when these items are designated as critical resources within the organization. The following factors [1] should be considered in each of these three pillars and are often key toward the successful implementation of an information security program within any organization:

- Information security documentation, to include policies, directives, guidance, and activities that reflect your business objectives.
- Approach and framework to implement, maintain, monitor, and improve information security that is consistent with your organizational culture.

- Visible support and commitment from all levels of management.
- Understanding information security requirements, risk assessment, and risk management (as discussed in Chapter 3—Security Planning).
- Effective marketing of information security to all managers and employees to develop security awareness.
- Funding of information security management activities.
- Establishing an effective information security incident management process (as discussed in Chapter 9—Emergency and Contingency Planning).
- Implementation of a measurement system used to evaluate the current information security program and suggest improvements (as discussed in Chapter 4—Security Administration).

In Chapter 2—Safety and Security Principles, we discussed the security fundamentals that are instrumental to any good safety and security program. All of these fundamentals are important to each area within your safety and security program, with particular emphasis on layering defenses or defense in depth, performing cost-benefit analysis, keeping things simple, securing the weakest link, using choke points, and segregating duties. Within information security, however, there are some additional fundamentals that should be also considered specifically in regard to the protection of information and data [2]:

- Principle of least privilege, which stipulates that an organization should "not give any more privileges than absolutely necessary to do the required job."
- Minimization of your system's information system configuration so that you do not run any software, applications, or services not strictly required to do the entrusted job.
- Compartmentalization to limit damage and protect other compartments when software in one area is malfunctioning or compromised.
- Incorporation and use of the concept of failing securely, which means that if a security measure or control has failed, that portion of the information system is not placed into an insecure state. For example, when a firewall fails, the system should default to a "deny all" rule rather than a "permit all" rule.

In addition to the three pillars of information security and the security fundamentals, there are also three primary system components that should always be considered in any information security systems initiative:

- Hardware, which includes physical devices and equipment, such as desktops and laptops.
- Software, which includes applications that act as conduits for the information contained within the hardware to a usable interface between the system and humans.
- Communications, specifically your organization's standards and policies that act as the guidance to protect the system, prevent mishaps, and tell your employees how to use products while ensuring information security within your company.

We will be looking at all these various factors: the three overarching pillars of information security (confidentiality, integrity, and accountability), information security fundamentals, and the components within an information system (hardware, software, and communications). We look at what is necessary for you to implement an effective information security program.

7.2 Confidentiality

Confidentiality is defined as "ensuring information is accessible only to those authorized to have access." [1] To ensure that only authorized individuals truly do have the appropriate access to your organization's sensitive information, it is necessary to provide appropriate security measures within both physical and information security areas for all confidential and sensitive information. To accomplish this, one of the first things every organization must do is to ensure every employee who comes into contact with that information must understand the added responsibility he or she has to maintain its confidentiality. With this inherent responsibility, persons who are provided access should be given several tasks through their initial training and indoctrination to the company:

- They must ensure they can identify and understand the information is designated as confidential or sensitive.
- They understand their responsibility to help protect that information.
- They can communicate their responsibility when accessing the sensitive information.
- They will maintain the information in accordance with any requirements for handling sensitive information.

7.2.1 General Considerations for Protecting Confidential Information

To assist your employees and provide them the necessary tools to ensure they can meet their responsibilities regarding sensitive and confidential information, there are some general considerations for your organization that should be disseminated to personnel. These considerations not only provide the means to protect information, they also ensure your employees have the necessary resources to accomplish their tasks and responsibilities regarding all confidential and sensitive information, whether it is in hard copy or in electronic format. We will look at each of these considerations over the next several paragraphs.

Sensitive and confidential information must never be left unsecured and unattended, and any storage containers for this information must be able to be locked and secured when not in use either during or after business hours. Many businesses provide open access during normal business hours to provide easy availability to frequently reviewed documents—an example is the practice regarding employees' personal information files contained within human resources records. Because this sensitive information is routinely and frequently accessed, many companies leave these files unlocked during operating hours; however, this should not preclude the need for security measures to ensure confidentiality, such as ensuring at least one trusted employee maintains control over the files and the area while this information is unsecured. Thus, in addition to providing locked storage containers for information, your organization must also designate an individual to maintain and control access to ensure some redundancy or defense in depth. It is also important that this employee not only understand his or her responsibility, but that he or she is trained on his or her duties to maintain this information so that even if he or she departs for short periods, he or she understands he or she must lock all storage containers if the information is left unattended.

Your organization should also develop and provide a process to formally identify who is authorized access to the sensitive information. This process should include a method that designates his or her ability to access specific information—usually accomplished through some form of identification or credentialing to access the information. The following list provides several different methods that can be used separately or in conjunction with one another, to ensure only authorized personnel have access to sensitive and confidential information.

- A list of authorized personnel should be developed and maintained. This list should be approved by the appropriate level of supervisor (normally the individual who maintains the information itself). As individuals attempt access to the sensitive information, they are checked against the list by the employee who controls access to the sensitive and confidential information.
- Sensitive and confidential information is kept in a secured location (e.g., safe or vault), and only individuals authorized to access the information are provided with the combination, key, or means of entry.
- Any physical safeguards for the sensitive and confidential information—keys, cipher locks, and passwords—should be changed on a periodic basis. These safeguards should also be changed when an individual who formerly had access either departs the company or moves into a position that no longer requires access.

We have previously discussed an employee's responsibilities regarding sensitive and confidential information and the need to ensure employees are regularly trained on these responsibilities. This training should include the following:

- Ensuring information is only accessed by authorized individuals.
- Updating combination locks and passwords as required by company policy and procedures.
- Not disclosing or sharing personal authentication credentials, such as user identification, passwords, key cards, or other forms of electronic authentication, with any other individuals.
- Not using personal authorization to sensitive information to provide to other individuals, even those they think may be authorized.
- Reporting requirements and procedures of any violations of the company's information security requirements.

These considerations, never leaving confidential information unsecured or unattended, credentialing identification for authorized individuals, and training, should be used to secure sensitive information in any format. We will next look at protecting computer systems and the information stored on laptops, desktop computers, and servers.

7.2.2 Confidentiality and Computer Systems

There are three areas we will discuss to ensure your computer and information systems maintain confidentiality. The first area is providing access control to the information contained within your electronic files, the second is ensuring any transmitted data remain secure, and the third is ensuring the proper administration and maintenance of your computer system security.

7.2.2.1 Computer System Access Control Methods

There are several simple solutions that can help minimize access to your organization's computer systems that should be communicated and accomplished with each and every employee within your organization.

- Position monitors and printers so that others cannot see or obtain confidential or sensitive information.
- Log out, shut down, or lock the system whenever an individual leaves his or her computer unattended at any time.
- Keep portable equipment and storage devices, such as CDs, DVDs, zip disks, USB drives, and other removable storage media, in locations with limited access.
- Do not leave computer equipment or portable storage devices unsecured or unattended.

Along with these simple procedural solutions that can be practiced by every employee, there are several additional security measures that are accomplished by your information systems department or point of contact. These include use of user identifications and passwords, two-factor authentication, and biometric verification. We will look at each of these information security measures over the next several sections.

The first security measure within an information systems department we will discuss is to require use of user identifications and passwords for all information systems within your organization. Use of user identifications and passwords constitutes a standard procedure that virtually everyone in the world is familiar with and so many of the rules governing these items are fairly standard. As discussed under an employee's responsibilities regarding sensitive and confidential information, it is necessary your department responsible for information security develop procedures and provide guidance to never share these passwords and also contain in-place controls to ensure these passwords are changed on a periodic basis for all employees. Your procedures should also dictate that these passwords are not simple words—particularly ones that may have a meaning for the individual, such as a pet's name or birth date. Because there are many different types of programs that can attempt to determine an individual's passwords, it is necessary that your business require passwords to use a mix of alphabetic and numeric characters, special characters, and mixing uppercase and lowercase letters in each password. With these simple and inexpensive information security measures, you can greatly enhance the security of information on each individual employee's computer.

The next information security measure we will cover is the use of a two-factor authentication process. Two-factor authentication is a process in which the user provides two means of identification. One source of identification is typically a physical token, such as an identification card with an electronic code that can be read by the computer. The other source of information is normally something memorized by the employee, such as a security code. With this in mind, the two factors are sometimes referred to as *something you have* and *something you know*. The most common example of a two-factor authentication process is your ATM bank card. The card itself is the physical item, while your personal identification number, or PIN, contains the memorized piece of data that must match the information contained within the card. Several government agencies have incorporated the two-factor authentication process for several years to further ensure authorized access to their computer systems—in this process, the individual must first place his or her identification card in a card reader and then use his or her computer password to ensure access—both items must match and the identification card must continually be inserted to use a government computer. Only after both identifications have been verified within the system can the authorized individual gain access to the computer system and the stored information. The advantage of such a system is the added security when compared with a simple user password logon; however, this process is also more expensive because your computer system must incorporate several additional components: an identification card containing employee information, card readers for every employee, and the necessary software application to ensure the system reads the personal information contained on the card and can check these data against the individual's password. Even with these disadvantages, the technology for many two-factor authentication processes has been available for some time and these systems have shown reliability and consistency because of the time they have been in service.

The last information security measure we will look at to provide improved access control to your organization's computer systems is biometric verification. This method uses any means by which a person can be uniquely identified (e.g., fingerprints and hand geometry, retina and iris patterns, voice waves, DNA, and signatures) by evaluating these identifiers against other distinguishing biological traits. We see an example of biometric verification every time we go shopping with the electronic signature pads that are normal in many retail businesses. In fact, this technology is extremely ancient—the oldest form of biometric verification is fingerprinting, which historians have found examples of thumbprints being used more than 2000 years ago as a means to uniquely identify certain officials and rulers on clay seals in ancient China [3].

Biometric verification has advanced considerably with the advent of computerized databases and the digitization of analog data, allowing for almost instantaneous personal identification. Although this is one of the more secure methods to control access, it can also be the most expensive and can cause a variety of problems due to the complexity of the equipment and difficulty in consistently reading an individual's biometric identifier. One system I have personally worked with in daily use accomplished personnel identification through hand geometry; however, various factors—weather and environmental conditions to name a few—could negatively affect the system to the point that it would not recognize the authorized individual. Technology continues to improve within this area, however, and with these gains, biometric verification provides greater and greater reliability to these security systems.

7.2.2.2 Data Transmission Security

To ensure you can maintain the confidentiality of sensitive and confidential information when it is sent and received across your organization's computers and networks, data encryption is the primary method used to accomplish this. Data encryption must incorporate both encryption, which is the conversion of that data into a form that cannot be easily understood, and decryption, which is the process of converting encrypted data back into their original form.

Much, if not all, of the information used in business today is transmitted through e-mail or obtained through access to the Internet. To maintain security of your sensitive and confidential information during these types of transmissions, there are some standard considerations that your organization's information security program should use. These include secure e-mail capability and information security awareness among your employees.

Securely sending e-mail messages can be accomplished using any number of vendor-offered products that encrypt these messages. Many of these programs are web based and easy to use, and they provide the ability to send private information, including attachments, in a secure manner. Typically with these programs, the recipient can also respond to your message using the same encryption method, so both sent and received messages remain secure.

The other consideration regarding security of e-mail messaging is to continually promote security awareness through emphasis by senior management and supervisors, and training among your employees. Training employees to conduct simple checks of their e-mails is easy. For example, they can ensure their addressees are who they actually intend the message is sent to rather than quickly typing in an address and allowing the e-mail service to complete the address, which can potentially allow a message to be sent to an individual who was either not authorized or should never have received the message. In addition, your employees should be provided awareness training to use caution when accessing e-mail—particularly if it is unexpected or from an unrecognized source. This training should include that an employee should never open these types of messages or access an attachment, without first verifying its authenticity and checking it against an antivirus program. Furthermore, their training should ensure employees understand if they remain in doubt regarding the safety of a particular e-mail message, they should contact their system administrator.

Another important aspect of data transmission security is to secure information from external Web sites, ensuring your own company's Web site is secure from hacking or interference. When entering or collecting sensitive information with another Web site, the same caution should be applied among employees as with their e-mail correspondence. There are several items employees should ensure when working with an external Web site:

- Individual employees should make sure that a secure connection has been established before downloading any confidential information.
- After working with any sensitive information over the Internet, they should close their browser and restart a new browser session before accessing an insecure Web site. This can prevent others from accessing nonpublic information, which may be stored in the browser's cookies.

By using these methods in their use with other Web sites, employees can greatly increase the security of any information your organization uses within both e-mail messaging and the web.

In addition to these methods to secure information obtained from external Web sites, you will also need to ensure your own company's Web site remains secure—especially if your organization uses the web to collect and transmit confidential information to customers or other companies you may work with. The general standard to secure a Web site is through the use of secure socket layers, or SSLs, which encrypt data transmitted over a Web site. When an employee opens an Internet browser, an open or closed lock appears in the lower right hand corner of the Web site. Your organization should ensure employees look for this lock to be closed, which means that the data transmitted over the Web site are secure, generally by SSLs. This allows for the transmission and collection of private data without worry that a hacker may be able to access or interfere with them. In addition to SSLs, secure Web sites are another method to ensure the confidentiality of our own company's Web site. These types of Web sites can be established by experts, such as internal web designers, analysts, and programmers, or by working with a vendor who has expertise in creating an appealing and secure web presence. Of course, there is no such thing as security without risks, but use of SSLs and secure Web sites significantly reduces the risk of information being inappropriately intercepted.

7.2.2.3 Computer System Security Administration

Companies today have found the benefits in using a professional computer systems administrator who is fully trained and an expert in maintaining and protecting information systems. Whether your business has an in-house employee performing these tasks or you use outside vendors to provide your organization with its computer services, it is important that these system administrators ensure your particular information security policies are observed. This can be done by clearly delineating system administrator responsibilities, training employees, and monitoring users. When working with a system administrator, your organization should ensure it accomplishes the following information security considerations and always keeps these items at the forefront of their tasks:

- Maintain up-to-date security software for all your organization's computer workstations, laptops, and software applications.

- Install and maintain antivirus software on all computer workstations and laptops and set them to auto-update and install the latest antivirus signatures.
- Use boot-up Basic Input/Output System (BIOS) passwords for all computer systems and set strong authentication methods for all user accounts, particularly any accounts that have administrative rights.
- Ensure all computer systems are enabled with screen savers that require password authentication when logging back onto the system.

With these considerations, your system administrators can continue to protect your sensitive and confidential information.

7.2.2.4 Networks and Wireless Confidentiality

Probably the most challenging arena in which to ensure confidentiality of any sensitive information is over networks—particularly wireless networks because of the significant potential for unauthorized individuals to obtain information over these means. With the increasing risk that sensitive or confidential information can be either misdirected or monitored over wireless networks (along with all the other public Internet access services, such as Internet cafés and cloud computing), it becomes even more imperative to ensure your systems are able to continuously maintain confidentiality by ensuring your company's sensitive information will only be available to those individuals who are authorized access. Unfortunately, this can be extremely difficult to accomplish because wireless networks by definition are particularly easy to access and monitor, and because the range of wireless networks can be difficult to control because radiowaves are not confined to secure areas. Providing for measures that ensure confidentiality over these types of networks is vital, even if your organization does not use wireless networking due to the explosion in third-party wireless resources that can still be used to access your company's sensitive information. These third-party resources, such as an Internet café or hotel networks, when used by your employees to access information, will increase the risk for unauthorized monitoring by other individuals. We will look at methods that can assist you in ensuring your sensitive information remains available only to authorized personnel, even with the risks that can be inherent in these networks.

7.2.2.4.1 ENCRYPTION

Because information moving over wireless networks is similar to any type of transmitted data, the primary security measure that protects this information is exactly the same used to protect information sent and received between users—encryption. Encrypting all sensitive and confidential information, because any of this information could be transmitted between wireless devices, is the best method to prevent inappropriate disclosure of confidential information.

7.2.2.4.2 REMOTE USER COMMUNICATION

Many of your employees, and in particular your managers and senior executives, will typically need to work from home or other locations outside your company's facility. These remote users present an additional security risk, because they are often using systems outside your own network to communicate between their location and the company's information. This means you and your information security team must not only need to be aware of how to provide for secure data transmission, but also how to minimize the information security risks associated with remote access to confidential information. To secure communication with remote users, installation of a virtual private network, or VPN, should be accomplished. This VPN encrypts all information traveling between the users using technology that is readily available on the market. Your organization should look at installation of a VPN if your employees require remote access to company information because the repercussions can be severe without such a network.

7.2.3 Information Security Measures to Maintain Confidentiality

Over the last several sections, we have looked at several security measures that will assist your information security program to maintain confidentiality. The first of these is establishing procedures that ensure sensitive and confidential information must never be left unsecured and unattended. Along with this, it is advisable for your organization to develop a process to identify authorized individuals who have access to this type of information and conversely make it easy to identify employees without the necessary access. We discussed several basic security measures that all employees should be trained on to minimize access to company information to include several different methods of user identifications and passwords. A significant security measure that not only protects data as they are transmitted but also any information that could be sent over wireless networks was the use of encryption. This security measure should be used throughout your information security program to protect information contained within your company Web site but also any sensitive or confidential information that could be available over third-party networks.

7.3 Integrity

The next pillar within information security is that of integrity. Integrity involves maintaining consistency, accuracy, and trustworthiness of critical information and data over the entirety of their life cycles. Integrity means that information must be able to remain unchanged throughout transmission, integration with other data, or other instances when the data are sent. This pillar not only includes information as it is being transmitted but also should include data that are maintained within your company's storage devices to include computers and servers. The concept of data integrity, along with its importance, can be shown through the following hypothetical example. A hospital patient is in treatment and is prescribed a daily medication dosage of 10 mg by his or her physician. This hospital maintains its information on a computer system, so the physician indicates the correct dosage and medication into that patient's electronic medical record. Unfortunately, the integrity of the hospital's information system is poor and a glitch in the program that transmits the electronic record adds a 0 to the dosage amount so that the patient's dosage now reads 100 mg. With the critical nature of medication dosage, this lack of integrity within the hospital's information system could result in fatal consequences for this particular patient. To preclude this incident from occurring within your own information system and ensure data are correctly maintained throughout transmission and storage, data integrity must be a critical component of any information security program.

There are some key security measures that every information system should adhere to, to provide for integrity of the system's information and data. These measures include the following:

- Equipping and maintaining up-to-date hardware.
- Using the right software that is maintained and updated with easy-to-use and automated techniques.
- Developing the right policies to guide business practices.

As we look at these security measures that need to be in place, we will also discuss the steps necessary to ensure transmitted data cannot be altered by unauthorized individuals, all of which will help to ensure critical information cannot be changed, either in transit or in storage throughout this section. We will also cover security measures that protect against and detect any changes in data should a problem arise either as a result of non-human-caused events, such as an electromagnetic pulse (EMP), or a server crash. Last, we will look at a key component of integrity, which is to provide backup copies of your data to restore any affected information back to its correct state in the event that an unexpected change occurs.

7.3.1 Up-to-Date Hardware

Ensuring the integrity of your information systems requires your organization to continually procure up-to-date hardware so that your employees can work on equipment that is able to support the most recent versions of software and hardware upgrades—particularly when dealing with information protection applications. We all know that upgrades and advances in information systems continue to expand at an exponential pace—both during the past several decades and into the foreseeable future. Unfortunately, this astonishing growth has also resulted in newer innovations from hackers and other individuals with malicious intent, which has led to more and more risks and vulnerabilities to these systems. To ensure your systems can combat these emerging threats and maintain data integrity, it is necessary your equipment can support the latest hardware and software upgrades because they are better designed to combat these ever-evolving threats. Without up-to-date hardware, your information system equipment could become obsolete and, in turn, increasingly vulnerable to the ever-increasing number of threats because it cannot support upgraded defenses.

Not only can up-to-date hardware help defend against malicious attacks by evolving initiatives by individuals, it can also help protect against environmental threats to your information systems. One such environmental threat is EMP, which is an intense burst of electromagnetic energy. Although the most frequent EMP incident occurring in movies is caused by the explosion of a nuclear warhead, a more likely scenario that your organization could experience this phenomenon is through a lightning strike. This event can also produce a localized EMP and result in extremely large electrical currents in nearby wires, which can easily damage or destroy sensitive hardware, such as computers and peripherals. For this reason, your information system hardware should also include protection against the effects of an EMP, such as surge protectors, AC outlets, and modem jacks.

7.3.2 Updated and Maintained Software

In addition to maintaining up-to-date information system hardware, it is also important to provide consistent software applications that are properly updated and maintained to protect and run your entire information system. There are two primary reasons that your systems should maintain the same software and version. The first reason is that it is much easier and more efficient when all your employees use the same software applications and versions across your entire organization. We have probably all seen the problems that can occur when companies run various word processing and spreadsheet programs across their organizations. Using the same applications alleviates these issues. Although this solution will likely result in higher upfront costs—especially if your organization is fairly large—these costs in both money and time can typically be gained through the subsequent improvements achieved in work output, along with the resultant fewer problems that occur when employees are working with the same programs and applications across the entire company. A second reason to maintain current software versions across a company is the added protection from your organization's protection software (e.g., antivirus and firewalls). Current versions of these applications will ensure your information system can keep pace with emerging risks and vulnerabilities. For these reasons, providing consistent and maintained software applications across your organization will greatly enhance integrity of information and data.

7.3.3 Proper Policies to Guide Business Practices

As with any area within your safety and security program, data integrity requires that appropriate policies and procedures are well documented and fully understood across your organization. These documents should address responsibilities across three different areas: the overall business and its employees, the information technology (IT) staff, and internal audits.

7.3.3.1 Business Responsibilities

There are three main responsibilities that your organization has in relation to integrity within the information system. These three responsibilities—accountability, access rights, and separation of duties—will be discussed in detail over the next several paragraphs.

As with several aspects not only within information security, but within the entire safety and security program, it is imperative that every employee takes ownership of sensitive and confidential information and he or she understands his or her accountability.

No single individual within your organization can do this to ensure success across the entire organization. Instead, it is necessary that each and every employee knows he or she is accountable for the correctness of any information he or she works with and that he or she understands his or her need in ownership of this task—particularly because each individual will be able to understand and verify the integrity of the information within his or her work better than anyone else. Training and emphasis by management can assist employees to better understand their role and subsequently increase awareness. It can also be useful to remind employees that failure to ensure their own ownership responsibility in data integrity can result in potential costs due to errors or problems, as shown in our hypothetical hospital example. These potential costs can be severe and include direct financial losses from fraud or operational disruption, legal costs due to errors in data, or damage to the company's reputation. It is also important that employees do not think that their responsibility is transferred to the individuals within an information system department, because much of a company's information and data may be stored electronically on computers and servers. With the increases in electronic record keeping, many employees may form the mind set that this information is primarily owned by the IT staff, rather than the individuals who actually developed and maintained the data. With some employees, this may be the easy thing to do—passing off ownership of the information to the IT department—because they want to pass the buck of their own responsibility to maintain the confidentiality and integrity of the information they developed for the organization. This problem is fairly simple to resolve through senior management working to engender the correct security awareness in all employees—specifically that this mind set is not the case and instead that responsibility for not only information security, but all aspects of safety and security, resides with everyone in your organization.

Another aspect of ensuring integrity for your organization's data is through proper policies and procedures that ensure appropriate access rights and privileges to this information. Along with the principle of least privilege discussed in the section on confidentiality, continuous verification of an individual's need to know must also be accomplished to ensure the correct access rights and privileges are adhered to. Several methods help to validate the appropriate access rights and verify individual privileges are reasonable. First, there should be an organizational process to request, change, or remove an individual's access rights. This process should be formalized, documented, regularly reviewed, and audited to ensure it is up-to-date with company policies and any emerging information security vulnerabilities. Failure to provide and follow such a process can result in privilege creep—individuals who have changed jobs and responsibilities but continue to carry forward privileges based on past history. This privilege creep can constitute a serious business risk that can undermine not only data integrity but also confidentiality of sensitive and confidential information. Second, ensure your organization develops and maintains an updated log or inventory of specific individuals with access to information along with a complete list of user privileges. This inventory can be maintained through the use of several methods—a database or spreadsheet to name a few simple ones—or there are several vendors that offer products that provide a computerized system that integrates individual authorizations with employee database listings or electronic identification cards.

The last business responsibility that helps to provide for integrity of data is the separation of individual duties. We discussed this security fundamental in Chapter 2—separation of duties avoids the possibility of one individual being responsible for different functions within an organization, which, when combined, may result in an undetected security violation. This is a well-proven concept and is something many audits insist on when looking at sensitive and confidential information systems. Separation of duties, as it relates specifically to information security, has two primary objectives. The first is to prevent any conflict of interest or even the appearance of conflict of interest, wrongful acts, fraud, abuse, or errors when looking at access to sensitive or confidential information. The second objective is to provide a system of checks and balances to detect any failures in the information security system such as security breaches, information theft, and circumvention of security controls. Because separation of duties also restricts the amount of power or influence held by any one individual, it ensures that employees do not have conflicting responsibilities and are not responsible for reporting on themselves or their superiors. There are some easy tests to ensure your organization properly separates duties. One particular test is to ask if any one employee can alter or destroy a specific electronic information area (such as financial data) without being detected and follow this up by asking if any one employee can steal sensitive information. Another test is to ask if any employee has influence over the design and implementation of security controls as well as over the reporting of the effectiveness of the controls. If the answer to either of these questions is yes, then you need to take a hard look at establishing some processes that provide for the separation of duties through implementing checks and balances into that area or by reestablishing the individual's roles and responsibilities within the organization.

7.3.3.2 IT Support Responsibilities

Depending upon the size and expertise within your organization; the responsibility for information systems and technology services could reside with internal individuals, groups, departments; or this responsibility could potentially reside outside the company with an external provider. Regardless of whoever provides these services and accomplishes these tasks, this group must provide and demonstrate they are meeting their responsibilities through appropriate measures and business metrics. These measures and metrics must be reported to company management on a periodic basis throughout the course of their work to ensure they are meeting their objectives. Some examples of appropriate measures and metrics that specifically apply to information integrity include the percent of user satisfaction with the availability of data, percent of successful data restorations, and the number of incidents where sensitive data were retrieved after media were disposed [4]. Regardless of what measures and metrics are tracked and reported, it is necessary that the group responsible for information systems and technology services collects, monitors, and reports these appropriate performance and risk metrics not only to assess their own performance but also to continually assess integrity of your system's data.

7.3.3.3 Audit Responsibilities

Your organization should conduct an in depth audit every 3–5 years to assess not only integrity of your data but also your entire information security program to identify any areas for improvement to improve efficiency or any corrective actions before they become significant problems. The role of auditors is to provide independent and objective assessments of your organization's policies and procedures. This can include an evaluation of how employees currently adhere to the organization's policies and procedures and can also provide an assessment of how effective the current policies ensure the effectiveness of your organization's information security program. Audits can be conducted by either internal employees with the knowledge and expertise in a particular area or they can be brought in from outside the organization to provide an evaluation of your organization's information security program. If you choose to use internal employees to accomplish any audits, it is recommended that the individuals performing the audit should not evaluate their own area due to the potential conflict of interest (and as discussed within the separation of duties). The same individual will also have difficulty to remain objective when assessing one's own work area.

7.3.4 Security Measures to Ensure Data Integrity

There are three main security measures we discussed to ensure integrity of your organization's data and information is maintained. The first is to provide up-to-date information systems hardware and properly maintain this equipment. The second is to provide consistent software applications across your company to minimize problems both with use across varied teams and sections and to ensure better protection through updated patches and versions. The last security measure is to develop procedures and policies that delineate the responsibilities across your organization, its employees, the IT staff, and audits. These three areas will dramatically increase your company's ability to ensure its sensitive and confidential information is properly maintained and remains consistent.

7.4 Availability

Availability, in regard to information systems, relates to the proportion of time your organization's system is in an operational condition and that the data contained within the system is available for use. In other words, availability describes your organization's information system's ability to deliver the correct data and information to the correct person within the bounds of the correct policies for your organization. Security measures that must be taken to ensure your information system ensures availability, both to your employees and to outside vendors and clients, include:

- Ensuring proper maintenance for all hardware
- Providing redundancy in your information systems
- Providing adequate communications bandwidth
- Guarding and protecting against malicious actions

We will look at each of these security measures in detail over the next several sections to provide you with the information necessary to ensure your system meets information availability requirements.

7.4.1 Hardware Maintenance

Availability within any information system is best ensured by rigorously maintaining all hardware and by performing hardware repairs immediately when the need arises. Two groups of individuals can assist in maintaining hardware; your organization's information system points of contact and your employees themselves. Hardware maintenance can be accomplished by either your system administrator or your IT department by conducting frequent checks of the system that ensure all system components are in proper working order. Employees also have a key role in ensuring information systems are maintained and available because they are the personnel using the information systems hardware and software on a daily basis. In the event they see any problems or issues with the information or data they are working with, employees must understand they have the responsibility to notify the appropriate personnel. With both system checks that are accomplished by systems administrators and notification by employees when they see any issues, it is much easier to ensure hardware is properly maintained and in operational order.

7.4.2 Redundancy

Redundancy is a must, to ensure availability of your organization's information system. One method to ensure redundancy is to have multiple pieces of equipment performing the same task. Although this is a relatively fool-proof method, it can also be expensive and time-consuming because it could result in the need to procure more equipment than is necessary to do the job. Still, for areas that are truly critical portions of your information system this may be the most viable option to ensure no loss or damage; however, there are other options that can be used to provide for redundancies in information systems.

Backup is another method that can provide redundancy—one that many organizations use within their information system. Regularly accomplishing off-site backups can limit the damage caused by any potential damage to information systems hardware or software through inadvertent accidents or natural disasters. In addition, having an off-site location or data center that is ready to restore services in case anything happens to your primary location will significantly reduce the downtime in case of any unexpected event that could occur. This backup can be accomplished using either your own resources, such as purchase of an additional server or other storage device, or by working with a vendor that provides information storage services.

Failover is another option to help provide for redundant information systems. Failover is a backup operational mode in which the functions of a system component (such as a processor, server, network, or database) are assumed by secondary system components when the primary component becomes unavailable through either failure or scheduled down time. A good example to illustrate failover is an emergency generator system that senses any type of electrical power interruption and provides continuous power with no break in electricity to the location it protects. Failover is used to make systems more fault-tolerant and is typically an integral part of mission-critical systems to ensure they are constantly available and can apply to any aspect of a system. Within a personal computer, for example, failover might be a mechanism to protect against a failed processor; within a network, failover can apply to any network component or system of components, such as a connection path, storage device, or web server. The procedure involves automatically offloading tasks to a standby system component so that the procedure is as seamless as possible to the end user and ultimately can provide redundancy to critical portions of your organization's information system.

Although there are several options that are available to ensure redundancy with your information system—it is up to each organization to determine the criticality of the information and equipment and balance against the cost of the various options.

7.4.3 Bandwidth

In information systems and computer networks, bandwidth is often synonymous with the data transfer rate of the overall system. In other words, bandwidth describes the amount of data that can be carried from one point to another in a given time period (usually a second). In general, the more information your organization sends across your network, the higher the bandwidth your information system will require.

Communications paths within your information system consist of a succession of links across the network and each link has its own bandwidth. If any one of these links is slower than the rest, that specific link is considered to be a bandwidth bottleneck. These bottlenecks should be prevented by attempting to provide for consistent bandwidth across your entire system. In addition, to ensure proper availability of your information system an adequate communications bandwidth for your requirements and usage should be provided for.

7.4.4 Protection

The last security measure to ensure availability within your information system is protection. This includes maintaining currency with all necessary system upgrades—both in relation to hardware and software. The other method to provide protection is to ensure your organization's information system can guard against malicious actions, such as denial-of-service (DoS) attacks. As we have already discussed the need to maintain and upgrade your information system's hardware and software, we will go into more detail on DoS attacks.

7.4.4.1 DoS Attacks

A DoS attack is accomplished when a malicious hacker exploits flaws or vulnerabilities in a computer system (often a Web site or web server) to be able to fool the location into thinking that they are the master system. Once they hacker can pose as the master system, they are able to identify and communicate with other areas within your overall information system for potential further compromise. Once the intruder has control of multiple compromised systems, they can instruct the machines to launch attacks that can flood the target system is with bogus traffic requests, which will cause a DoS attack for users of that system by causing the targeted system to shut down.

Although some DoS attacks result in theft or loss of security measures within your information system, many DoS attacks are only intended to disrupt communications or shutdown an organization's Web site or email system. These are still unwanted because they still result in costing the targeted organization a great deal of time and money. The loss of service from such an attack can disable a particular network service, such as email, to be available or the temporary loss of all network connectivity and services. As alluded to earlier, there are more adverse DoS attacks that can destroy programing and files in affected computer systems and in some cases, DoS attacks have forced Web sites to temporarily cease operation. We will look at the most common forms of DoS attacks, and their implications, over the next several paragraphs.

7.4.4.1.1 BUFFER OVERFLOW ATTACKS
This is the most common kind of DoS attack. A buffer overflow attack simply sends more traffic to a network address than the programmers anticipated someone might send. The attacker may be aware that the target system has a weakness that can be exploited or the attacker may simply try the attack in case it might work. The result is that the system is overloaded and either slows down significantly or shuts down completely.

7.4.4.1.2 SYN ATTACK
When a session is initiated between the Transport Control Program client and server in a network, a small buffer space exists to handle the usually rapid "hand-shaking" exchange of messages that sets up the session. These messages, or session-establishing packets, include an SYN field that identifies the sequence in the message exchange. In an SYN attack, the hacker will send a number of connection requests very rapidly and then fail to respond to the reply. This leaves the first packet in the buffer so that other, legitimate requests cannot be accomplished. Although the packet in the buffer is dropped after a certain period of time when no reply occurs, the resulting effect of several of these bogus connection requests makes it very difficult, if not impossible, to establish the session, which results in slowdown or crash of the system. The method to combat this type of attack is to ensure your operating system provides the correct settings or allows the systems administrator to tune the size of the buffer and the timeout period.

7.4.4.1.3 TEARDROP ATTACK
Internet protocol, or IP, requires a packet that is too large for the next router to be divided into fragments that will be reassembled by the receiving system. The teardrop attack exploits this process by submitting a confusing value in the second or subsequent fragments. Because the next router cannot reassemble the overall packet, the system can crash, unless the receiving operating system does not plan for this type of situation.

7.4.4.1.4 SMURF ATTACK

In this attack, the perpetrator sends an IP ping (or "echo my message back to me") request to a receiving site. This ping packet specifies that it be broadcast to a number of hosts within the receiving site's local network. The packet is then sent out within the local network from the original receiver stating this individual, typically called the spoofed host, receives the denial of service. The result will be lots of replies to the original receiver of the IP ping and if the flood is great enough, the spoofed host will no longer be able to receive or distinguish real traffic.

7.4.4.1.5 VIRUSES

Computer viruses, which replicate across a network in various ways, can be viewed as DoS attacks where the victim is not usually specifically targeted but simply a host unlucky enough to get the virus. Depending on the particular virus, the denial of service can be hardly noticeable ranging all the way through disastrous.

7.4.4.1.6 PHYSICAL INFRASTRUCTURE ATTACKS

This type of attack is an act against actual equipment comprising your information system, such as cutting a fiber optic cable or damaging a primary server. This kind of attack is usually mitigated by redundancies within your organization's overall information system.

7.4.4.2 Preventing against DoS Attacks

Preventing a distributed DoS attack can be difficult because it can be challenging to differentiate between a malicious traffic request from a legitimate one because they use identical protocols and ports. Even with this challenge, however, there are several steps you can take to protect your systems from distributed DoS attacks:

- Ensure there is an excess of bandwidth on the organization's Internet connection. Having more bandwidth than originally thought is one of the easiest defenses against DoS, but it can also be costly. By having a lot of bandwidth to service traffic requests, this measure can help protect against low-scale DoS attacks. In addition, the more available bandwidth within an organization, the more work hackers must accomplish to clog its connection.
- Be sure to use an information system intrusion detection system. Several intrusion detection systems available today are equipped with the technology to protect systems against DoS attacks by using connection verification methods and by preventing certain requests from reaching enterprise servers.
- Use a DoS protection product. Several vendors offer DoS protection and prevention appliances that are specifically designed to find and thwart the types of DoS attacks discussed.
- Prepare for a DoS response. The use of throttling and rate-limiting technologies can reduce the effects of a DoS attack.
- Maintain a backup Internet connection with a separate pool of IP addresses for critical users. This offers an alternate path if the primary circuit is overwhelmed with malicious requests.

7.4.5 Information Security Measures to Provide Availability of Data

Ensuring your organization's data is available and the overall information system is operational requires some of the similar security measures necessary to maintain data integrity and also includes some additional security measures. As with data integrity, providing appropriate hardware and ensuring this equipment is properly maintained will help to ensure your information is available. In the event of an emergency, your organization should provide redundant systems for critical components. In addition, it is necessary that your organization evaluates the necessary bandwidth needed to operate your information systems and ensure this is always adequately provided for. Last, your information system must provide hardware and software solutions that guard against potential attacks by hackers or other potential perpetrators. These four security measures will greatly enhance the availability of your organization's data.

7.5 Information Security Summary

Information security can be complex because of the technology and computerized information systems that are involved; however, looking at implementing a viable information security program one area at a time can make the task a little easier. To ensure your information security program properly mitigates risk, it is easier to develop the program by using the three pillars of information security as a guide—confidentiality, integrity, and availability.

Within these three pillars, we also need to consider the primary components of any information system. These components (hardware, software, and communications) provide the actual equipment and documentation that must be accomplished while ensuring the confidentiality, integrity, and availability of the overall program.

Confidentiality ensures that only authorized employees come into contact with your organization's sensitive information. To ensure your information security program meets this requirement, the following security measures should be in place:

- Secure all your organization's sensitive information.
- Develop a process to verify the authorization of employees attempting to access sensitive information.
- Provide procedures and equipment for information system access control. This should include organizational requirements for user identification, passwords, and possibly some additional means of personal verification.
- Provide data transmission security measures, such as encryption and SSLs, for your Web site.
- Identify a point of contact for system administration and ensure they understand their roles and responsibilities.

A primary aspect in ensuring confidentiality of your company's information is to develop security awareness among all employees so that they understand they have responsibility and accountability in keeping sensitive information confidential.

Integrity ensures data remain the same throughout all processes and transmissions. The measures to ensure your information security program provides data integrity include providing up-to-date hardware, using and maintaining the correct software, and developing appropriate procedures and policies throughout the company. By considering all three components of any information system, your organization can ensure data integrity.

Availability describes your information system's ability to deliver the correct information to the right person while meeting your company's policies and procedures. Several security measures assist with this information security pillar. First, information system hardware should be maintained in proper operational order. Second, it is necessary that your information system has redundancies along its critical points. Third, your information system should have more than adequate communication bandwidth across the system. Last, your organization must have protection against malicious actions aimed at your information system.

By keeping in mind the components of any information system—hardware, software, and communications—and ensuring these items meet the three pillars of information security, your program should greatly minimize any potential threats and vulnerabilities.

7.6 Information Security Checklist

Checklist	Yes	No
Does your company have an overarching information security policy and procedure and, if so, is it readily available to all employees?		
Does your information security policy, procedures, and training address employee responsibilities—specifically their ownership and accountability to ensure integrity with company data?		
Does your information system have adequate protections in place to include the following: • Current antivirus and protection software? • An intrusion detection system and a denial-of-service protection product? • Firewalls and using the concept of failing securely so that if a firewall is breached, the system defaults to deny access?		
Does your organization ensure sensitive information is never left unattended or unsecured?		
Does your organization have secure and lockable storage for personal information files of employees?		
Does your organization have an employee (or group of employees) who are responsible to maintain and control access to sensitive and confidential information, particularly if this information is routinely left unsecured?		
Does your organization have a process to identify and ensure only authorized individuals have access to sensitive information for both hard copy and electronic forms of information?		
Does your organization have procedures in place for computer passwords and screen saver locks?		
Does your organization encrypt transmitted electronic information?		

Checklist	Yes	No
Does your organization have measures to secure your company Web site?		
Does your organization ensure employees are not given any more privilege or access than is absolutely necessary, along with checks and balances in the process?		
Does your organization compartmentalize its information and data to limit damage or loss in the event of system malfunction or compromise?		
Does your company have a policy and process to minimize applications and programs on computers and servers?		
Does your organization provide controls to secure remote user communications?		
Does your organization ensure for separation of duties with regard to information systems?		
Does your organization provide redundancy in your information system?		
Does your information system have more than adequate bandwidth?		
Does your organization have a process to ensure all computer system hardware and software is maintained and current?		
Does your organization conduct periodic audits of your information security program? Has an audit been conducted within the past 5 years?		

Note: All items are listed in priority order so you should ensure each answer is "Yes" before expending funds or effort on the next question. This ensures an executive with minimal security expertise can easily move down the list to implement an adequate security program.

References

[1] International Standard ISO/IEC 17799:2005(E). Information technology—security techniques—code of practice for information security Management.

[2] Cryptome. Fundamental security concepts. www.cryptome.org.

[3] Barnes JG. The fingerprint sourcebook. https://www.ncjrs.gov. National Criminal Justice Reference Source.

[4] ISACA. Control objectives for information and related technology DS 11 – manage information ; 2013. www.isaca.org.

Recommended Reading on Information Security

Small Business Information Security: The Fundamentals by Richard Kissel, DIANE Publishing.

The Basics of Information Security: Understanding the Fundamentals of InfoSec in Theory and Practice by Jason Andress. Syngress.

8

Personnel Security

Personnel security is the last major area that should be covered in any organization's safety and security program. Many organizations are aware that this area is important because of the necessity to protect an individual's personal information; however, this is only a minor portion of an organization's personnel security program. A more important aspect of personnel security should ensure that all hiring and retention actions across your organization find employees that not only pose no risk to the organization, but that also meet your own company's business and moral interests. This aspect is critical since it can alleviate many problems that may occur without any process to determine individuals' interests prior to hiring new employees. Unfortunately, ensuring employees meet your organization's interests can be easier said than done—particularly since it can be extremely difficult to determine a person's character traits during a standard hiring interview. Thus, an effective personnel security program that provides an overarching process to determine if a potential employee meets the interests of your company is an important aspect of a personnel security program, and one that we will emphasize throughout this chapter.

In order to determine and monitor an individual's character traits, both prior to hiring and once an individual becomes an employee, the personnel security process should involve three primary steps:

1. Conducting pre-employment screening processes prior to the actual hiring of any potential employee.
2. Investigation of current employees suspected of violating company rules and regulations.
3. Protection of all employees from discriminatory hiring or termination, as well as guarding against unfounded allegations of illegal or unethical activities and conduct.

To develop this overarching process, it is absolutely critical that an effective personnel security program includes proper documentation—meaning company policies and procedures for your organization's personnel actions. Developing this documentation—as with any other area within an organization's safety and security program—is a critical task in order to establish an effective personnel security program and ensure that all personnel actions are consistently followed for every individual and throughout the entire organization. This documentation must detail your methods to implement the various processes and procedures that are vital parts of an overall personnel security program—to include your organization's Human Resources processes, details on the conduct of pre-employment screening, the process for hiring new employees, and how your organization reacts to allegations and conducts investigations. By consistently following these processes through the help of formalized policies and procedures, different supervisory personnel located throughout various sections within the company can consistently follow all Human Resources processes. This will not only ensure that all potential and current employees are the best fit for the organization and that they meet your company's interests, but also will protect your organization against lawsuits and other legal issues that can arise from personnel actions. All of these formally documented procedures ensure greater consistency across the entire organization and ensure that supervisors can make the best informed decisions regarding their employees.

8.1 Conducting the Pre-employment Screening

Prior to even considering whether or not to hire an individual, it is critical to conduct some screening in order to begin assessing whether that particular individual's character traits fit those of your company. The primary purpose in conducting pre-employment screening is to identify potential employees who may be bad risks or do not fit with the team before they are even hired and working. To help simplify the process and break it down into manageable tasks, it is useful to look at the overall pre-employment screening as a four-step process:

1. Define what character traits, experience, and other factors your organization wants the screening process to look at in a prospective employee. These areas can include specific job qualifications, character traits, education, level of experience, or other areas that are important to your specific organization's personality and work ethic.
2. Develop specific methods that test these abilities and characteristics that you want to measure.
3. Compile the information in a uniform and measurable method in order to determine the candidates who best meet your organization's requirements for the position in question, but also how their personality fits with that of your company.
4. Ensure usage and maintenance of this information when making an informed hiring decision.

These screenings must follow an established and consistent set of standards within your company for each and every individual being considered for a position in your company. As we have previously discussed, the method to ensure consistent application across the entire organization is to formally document these standards in an easy-to-follow process for any individual that conducts hiring within your company. Once you have established these sets into an overall set of procedures, you can move forward with your hiring choice.

8.1.1 Step 1: Determining Organizational Traits in Prospective Employees

This is probably the most important step and should be done prior to conducting any hiring actions. Fortunately, it should also be relatively easy to accomplish since your organizational traits should be readily identifiable to everyone that is a part of the company's leadership team. Every senior manager in the company should have a very good concept of the organization's character—they likely wouldn't be in their position if they didn't synch-up with the organization they work for! A brainstorming session, hopefully accomplished in a single meeting with senior management, should enable everyone to get these traits on paper and documented for further use.

Once these traits are formally documented and are at the forefront of everyone's thoughts, further discussion amongst the executive management team can produce an easy-to-understand listing of the organization's desired traits and characteristics. This document should be incorporated into your personnel policies and can now be referenced and used by everyone when considering any prospective employee.

8.1.2 Step 2: Developing Methods to Measure Traits

Once the organization's traits and characteristics are documented, the next step is to develop methods that measure and determine how well a potential candidate meets these traits. In order to accomplish this, it is necessary to obtain some information—preferably prior to an actual interview—on the potential candidate. There are a variety of methods to obtain this basic information and they include the initial employment application, information obtained through the potential employee's background investigation, and through interviews with the actual candidate.

8.1.2.1 *Employment Application Form*

We will look at the specific items that should be included in an employment application later in this chapter. Suffice to say, an effective employment application will provide a great deal of information on any prospective employee, either directly from the form itself or from research that can be conducted based upon information contained within the form. To use one obvious example of the information available from an application, an organizational trait many companies will look for in a candidate is if that individual has the necessary experience and expertise in the specific subject area related to the particular position in question. This information is easy to determine from information contained in the employment application to include the candidate's previous positions, education, and years working in related jobs and fields. The employment application can also be used to determine some fairly subjective character traits by using some forethought during the development of your organization's specific application form. For example, if communication skills are a characteristic deemed necessary for any potential employees, your organization can ensure the application form includes sections that require a prospective employee to demonstrate their writing skills, such as having the individual complete a short essay on a subject relevant to the position, or by including several sections that require the candidate to answer questions in complete sentences and paragraphs rather than by simply checking a box. In this manner, your organization can use the form to better assess that potential employee's ability to communicate, rather than by simply reading bullets in one's résumé that state their exceptional communication skills with no real proof of this ability. This is only one example of a trait that can be determined through some innovative use of an employment application form. By using this document to its fullest potential, it can help to better determine if an applicant meets your organization's key traits and requirements and can provide you with a better perspective on that individual's ability to fit in with your company prior to the taking it to the next step—the potential candidate's interview.

8.1.2.2 Potential Candidate Interview

Because of the interactive nature of the interview and the advantage of meeting a candidate face-to-face, many of the desired traits and characteristics an organization has designated and identified as important can be ascertained during this meeting. The interview provides one of the best opportunities to determine whether an individual meets your team's characteristics and traits based not only upon the verbal responses of the candidate, but also form the nonverbal communication you can see during the interview. A potential candidate's body language, pauses in response, and eye contact can provide a great deal of information on what that individual is like and how they would fit into your organization.

With this in mind, asking questions that help to determine if a candidate meets your desired character traits can and should be part of any interview. For example, if your organization has placed a premium on honesty and integrity, there are several questions that can be asked during the interview to gauge a candidate in these areas through their answers. Examples of questions that can help to assess an individual's honesty and integrity include:

- Describe a time when you admitted a mistake to a coworker.
- Would previous coworkers describe you as a person of integrity? Why did they reach that conclusion?
- Can you describe a time at work when you brought bad news to your manager?

There are many other questions to evaluate a potential candidate's honesty and integrity, and there are also questions that can assess other various traits that your organization may place importance on. Including these questions into your organization's interviews and seeing how a candidate responds to tough questions related to your company's specific traits can be a great way to determine how a potential employee will fit into your team before they are actually working for your company.

Another method during the interview that can determine the suitability of a potential employee and how they line up with your organizational character traits is to provide the individual with scenarios or tests to see how they might react to certain situations they may find in the typical work environment within your company. Most supervisors should be able to easily develop scenarios from their own recent experience. These can then be posed as questions to the potential employee to see what decision they might make in given situations and determine their rationale for doing so.

There are many methods to ensure the interview is a valuable feedback into a potential employee's traits, particularly with some preplanning and forethought prior to the actual meeting. It is up to your organization to develop these questions and a process to ensure their consistent use, so that the interview is a valuable forum to not only determine how the potential candidate's experience fits with the job, but also how their character and personality fits with the organization.

8.1.2.3 Background Investigation

We will cover the specifics of what needs to be included with any good background investigation later in this chapter; however, we will touch on this process since it is the last method we will discuss that assists in determining if an individual would fit in with your organizational traits and characteristics. Background investigations provide a great deal of information on a potential employee to include basic information such as name, address, and phone number. In addition to this information however, a good background investigation will typically go much deeper than this, as it should include several other items of interest:

- Criminal records
- Arrests and convictions
- Sex offender listings
- Driving records and vehicle registration
- Bankruptcy and liens
- Past employers and military records
- Court records

Although a background investigation should not be the sole source to obtain information regarding a potential employee, the information obtained from this source—particularly when used in conjunction with information from the employment application and interview—can be a tremendous method to verify claims made by a candidate throughout the process, and can also help to assess how well that potential employee's traits fit in with your team.

By combining all three methods that measure a potential candidate's traits and characteristics—the employment application, interview, and background investigation—your organization will have much greater success in hiring the right individuals who not only fit with your team, but do not cause problems further down the road.

8.1.3 Step 3: Compiling Information on Candidates

We have already covered how to obtain information during the interview beyond the normal job experience and qualification; however, we had only touched upon the other two methods used in compiling information on potential employees within your organization: namely, the employment application and the background investigation. We will now look in detail at what needs to be included within these two items.

8.1.3.1 Employment Application

A completed employment application is the single most important information-gathering tool in the pre-employment screening process, and should be accomplished and reviewed prior to any other actions with a prospective employee. At a minimum, applications should request and obtain the following information:

- Name, address, and telephone numbers with any first and last name variations the applicant has used.

- Citizenship and, if applicable, green card number.
- Military service information to include a DD-214 (the form provided to all U.S. military service members upon separation, discharge, or retirement).
- A minimum of three personal references. The listed individuals should not be relatives, nor should the applicant reside with them.
- Any security clearance information to include current or past clearances held.
- Previous education to include the name of the school, years attended, and degree or certification earned.
- Former employment of all jobs held over the past 7 years to include supervisor's names, company addresses, and telephone numbers.
- Full and detailed explanations about prior convictions. Note that questions cannot be asked about prior arrests but only convictions.
- Previous residences.
- Hobbies.

With this information on the candidate now available, your organization can obtain additional information in order to determine if the potential employee meets the minimum qualifications for the position in question. You will also have the ability to verify any claims by the individual so that you can ensure you hire the individual you believe them to be, rather than find out the individual was able to mask their true character. Once a potential candidate has completed your organization's employment application, the next step should be to accomplish a background investigation.

8.1.3.2 Background Investigation

As discussed in Section 8.1.2.3, the purpose of the employment background investigation is to identify individuals who may be a risk in regard to employee theft, lawsuits, or losses to the company, and prevent these actions before they even occur. Conducting a background investigation on all potential employees verifies the accuracy and completeness of an applicant's statements, develops additional relevant information on the candidate, and determines the individual's suitability for employment.

The background investigation should look for inconsistencies between an applicant's statements made either in their application or interview. There are typically three common ways that applicants will falsify information within their application:

- Incomplete information contained in the application form.
- Omission of facts or job references, or providing incomplete or inaccurate contact information for listed references.
- Misrepresentation of education or employment history.

The importance for an organization to accomplish a proper background investigation can be found through the real-world example that created significant headlines and embarrassment. The incident occurred in 2001, when the University of Notre Dame hired their new head football coach. The individual, formerly the head coach at Georgia Tech, had exaggerated his accomplishments as a football player while in college, and in addition, he falsely claimed to have earned a master's degree in education [1]. Much to the chagrin of Notre Dame, they failed to accomplish a complete background check that would have identified these issues, and instead the background checks were done by a newspaper doing an article on the new coach. The paper identified these discrepancies and as a result, 5 days after he had been hired, the individual was forced to resign with a great deal of embarrassment for both the individual and the university. Unfortunately, and even with the potential for major embarrassment, many companies do not accomplish background investigations; however, it is imperative that your organization dedicate the time and resources to ensure that this is a part of your pre-employment screening process.

Earlier, we briefly covered a summary of information contained in a typical background investigation; however, there is a good amount of information that should researched in order to accomplish a proper investigation. The following includes a complete list of information and items that should be part of any employment screening background investigation:

- Check of any local security incidences and police files to determine if the individual has any derogatory information.
- Obtaining details on any gaps in employment history.
- Check of previous residences.
- Research of the applicant's consumer report and financial status.
- Check of civil court and criminal court records.
- Contact the candidate's personal references.
- Verify education background.
- Conduct interviews with former employees and work associates.
- Check of military history, professional certifications, and social security numbers.

One recent item that many employers now choose to consider when conducting a background investigation is to look at a potential employee's interactions and communications within various social media sites. This information can provide a very accurate source of information on an individual's actual persona and conduct, since many potential employees put forth a different face—and probably a truer glimpse into themselves—than that found throughout the application and interview process. In many cases, an individual's social media interaction will identify traits that are not representative of what many organizations are looking for, as seen by a recent survey accomplished by the Society of Human Resource Management. This study found that 30% of companies indicated that they used "social networking information to disqualify job candidates" [2].

It should be noted; however, that one should use caution when looking at an individual's social media interactions—particularly if an organization uses this to disqualify candidates. Currently, few court decisions provide guidance on the issue of using an applicant's social media interactions as a factor in the hiring process. With this in mind, the best decision would be to combine this information with all other sources in order to make the best determination on that individual's character prior to hiring.

8.1.3.3 Using the Employment Application and Background Investigation

The employment application, along with the background investigation, should typically be the primary sources of information to assess if a candidate should be offered an interview. This is in conflict with the process many organizations use. Instead, many companies conduct the interview and then accomplish a background check only on their top candidate(s). This divergence from the process of offering interviews based upon information from the employment application and background investigation is normally due to the cost of conducting background checks. Although cost may deter many companies from accomplishing the background check prior to offering an interview (and in many cases, from accomplishing the background check at all); it should be emphasized that the background check should precede the interview because it not only can filter out many poor candidates, but it can also alleviate problems that can occur later, as we will discuss.

There are several advantages in accomplishing both the application and background check prior to the interview, and we will look at these now. The first advantage is that your organization will likely be able to cut some candidates out because of issues or discrepancies between the application and background check, making the final choice easier. The second advantage is that if you have already been able to obtain the large amount of information from both the application and background investigation, then in your interview you can spend a great deal more time in determining the how a potential candidate's experience and character traits match those of your organization, rather than having to ask questions about their background (since this has already been accomplished). The last advantage is problems that can occur if the front-runner has issues as a result of their background investigation. It is human nature to pick a favorite, so once you have met with all the candidates as a result of the interviews, it will be much more difficult to consider issues with a front-runner that are found during the background check—unfortunately, there are likely significant concerns that may be raised in the event of any issues; however, many people may attempt to overlook them because of bias or sympathetic feelings based upon the interview with that individual, since they have already been conducted. If the background check is conducted prior to the interview, however, a potential candidate with issues would have probably been cut and there would not be as much consternation to look at another individual for the position. Although it may be a little more expensive, the costs are minimal when compared to the advantages gained by conducting both the employment application and background investigation prior to any potential candidate interviews.

8.1.4 Step 4: Making the Hiring Decision

Once the information from screening and background investigations has been compiled and the interviews have been conducted, it is likely that your organization has developed a short-list of potential candidates that you can decide upon for the position opening. When making any hiring decision, it is advisable that your organization use a standardized methodology each and every time in order to ensure consistency across the entire organization and amongst the various supervisors who will make these choices. If all the information from the application, pre-employment screening, and background investigation has been fully utilized to narrow down the list of candidates, hiring can be the most straightforward step in the process—although it may not be the easiest step if you have seen a great many exceptionally-qualified candidates during the application and interview process.

In order to make hiring a straightforward process and to alleviate any legal issues within the personnel arena requires that your organization to use a predetermined and documented methodology to pick the best candidate. Several methods exist in order to accomplish this, and we will cover two of these methods in detail. Your organization may choose to use one of these methods, or it may choose an altogether different method—the only requirement is that whatever method you choose to use within your company must have a documented process and is covered in your hiring procedure to ensure its consistent use.

The first method we will look at in helping to determine the best candidate from all the available individuals is a scoring system to compare all the potential employees included amongst the final selection. This scoring system will look at the traits your organization has already determined that you desire in any prospective employee (as accomplished in step 1 of the pre-employment screening process). A weighted scoring system can be developed from these traits in order to emphasize some of the more vital traits versus some of the others. Once you have determined the appropriate weights for each of the characteristics and traits, you simply scores each candidate based upon their own evaluation and total the scores. The individual who achieves the highest score then becomes your organization's selection for that position. It should be noted that scoring the candidates is a subjective process, and different supervisors will likely score potential candidates differently, so it is recommended that several supervisory personnel participate in this method. In this manner, the organization provides a more balanced and valid scoring of each of the potential candidates and can better alleviate concerns based upon prejudice and bias for the future. Table 8.1 shows an example of a scoring sheet accomplished for a mock position within an organization.

As can be seen in the example, there are different maximum scores for the various traits. This allows for more important areas (in the above example, self-reliance, initiative, and supervisory experience) to produce more points than other areas. In this example, candidate 3 has the highest score and should be selected for the position.

Another standardized method that can be used in hiring decisions is the utilization of a candidate matrix. Although similar to a scoring system shown in the previous example, this method is a little more subjective since most matrices will typically have fewer rankings (e.g., outstanding, above average, and average rankings versus numerical scores as compared to a strict numerical score) to differentiate between the candidates when considering the desired traits for the position being considered. The following matrix contained in Figure 8.1 shows an example of this method using the same traits used in the previous example:

This method differs from the previous scoring process in that it is difficult to place weights on different traits and areas to be evaluated. The candidate matrix is similar to the weighted scoring system, although, as it also subjective, so it is again recommended that

Table 8.1   Example Weighted Scoring Sheet

		Candidate 1	Candidate 2	Candidate 3
Supervisory experience (maximum of 25 points)	Supervisor 1	18	14	22
	Supervisor 2	22	18	23
	Supervisor 3	16	11	21
	Supervisor 4	22	23	24
Experience related to the technical requirements of the position (maximum of 15 points)	Supervisor 1	7	13	11
	Supervisor 2	11	14	12
	Supervisor 3	10	14	13
	Supervisor 4	10	14	11
Self-reliance and initiative (maximum of 25 points)	Supervisor 1	12	18	21
	Supervisor 2	18	23	22
	Supervisor 3	16	20	24
	Supervisor 4	19	21	24
Organizational management skill (maximum of 15 points)	Supervisor 1	14	10	13
	Supervisor 2	12	14	14
	Supervisor 3	11	12	13
	Supervisor 4	10	14	15
Honesty and integrity (maximum of 20 points)	Supervisor 1	8	16	15
	Supervisor 2	14	18	18
	Supervisor 3	12	20	20
	Supervisor 4	14	19	20
Total score		276	326	356

multiple supervisors be included in this process to ensure greater fairness and alleviate any possible perception of inappropriateness in the hiring process.

Regardless of what method your organization chooses to use in hiring new employees, it is important to remember the following considerations: First, ensure that you use consistent processes and that they are documented in your personnel policies and procedures. Second, use all the available tools—employment application, background investigation, and candidate interview—to ensure that a candidate doesn't have any hidden skeletons in their closet and that they truly are a good fit with your organization. Lastly, ensure everyone uses the consistent processes as documented to minimize the potential for issues arising as a result of legal or discriminatory allegations.

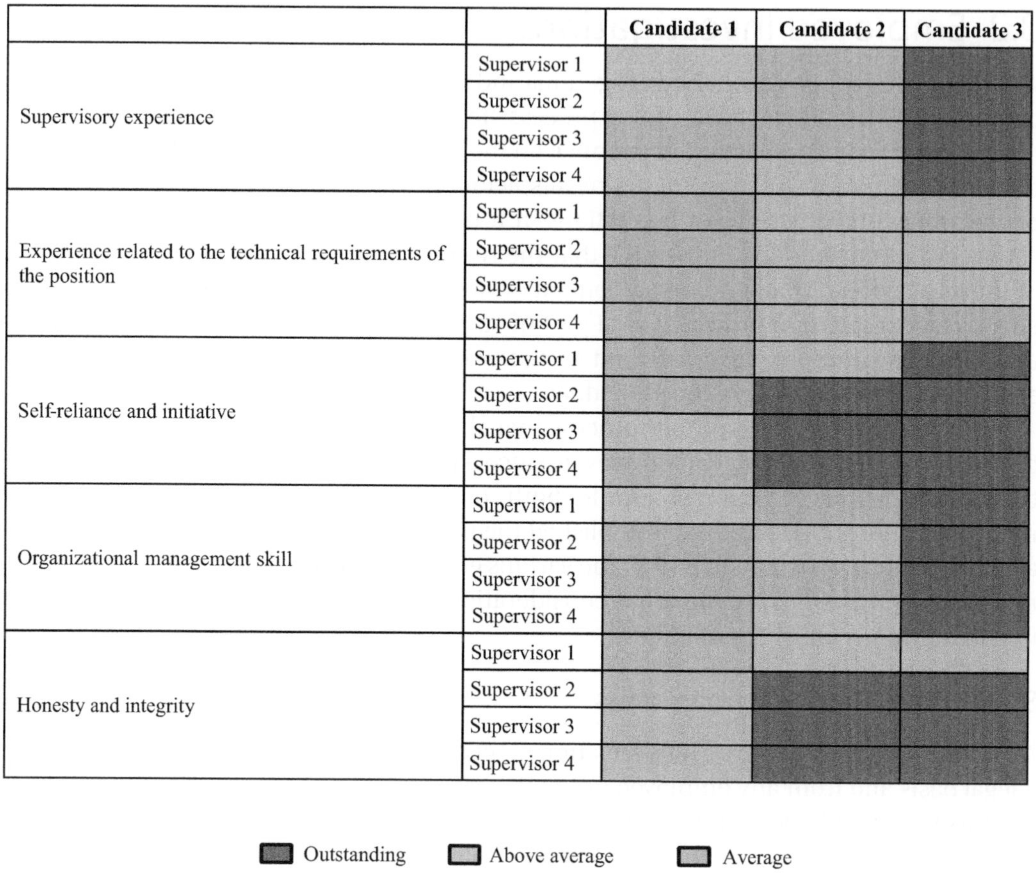

		Candidate 1	Candidate 2	Candidate 3
Supervisory experience	Supervisor 1			
	Supervisor 2			
	Supervisor 3			
	Supervisor 4			
Experience related to the technical requirements of the position	Supervisor 1			
	Supervisor 2			
	Supervisor 3			
	Supervisor 4			
Self-reliance and initiative	Supervisor 1			
	Supervisor 2			
	Supervisor 3			
	Supervisor 4			
Organizational management skill	Supervisor 1			
	Supervisor 2			
	Supervisor 3			
	Supervisor 4			
Honesty and integrity	Supervisor 1			
	Supervisor 2			
	Supervisor 3			
	Supervisor 4			

■ Outstanding   ■ Above average   ■ Average

FIGURE 8.1 Candidate matrix.

8.1.5 Conclusions on the Employment Screening Process

When looking at the overall employment screening process, the most important aspect is to ensure that your organization is looking at the big picture—or the whole person when applied to a potential employee—rather than one particular aspect in order to assess their abilities and fit within your team. Evaluating the whole person requires that you include all aspects of the hiring process—the pre-employment screening; the individual's employment application, their responses and conduct during the interview, and information gained during the background investigation. If an organization only uses one aspect to make their hiring decision, for example, the potential employee's social media interaction, this will not provide a true picture of whether or not that individual will be a good fit with your organization and be a productive employee. Only by using all the multiple tools available throughout the entire process will you have an adequate amount of information to determine that applicant's suitability for a job within your organization.

8.2 Employee Investigations

We have looked at background investigations and what information is obtained from these during the pre-employment screening process; however, there are other types of investigations that may need to be conducted once an individual has been hired. These investigations are conducted in the event of any suspicions or allegations that an employee may be violating company rules or regulations. If it is determined that an employee investigation be conducted, it is imperative that the results stand up to the necessary scrutiny of the legal system or any union agreements your company is subject to. This makes the employee investigation process a vital part of ensuring that your organization can maintain discipline and provide a safe and secure work environment, although still meeting any requirements to protect the individual.

We will first look at the proper process that should be followed in order to conduct a proper investigation against an employee, since a poorly or illegally conducted investigation can result in severe repercussions for both your company and any employees involved in the allegations. Once we have established the proper methodology to accomplish such an investigation, we will then look at the various employee misconduct incidents that normally occur in businesses and what considerations should be taken into account when investigating any concerns or issues.

8.2.1 The Investigation Process

As stated, it is critical that any investigation meets all necessary requirements—both from a legal basis and from any employee or union agreements your organization must follow. For this reason, it is best to follow specific steps prior to and throughout the conduct of an investigation in order to mitigate the possibility of an inaccurate or unsubstantiated investigation. These steps are not necessarily in order, as many of these tasks are done in conjunction with one another; however, each of these tasks should be accomplished in order to ensure that the investigation is conducted properly.

- Designate qualified investigators within your organization.
- Continually develop investigative resources.
- Follow established methods to collect, handle, and store evidence.
- Train and follow proper interview techniques with any eyewitnesses, supervisors, and suspects.
- Accomplish completed investigation reports in the proper format to ensure full documentation of the results of the incident.

We will cover each of these tasks in detail over the following sections.

8.2.1.1 Designation of Qualified Investigators

Finding and designating one individual within your organization, or a small cadre of individuals, who has the experience and necessary traits to conduct a thorough investigation, is a necessary first step that should be accomplished in order to accomplish employee investigations. Without this step, it is impossible to conduct a thorough and proper investigation without a trained and qualified individual. Many organizations will wait to designate an individual to conduct an investigation until an incident has occurred—this is normally not a good idea, as the selected employee may not have any training or qualifications to conduct an investigation and, because of the last-minute notice, definitely will not be prepared to accomplish a thorough investigation. By designating specific individuals to accomplish investigations within your organization prior to their occurrence, you will lessen any potential issues that could occur due to an inadequate or improper investigation.

When looking at what individuals within your organization should be identified to work on any investigations, there are several traits that typically ensure successful investigators. A good investigator should ideally have some experience in conducting investigations and should be:

- Unbiased, unprejudiced, and not allow personal likes or disliked to interfere with the investigation.
- Have high ethical values and adhere to the principles of honesty, goodwill, accuracy, discretion, and integrity.
- Exhibit faithfulness, diligence, and be able to conduct themselves in an honorable manner while carrying out assignments.

It will likely be necessary to designate more than one individual within your organization with the responsibility to conduct investigations. Multiple investigators will ensure redundancy in case of any absences of the primary investigator at the time of an incident, or minimize any potential conflicts of interest that could preclude the primary investigator from conducting an investigation. For example, if your organization's primary investigator is the supervisor of an employee who is alleged of wrongful behavior, it would be inappropriate to have them conduct that particular investigation. For these reasons, it is a good idea to have more than one individual, or a small group of people, who are designated and qualified to conduct an investigation.

Once you have designated your organization's primary investigators, it is highly recommended that they obtain training on investigatory procedures (if they are not already certified or have experience as an investigator) and coordinate together to keep each other informed of any lessons learned or changes in procedures from recent investigations. There are a variety of resources where you can obtain this training that include many local law enforcement agencies, schools, and training seminars. In addition to training, all investigators should coordinate on any ongoing investigations. This will not only provide for an alternate investigator should the primary become unavailable over the course of the investigation, but it will also ensure that any issues, concerns, and lessons learned from recent investigations strengthen the overall investigative process. Once these individuals are trained, certified, and develop a system to periodically coordinate with each other, your investigative team will be fully prepared and qualified to handle most investigations within your organization.

8.2.1.2 Obtaining Information from Available Resources

There is a variety of information that can be useful to an investigator during the course of any investigation, and investigators must be aware of where to obtain this information. In order to obtain this information, they should constantly develop sources and become aware of available resources so that they can quickly and accurately obtain information on individuals involved in the investigation or the incident in question. These resources can include any reference material that is relevant to your company's industry and workforce, or sources that provide personal information on individuals. Many of these reference materials can be found in such obvious locations as the public library or local newspapers and magazines, whereas other useful information pursuant to the investigation can be obtained from informants who are known to provide reliable information based upon the investigator's knowledge and development of these sources. Table 8.2 provides a list of many different sources that can provide information and material relevant to many different types of investigations—although this list is not complete, it provides a starting point for your organization's investigative team to begin to develop their own information sources.

Table 8.2   Investigation Resources

Agency	Available Information
Public library	• Periodicals and newspapers • *Who's Who* listings • Professional directories (e.g., medical directories, law directories, banking directories, etc.) • Encyclopedias • Telephone books
City and county offices	• Business licenses and permits • County clerk office for citizenship, marriage licenses, and divorce decrees • Weapons permits • Felony and misdemeanor charges • Bankruptcy and other civil records • Real-estate transactions and property tax payments
Local law enforcement	• Incident reports • Accident reports • Criminal reports
Worker's compensation bureau	• Job-related injuries • Previous employers • Listing of dependents
Credit reporting bureaus	• Individual financial history • Social security number • Personal information to include current address, date of birth, employment, and marital status

8.2.1.3 Evidence Handling

During any investigation, it is normal that evidence pursuant to the incident will need to be collected. In conjunction with obtaining information from the necessary resources throughout the course of an investigation, the investigator must also ensure they know the proper procedures when collecting, handling, and storing any evidence relevant to the issues at hand.

The basic rules for collecting and handling evidence must follow the same chain of custody that is required and used in a court of law, since it is never known at the outset of an investigation if actual criminal action occurred. For this reason, all evidence must be properly collected to ensure there is no break in the accounting and possession of any item of evidence from the time it is collected at the scene until the evidence could be used in court. The purpose of maintaining the proper chain of custody for any evidence collected is to be able to show that the evidence is in the same condition as found at the crime scene and has not been tampered with. When the investigator first identifies an item as evidence, the following steps must be taken:

- Photograph the crime scene and document where each piece of evidence was found. This documentation should include the date, place, and time of discovery.
- Mark the evidence with a distinctive mark, being careful not to damage or alter the item in any way.
- Place the evidence in a proper container that is appropriate for that item (e.g., fibers in a plastic bag, liquids in their original container, medication in pill boxes, etc.). The container should be marked with the date, place, time of discovery, and identification of the individual who collected the item. If at all possible, witnesses should be present when packaging any evidence.
- Maintain a chain of custody log that documents the identity of any individual who takes possession of the evidence during either transport or storage of the item. This information should include the individual's printed name, signature, date, and time where they took possession.
- Place the evidence in a secured evidence locker until the item is to be presented.

It is best to keep the chain of custody, or the number of individuals who come into contact with each piece of evidence, as short as possible. Ideally, it would be best for the same individual who collected the evidence to be the person who eventually places the item into secured storage.

8.2.1.4 Interviews

It is critical that the investigator obtain as much information from other persons who were eyewitnesses as possible; in order to determine the circumstances and facts surrounding the incident they are investigating and one of the best methods to obtain this information is through interviews. A trained investigator will typically interview all individuals who are believed to have information regarding the incident in question and then obtain additional names of other eyewitnesses or potential suspects over the course of their initial interviews. It is not unusual for an investigator to conduct multiple interviews with key eyewitnesses based upon subsequent information they may obtain over the course of their investigation. In order to ensure that they can completely explain the incident, a thorough investigator will continue to conduct interviews until they are satisfied they have knowledge of all the facts and can successfully close the case.

The purpose of these investigation interviews is to gain information in order to establish facts surrounding the incident. Some of the basic information an investigator will want to obtain or confirm with the witness during any interview includes:

- Developing background information on the specific incident.
- Identifying additional witnesses for further interviews as necessary.
- Identifying suspects and accomplices.
- Eliminating suspects and discovering details of other offenses.
- Verifying statements and physical evidence obtained from other interviews.
- Obtaining additional evidence.

As discussed earlier, it is sometimes necessary for an investigator to conduct follow-on interviews with the same individual in order to reaffirm and reestablish the facts obtained from the initial interview. These follow-on interviews can provide new perspectives on evidence, jog the witness's memory, or identify other suspects who were missed due to information the investigator has gained since the original interview.

Documentation of the interview, normally called a written statement, is necessary in order to legally preserve the information provided by the eyewitness. These written statements not only provide a record of the interview, but they are also useful to refresh recollection of a witness and discourage the witness or suspect from changing their story. A written statement can be hand-written or typed and should include the following elements:

- Start and end time of the statement.
- Eyewitness's personal information (e.g., name, address, telephone number, position, and section, etc.).
- Statement that the information was provided freely, voluntarily, and was not coerced by threats or promises.
- In the conclusion, the statement should contain an affirmation that the contents are true, correct, and voluntarily provided.
- Signatures of both the eyewitness and investigator.

In the majority of investigations conducted in the corporate arena, interviews are the most critical portion of any investigation. In order to ensure that the information obtained during these interviews is admissible and useful, following the steps previously discussed will greatly enhance your organization's ability to bring these incidents to a successful conclusion as quickly as possible, so that everyone can then concentrate on the real business at hand.

8.2.1.5 Investigation Results and Reports

The objective of any investigation report is to provide a professional, accurate, detailed, and easy-to-understand account of the events that took place based upon information obtained over the course of interviews and the investigator's personal observations. This account should be compiled into an investigation report that should always include the five W's and one H: the Who, What, Where, When, Why, and How. The report should concentrate on the facts and report, in chronological order, the correct sequence of events as they occurred, based upon the information obtained during the course of the investigation.

The investigation report should include all information from the investigation, such as a list of evidence, copies of documentation, and the written statements from all interviews. A standard format for the investigation report is as follows:

- Executive Summary. This section includes a brief synopsis of the incident. It should provide a brief overview of the incident as it occurred in chronological order. It is meant to be an overall summary for executive managers to be able to rapidly understand the facts surrounding the incident and to obtain the necessary information in order to make their decisions, without having to read the entire report.
- Detailed Investigator Log. This section is an in-depth list of all actions taken by the investigator over the course of the investigation. It should be accomplished in chronological order and includes notes on all tasks that were accomplished during the investigation of the incident, such as their notification of the incident, investigation of the crime scene, evidence collected, interviews, and conclusions based upon the facts found.
- Complete List of Interview Statements. This section includes all statements obtained from the interviews conducted during the investigation. These interview statements should usually be in a "question and answer" format and they should include the signatures of both the witnesses and interviewer.
- Evidence Log. This section is a complete list of each item of evidence collected. It is normally accomplished on a worksheet and includes a brief description of the evidence, where it was found, the date and time it was collected, and its current status (e.g., stored in a secured evidence locker, turned over to law enforcement, etc.).

8.2.2 Employee Misconduct Investigations

Now that we have covered the necessary steps to conduct an investigation, we will look at the various types of employee misconduct typically found in business. Within all of these incidents, an employee misconduct investigation must be accomplished in order to assist in determining if an individual has violated company rules and policies or state and federal laws. Several different employee misconduct issues are listed below, along with the considerations specific to that particular issue.

8.2.2.1 Sexual Harassment

Sexual harassment, or unwelcome sexual advances, is defined by the United States Equal Employment Opportunity Commission (EEOC) as "any requests for sexual favors, and other verbal or physical harassment of a sexual nature" [3]. Prior to any incident within this area, every company should establish a zero-tolerance sexual harassment policy and post the policy to ensure that employees are aware that sexual harassment will be promptly investigated. Furthermore, employees should be made aware that assistance in sexual harassment investigations will not be subjected to any form of retaliation and all matters regarding the case will be kept confidential. Along with the definition listed above, the EEOC has two defined conditions of sexual harassment [4]:

- *Quid pro quo* harassment describes a claim that arises from a supervisor offering employment opportunities in return for sexual favors.
- Hostile environment harassment is a claim that arises from a supervisor creating or allowing a pattern of conduct pertaining to sex that causes an unpleasant or hostile work environment.

Investigations into any sexual harassment claims should follow the investigative process and include well-written reports and complete records, particularly if the investigation led to termination or the claimant files a sex discrimination suit.

8.2.2.2 Theft Investigations

Employee theft accounts for billions of dollars of loss for businesses every year. Typically, theft is more prevalent at smaller and medium-sized businesses because these organizations have less supervision and rely more on the employees' trustworthiness, which in turn allows individual employees greater freedom of movement than at large companies with well-established bureaucracies.

Major factors that contribute to employee theft are the lack of proper security measures, the lack of a control and oversight program, and few checks and balances within certain financial processes. Without these controls in place, along with the lack of a strict policy against theft, many employees could be undeterred from stealing since they might not think there is any risk of criminal prosecution or the company's recoupment of lost money or assets. In order to provide the necessary deterrence against employee theft, developing an effective loss control program policy should provide for and emphasize the following areas:

- Development of checks and balances, safeguards, and preventative aids such as security inspection checklists.
- Conducting physical inventory inspections of goods and merchandise and daily audits with prompt reporting of missing items.
- Employee integrity and honesty testing.
- Employee education and motivation.
- Taking immediate steps toward apprehension and recovery to include prosecution and remedial actions.

8.2.2.3 Embezzlement Investigations

Unlike external theft, which can normally be identified to management and company employees fairly quickly, internal theft, or embezzlement, is stealthy and can go undetected for long periods of time. Embezzlement occurs when someone holds a position of trust and misappropriates money or converts company merchandise for personal use or advantage. Many of the actions that help to deter employee theft can also assist in deterring and detecting embezzlement.

Suspicious activities that are common in embezzlement and can help to identify potential problems include:

- Changes in spending habits or increases in an employee's standard of living.
- Apparent devotion to work, such as working later hours or refusing vacations. This is done in order to minimize exposure with other coworkers.
- Account discrepancies or questionable transactions such as "padding" to cover up losses or "skimming" before cash entries are made.
- Complaints or allegations of misconduct by coworkers, customers, and contractors.
- Noticeable behavior changes.
- Objection to any procedural changes that will lead to closer supervision and scrutiny.

A disciplined environment with appropriate checks and balances and other safeguards is one of the most effective countermeasures against embezzlement. As covered in Chapter 2, one of the security fundamentals is redundancy, or separation of duties, which covers many of the areas meant to deter or detect embezzlement. Some of the specific methods to combat this threat include:

- Separation of duties and audit trails.
- Periodic financial and operational audits.
- Gathering information on lifestyles and personal habits of employees.
- Interviewing coworkers.
- Searching e-mail and quality checks on company phones.
- Suspicion—if any employee exhibits traits consistent with possible embezzlement, further investigation may be required.

8.2.2.4 Fraud Investigations

Fraud can be defined as improperly obtaining an asset or item by providing false information. Both theft and embezzlement are considered fraud, so many of the considerations and mitigating actions from these threats can also be used and applied to mitigate the potential for fraud. In addition to simple theft and embezzlement, other types of fraud include: corporate fraud, computer fraud, medical fraud, theft of intellectual property rights or counterfeiting, financial fraud, credit card fraud, economic fraud, personal injury and vehicular accidents, and fraudulent disability claims.

In addition to the guidelines used to deter theft and embezzlement, some additional guidelines that can assist to prevent fraud include managerial controls, employee screening, forensic accounting, and financial controls.

8.2.2.5 Employee Absenteeism

Employee absenteeism is a subtle form of theft that costs businesses millions of dollars each year. Although closer supervision is one of the first responses many organizations will consider when minimizing absenteeism, other more effective methods can include:

- Developing ways that make employees feel important and significant to the company.
- Personalizing management's relationship with employees.
- Recognition of employee excellence and dedication.
- Proper training.

With all these options, however, the best method to reduce employee absenteeism is simply good leadership and supervision by managers with their employees.

8.2.2.6 Drug Abuse Investigations in the Workplace

Improper use of alcohol and drugs in the workplace can create significant costs to businesses due to lost work and inefficiencies sustained by the affected employee. Although it can be difficult to clearly identify employee drug abuse, a supervisor may consider this issue if an employee exhibits absenteeism or attendance problems from work, financial problems, trouble with local law enforcement or arrest, relationship issues with other employees, or unusual circumstances surrounding accidents at work. Physical symptoms of drug abuse may include trembling hands, sallow skin, wan cheeks, runny nose and eyes, and dilation of the pupils.

When conducting drug abuse investigations, the following items should be considered:

- Drug abusers commonly feel that they cannot manage without support of their habit.
- Chronic drug use generally indicates mental or emotional illness.
- Drug abusers commonly have a history of social maladjustment and find it difficult to get along with others.
- Drugs may not be easy to spot, as they can be carried in a number of ways, including within prescription bottles, fountain pens, toothpaste tubes, etc.

8.2.2.7 Gambling Investigations

Gambling addiction can take the employee away from their job because of the lure of dice, cards, horse and dog betting, and other games of chance. In addition, any employees suffering from gambling addiction can become higher risks to attempt theft or embezzlement because of the financial strain they continually place themselves under.

Some considerations for investigation of employee gambling issues include:

- Use of undercover operators.
- Evidence of gambling, such as IOUs, and lists of athletic or payroll pools.
- Cooperation with law enforcement agencies.
- Use of handwriting and fingerprint experts to examine documentary evidence.

8.2.3 Summarizing Employee Investigations

We have gone over a great deal of information within our discussion on employee investigations, so it will be beneficial to briefly summarize the main points. We initially went over the considerations your organization should look at prior to conducting any investigation. These included the designation of investigators, development of sources of information to be used in investigations, methods to properly handle evidence, how to properly conduct interviews, and methods to develop a complete and accurate investigation report. We then covered a variety of employee misconduct issues commonly found in corporate America. During this discussion, we looked at individual types of misconduct and provided some considerations that can minimize the threat of a similar incident within your organization. By ensuring that your company is prepared to properly investigate any issues and taking action to mitigate the likelihood of specific types of misconduct, you will ensure that your organization is prepared for these types of eventualities.

8.3 Protecting Employees from Discrimination and Unfounded Allegations

The last area that we will cover within the personnel security realm is providing protection to your organization's employees from discrimination and unfounded allegations. In order to adequately discuss this area, we will first look at the many different legal considerations and restrictions that your organization must comply with during both the screening and investigation process. These considerations and restrictions are derived from a number of laws and regulations that your Human Resources point of contact should be intimately familiar with. These laws and regulations include:

- Age Discrimination in Employment Act—1967
- Americans with Disabilities Act (ADA)
- Civil Rights Act—1964
- Consumer Protection Act—1976
- Department of Justice Order 601-75
- The Electronic Communication Privacy Act of 1986
- Employee Polygraph Protection Act of 1988 (EPPA)
- Fair Credit Reporting Act
- National Labor Relations Act (NLRA)
- The Omnibus Crime Control and Safe Street Act of 1968 (Title III)
- The Privacy Act—1974

We will look at the two areas where these rules and regulations best apply and can be most easily abused—employee screening and investigations—and discuss methods to ensure that your organization adequately accounts for each of their respective restrictions and considerations.

8.3.1 Considerations and Restrictions on Employee Screening

Under various provisions of several of the laws and acts listed above—namely the Civil Rights Act, Privacy Act, and Consumer Protection Act—the following questions or actions cannot be taken during the employment screening process:

- Ask the applicant to disclose their original name if a name change has been made.
- Inquire of the applicant's birthplace if it is outside of the United States.
- Require the applicant to produce military discharge papers prior to employment or inquire into the applicant's foreign military experience.
- Ask age if it is not an occupational qualification or otherwise required by law.
- Inquire about racial background and religion.
- Ask questions about organizational affiliations from which race, religion, or national origin can be obtained.
- Ask a male applicant for data regarding maiden name of spouse or mother.
- Ask for the place of residence of the applicant's spouse and relations.
- Make inquiries regarding the naturalization status or citizenship of the applicant's spouse or parents.
- Require photo with the application.

This list contains requirements from multiple laws and regulations; however, each individual act discusses requirements that your organization must adhere to throughout the employment screening process. We will look at each of these laws and regulations, along with any specific requirements that your organization must be aware of.

8.3.1.1 Age Discrimination in Employment Act—1967
This Act bans discrimination against applicants who are at least 40 years old on the basis of age.

8.3.1.2 Americans with Disabilities Act
The ADA prohibits employers from discriminating against a "qualified individual with a disability." An individual with a qualified disability is one who, with or without reasonable accommodation, can perform the essential functions of an assigned position.

8.3.1.3 Consumer Protection Act—1976
The Consumer Protection Act prohibits the following:

- Inquiries regarding records of arrests, indictments, or convictions of a crime where the information is more than 7 years prior to the application date.
- Inquiries regarding any bankruptcies that took place more than 14 years before the application.
- Inquiries regarding any paid tax liens, legal suits, or judgments with harmful effects.

8.3.1.4 Department of Justice Order 601-75
This Department of Justice Order prohibits a criminal justice agency from confirming or denying the existence of criminal history data for employment purposes.

8.3.1.5 Employee Polygraph Protection Act of 1988

The EPPA restricts the use of lie detectors by most-private sector employers in applicant screening. Exceptions allowing administration of lie-detector tests include:

- United States Government employers and any state or local government employers and employees.
- Certain job candidates in private business who will handle large sums of money or engage in security services.

8.3.1.6 National Labor Relations Act

The NLRA prohibits discrimination in hiring based on union affiliations. Furthermore, this Act ensures employees with the following rights:

- Form, join, and assist in unions and union activities.
- Engage in concerted activities, which are usually defined as collective bargaining to improve work conditions and wages, grievances, on-the-job protests regarding unfair labor practices, picketing, and strikes.

8.3.1.7 The Omnibus Crime Control and Safe Street Act of 1968 (Title III)

This Act prohibits private individuals and employers from intercepting wire or oral communications.

8.3.2 Considerations and Restrictions in the Conduct of Investigations

Employee rights must be maintained throughout the course of an investigation. For this reason, the restrictions listed in the previous section regarding employment screening must be adhered to with some exceptions:

- Use of Lie Detectors. Employers conducting investigations of economic loss or injury may be able to administer a lie-detector test. The test should be conducted in connection with an ongoing investigation involving theft, embezzlement, misappropriation, or an act of unlawful industrial espionage or sabotage. In addition, there must be reasonable suspicion that the employee being considered to take the lie-detector test was involved in the incident and had access to the property in question.
- Intercepting Wire or Oral Communications. Wiretapping may take place in a one-party consent state, meaning that only one party to the communication needs to consent. Wiretapping may also be conducted with a court order.

8.4 Summary

We have looked at the primary areas within an effective personnel security program— pre-employment screening, investigations, and ensuring that your employees are protected from discriminatory hiring and unfounded allegations of improper conduct.

As discussed throughout this chapter, it is critical that you develop formalized documentation that outlines all these areas in order to ensure consistency and minimize any possibility of placing your organization in a situation that violates the myriad of laws and regulations covering human resources actions.

The purpose of conducting a pre-employment screening is to identify potential employees who are bad risk or do not fit with your organization's characteristics and traits. This screening is easy to develop by following these four steps:

1. Define the qualifications, characteristics, and traits that your organization wants in prospective employees.
2. Develop a method to test these qualifications, characteristics, and traits.
3. Consolidate the information and compare across all candidates. This step will typically include reviewing a candidate's completed employment application, conducting a background investigation, and interviewing the potential employee.
4. Use this information in making a decision on a single candidate.

We also discussed employee misconduct investigations—both regarding the process to conduct an investigation and various types of investigations. In order to effectively conduct employee investigations, it is necessary to identify investigators within your organization, available resources used to obtain information, methods to properly handle evidence, how to conduct and document interviews with witnesses and suspects, and how to document the results of the investigation into a final report.

Finally, we covered various laws and regulations that govern protection of employees from discrimination and unfounded allegations. These requirements must be adhered to in order to ensure that your organization meets all legal agreements with your employees.

8.5 Personnel Security Checklist

	Yes	No
Does your organization have a written procedure to cover the overall hiring process?		
Does your company have a sexual harassment policy? Is it posted?		
Does your company have a documented process when making any hiring decision?		
Does your company conduct pre-employment screening on all potential employees?		
Does your company have a standardized employment application that contains all necessary information?		
Does your company conduct background investigations on all potential employees?		
Has your company determined the desired traits that your organization values in its employees?		
Does your company have methods in the pre-employment screening process to measure these traits?		

	Yes	No
Does your company have a designated cadre of investigators to conduct any investigations as needed?		
Have your designated investigators gone through a training program? Does this training program include investigative resources, evidence handling, interviewing, and report writing?		
Does your company have checks and balances in place to help identify employee theft?		

Note: All items are listed in priority order, so you should ensure each answer is "Yes" prior to expending funds or effort on the next question. This order ensures that an executive with minimal security expertise can easily move down the list in order to implement an adequate security program.

References

[1] Fountain JW, Wong E. Notre Dame coach resigns after 5 days and a few lies. The New York Times; December 15, 2001. www.nytimes.com.

[2] Gates M. Pre-employment screening and social Media. Security Management Magazine; September 3, 2013.

[3] U.S. Equal Employment Opportunity Commission. Sexual harassment definition; 2013. http://www.eeoc.gov.

[4] United States Equal Employment Opportunity Commission Enforcement Guidance. Policy guidance on current issues of sexual harassment Number N-915–050; 1990.

Recommended Reading on Personnel Security

Case Studies in Personnel Security by Adam Yarmolinsky. University of Pennsylvania Law Review.

The Art of Investigative Interviewing by I Sebyan Black, Butterworth-Heinemann.

Emergency Response and Training

The last major section within this book that we will cover deals with the response effort your company should take in the event of an actual emergency along with the ongoing training to ensure employees understand their actions and responsibilities in regard to your organization's safety and security program. We will first look at the preplanning and preparation that are necessary to mitigate potential emergencies and conclude with a discussion on implementing a viable training program within your organization.

9

Emergency Response and
Contingency Planning

Developing and directing the response during an emergency situation is one of the most demanding actions any executive can ever accomplish; however, it has not always been emphasized or practiced. Although emergency planning has always been part of most safety and security plans, the growth of terrorism and the increasing number of security incidents has resulted in the importance of adequate planning of emergency situations to take on a much greater urgency. This chapter will provide you with the preplanning and preparation to potential emergency incidents that can greatly increase your organization's ability to effectively respond to these emergencies and help to minimize damage, injury, or even loss of life. Over the course of this chapter, we will discuss planning factors that can significantly decrease the impact of these incidents, identify various emergency incidents that your plans should address, and finally will look at procedures that assist in your response to potential emergencies.

9.1 Emergency Response Planning Factors

Emergency response planning factors are considerations that every organization should take into account when developing its own response procedures. These planning factors are designed to accomplish several objectives: provide a safe environment for staff, visitors, and community members; provide guidance for your employees to effectively prepare for, respond to, mitigate, and recover from emergencies or disasters; and reduce the potential for damage, injury, and loss of life in the event of an emergency. With this in mind, the four emergency response planning factors that any good emergency response plan should consider are as follows:

- Mitigations, which are the efforts taken before any type of emergency incident in order to lessen the impact of an event.
- Preparedness, the efforts exerted to prepare your organization's staff for response and recovery requirements.
- Response, which includes the activities necessary to address situations as they arise in the course of an emergency.
- Recovery, after an emergency has occurred, includes the necessary actions to return the organization to full, preevent operation.

We will be looking at each of these separate planning factors over the next several sections.

9.1.1 Mitigations

Many of the mitigation actions to assist with emergency response planning are accomplished throughout the security planning process; the specific details on these areas have been covered in previous chapters. These include identification and assessment of risks to your organization, which were covered in Chapter 2 – Safety and Security Principles, and security measures that your organization has implemented relating to your physical security, information security, and personnel security programs as discussed in Chapters 5–7. By identifying the risks that pose the greatest threat to your organization and taking proactive action to mitigate these risks with security equipment and procedures, you have taken a significant jump toward mitigating potential emergencies that could occur.

Once you have accomplished an assessment of risks particular to your organization, you need to ensure you focus on these in order to spend your limited time and effort planning emergency response actions against the most viable emergencies. For example, if your business is located in Phoenix, Arizona, on high ground, it would be a waste of time and effort to take time to develop emergency response procedures against flooding. Although this is a very obvious example, it is amazing how many organizations will try to focus on events that are very far down the priority list of potential risks and vulnerabilities because of knee-jerk reactions based on a recent event in the local area or even the country—this is why it is so important to develop a prioritized list of risks and follow it when developing your own organizational emergency procedures.

The security measures—including safety and security equipment, processes, and procedures—your organization has procured and developed will also assist in mitigating against potential emergencies. The likelihood of a security incident—such as an unauthorized visitor that could evolve into an active shooter or hostage situation—is much greater without any access control systems or procedures within an organization than if there are entry controllers present, employee access cards, cameras, and other systems that can mitigate the potential for unauthorized access into a facility. As discussed in previous chapters, it is prudent to have several redundant layers of physical security measures protecting your facility that can provide greater deterrence and increased ability to lessen the impact of an actual incident—all of which will ultimately help to mitigate any potential emergencies.

9.1.2 Preparedness

Preparedness is the next emergency response planning factor that we will discuss, and there are several areas that should be considered when preparing your organization's response against potential emergencies. These preparedness areas can be divided into the following five items: command and control, communications, collection and distribution of resources, coordination, and congestion. We will look at each of these areas separately over the following sections.

9.1.2.1 Command and Control

Someone must be in charge of the response to any emergency incident and the command and control area within preparedness ensures this requirement is provided for. This area also provides the designation, regulation, and coordination of the many responsibilities and tasks required to accomplish the emergency response plan. The easiest and clearest method to provide for command and control is to designate an emergency response team within your organization, along with a chain of command that includes a listing of tasks and responsibilities before any emergency. Major tasks and responsibilities that must be included in the emergency response team are:

- Identify the individual responsible for the overall response efforts. This individual is typically called the incident commander (IC). The IC can be any employee, but a member of management with the authority to make decisions is typically the best choice because this individual must have the capability and authority to accomplish his or her responsibilities, which include:
  - Assume command and assess the situation.
  - Implement the emergency management plan and activate the organization's emergency response team.
  - Be the primary focal point with local law enforcement and fire department first responders.
  - Determine response strategies and order an evacuation if necessary.
  - Determine response strategies and oversee all incident response activities.
  - Declare the incident is "over."
- Identify the primary communications focal point. This individual will not only work on communication efforts within the organization but will also act as the primary conduit with local press agencies.
- Identify the individual responsible to coordinate any facility or maintenance issues. This person should be very familiar with the overall layout of the facility, utilities, and any mechanical and electrical infrastructure contained within the building.
- Is the individual responsible for conducting accountability of all staff and any visitors. This task is critical if the emergency involves injuries or loss of life, because the primary focus is always on the identification of employees who have sustained any significant injuries or death.
- Individual responsible to oversee any logistics and transportation issues.

This list is a minimum of the tasks that should be identified and will vary based upon the type of business and what functions your organization may have. If, for example, your business is very dependent upon information technology, it will likely be necessary to include an individual response for information systems within the emergency response team. With the addition of any other responsibilities you may identify, it is critical that you also identify a responsible individual before an emergency to ensure awareness of each necessary task.

9.1.2.2 Communications

Communications is the next area within preparedness and refers not only to the equipment necessary to allow your staff to talk to one another in the event of an emergency, but also that allows for understanding regarding the limitations and capabilities of your organization's communications system before disaster strikes. For example, during many major incidents, the amount of cell-phone traffic will typically overwhelm local and regional communications systems, causing them to crash and become inoperative. Thus, reliance on the use of cell phones during an emergency would not be the wisest course of action. The solution to ensure a viable communications system in the event of an emergency is to have several redundancies. In addition to, or even in lieu of cell phones, plan on using landline telephones; or better yet, purchase a radio and walkie-talkies for use during emergencies if your facility is small enough to use them. Other communication methods that may need to be used in the event of an emergency that compromises normal systems include messengers, FAX machine, local area networks, and hand signals.

Not only should your communications plan include actual equipment, it should also include procedures on how to conduct communications during the course of an emergency, both within your organization and within the community and local area. Some considerations include:

- Notification methods to ensure all employees are aware of the incident. This can refer to either a notification tree to identify any necessary personnel by phone or to a facility-wide notification system such as an audible alarm or loudspeaker. There should also be accommodations to ensure out-of-town employees are contacted or instructed to call their supervisor in the event of an emergency.
- Communications procedures to provide guidance on communications both within the organization and to outside agencies. It is critical that your plan identify what individuals, by position, should be talking with emergency responders (e.g., police, fire) or with the press. By identifying which personnel will accomplish this before the actual event, all other individuals can concentrate on their jobs and provide a more effective response to the emergency.
- Communication with the press and other media sources. Any emergency experienced by your business will likely result in media interest; it is imperative that you consider how your organization will react and respond to the press and community.

9.1.2.3 Collection and Distribution of Resources

Another area that is part of preparing for your organization's response to an emergency is developing processes to collect and distribute necessary resources during the incident itself. Trying to identify which resources are available and their location cannot be accomplished once the emergency has begun. Instead, it is necessary for you and your team to determine this information before any initiation of an incident.

Some items that must be included in this determination are:

- Personnel. In the event evacuation or transport is necessary, an individual must be designated to arrange for group transportation if necessary.
- Critical company information.

- Medical supplies to provide initial first aid for injured personnel before the arrival of medical responders.
- Emergency food supplies in the event that personnel are unable to leave the facility for an extended period.
- Emergency response "go-bags," which are preprepared bags for your organization's emergency response team. Equipment will typically include local area , diagrams of company facilities (including interior and exterior plans), additional radios, and a copy of the emergency response plan and any applicable checklists.

All these items, along with their locations, must be identified before the start of the emergency. Once this has been accomplished, you and your executive team must identify a responsible individual who will ensure this resource is secured and safeguarded until resolution of the emergency incident.

9.1.2.4 Coordination

The area of coordination works in concert with the command and control area in the preparation of your organization's response to an emergency. To best accomplish this coordination, it is necessary to not only identify the tasks and designate the responsible authority in the event of an emergency, but it is also critical that your organization form its emergency response team with the members discussed earlier. In addition to forming the team, it is also necessary to conduct periodic training and exercises so that this team ensures it develops the necessary coordination and can work together to effectively coordinate its actions during an actual incident.

9.1.2.5 Congestion

The last area within preparedness is alleviating congestion within your organization. Congestion refers to bottlenecks in the workflow of your organization. Within your organization, there may be *single-point failures* in which critical tasks flow through one individual or a specific section. These *single-point failures* are normally your superb performers that get an extraordinary amount of work done; however, because of these qualities the work processes become overly dependent upon them and over time the entire process can break down in their absence. During normal operations, this may not be a problem and thus there may be no need to provide for allowances or redundancies so that other work sections are familiar in accomplishing these critical tasks. In the event of an emergency however, this *single-point failure* can become quickly overwhelmed and the entire organization's response to the emergency can fail because there is no duplication of effort to assist with this critical task.

The best method to mitigate congestion in the event of an emergency is to identify all critical tasks that would be necessary to accomplish and ensure there are alternate people or sections identified and trained so that they can assist with, or even accomplish the work, should the primary personnel become unavailable or unable to accomplish that particular task.

9.1.3 Response

The next major area involved in an organization's ability to react to an emergency is response. This area refers to the actions, processes, and procedures that take place once an incident has occurred or is ongoing. The key elements of any response to an emergency are protecting human life, preventing or minimizing personal injury, reducing exposure of your organization's critical assets, and minimizing loss. To accomplish these elements, it is important to consider the following actions that must be taken in any type of emergency response:

- Command and management of emergency operations.
- Fire management and/or facility evacuation operations.
- Security and traffic control operations.
- Emergency medical operations to include preventive medicine and assistance to coroner operations.
- Staff care and shelter operations.
- Facility management and plant operations to include relocation efforts as necessary and resources and support operations.
- Internal rescue operations.

We will look at each of the actions separately over the next several sections.

9.1.3.1 Command and Management of Emergency Operations

Managing emergency operations provides for the overall management and coordination of the emergency response, whether it is the actual management of the staff in the facility or coordination of your organization's departments in conjunction with outside agencies supporting the response operation.

We have already discussed the most important task that assists in managing emergency operations—designation of your emergency response team and delineation of each member's tasks and responsibilities. Upon any notification of an emergency, it is necessary that the IC within your organization determine where the team will operate during the incident and clearly communicate this information to the entire team to begin the process of managing the overall organization's emergency operations. Another important action in managing the emergency response is to determine how the staff will accomplish staff recalls and communications throughout the response. You must clearly identify who performs the recall and have alternate plans in case the local phone system is down. Additionally, you must have the ability to notify personnel within your facilities to ensure employees take appropriate action. The next task in managing your organizational emergency response operation is the public information officer policy. We had earlier discussed the need to designate a point of contact who will handle all communication with the press. Not only is it important that this individual and the other members of the emergency response team are aware that the press should go through the organization's designated person, but it is also important that all employees understand this and are aware of any other public information officer policies. This can save a great deal of miscommunication during the actual response to an incident. The final task that is part of managing the emergency response operations is to develop and provide a reporting system for any necessary information during the course of the incident. This process should also ensure the organization conducts a critique and evaluation at the conclusion of the emergency response. With accurate record-keeping, both throughout the response and at the conclusion, your organization can evaluate problems in your current emergency response procedures and correct them. Although this task will be extremely difficult to do at the conclusion of an actual emergency, it is an important aspect of your emergency response and can not only improve your ability to respond to emergencies but can also make your entire organization better.

9.1.3.2 Fire Management and/or Facility Evacuation Operations

Fire management and facility evacuation operations are another area within the management of your organization's emergency response. This area limits the loss of life and property for your organization. To effectively accomplish this, it is important that your organization liaise with local fire departments before an actual incident to ensure both your company the local fire department are aware of each other's plans in the event of an emergency. Along with this liaison, your organization needs to designate specific personnel who would assist rescue units as necessary.

9.1.3.2.1 FACILITY EVACUATION OPERATION CONSIDERATIONS

A significant decision that must be made in any emergency situation is whether it is safer to evacuate personnel inside the facility or shelter-in-place. Although some situations are fairly straightforward—such as a fire that demands immediate evacuation—decisions in other situations may not be obvious. For example, it was thought for some time that in the event of any active shooter situation, the correct decision was for personnel to shelter-in-place and lock down the facility. In a lockdown, all personnel hide in the room they find themselves in at the outset of the incident, lock and barricade any entry points, and attempt to remain in the room and avoid detection by the intruder. From experience with several active shooter situations however, it has become apparent that resolution in the vast majority of these incidents occurs when the shooter either takes his or her own life or is killed by responding security or law enforcement personnel. With this result in mind, the original lockdown response to active shooter situations would place an individual inside the facility in an exposed position for an extremely long period. This has resulted in a revised response to active shooter incidents that directs individuals to evacuate the facility if they can safely do so without coming into contact with the intruder. This solution calls for a minimum number of personnel—specifically those in close proximity to the shooter—to go into lockdown. Although there are still personnel at risk, the number is significantly lessened and because these types of situations have normally been resolved when either the shooter runs out of ammunition or first responders arrive and locate the shooter; this has now become the more accepted practice. Within your own organization, you will need to make the determination on whether employees evacuate or remain in place in the event of not only an active shooter situation but many of the other possible threats your business could experience.

Another consideration in evacuations is to ensure you take into account the distance personnel would need to ensure their safety during the evacuation. To account for all scenarios, evacuation procedures should include both short- and long-distance scenarios. Short-distance evacuations are normally accomplished in the event immediate evacuation from the building is necessary but distance from the building is not necessary to ensure safety—the primary example being a fire drill. Long-distance evacuations are defined as evacuations that, because of longer distances involved, require alternate transportation. These types of evacuations may be due to bomb threats, radiological concerns, or chemical contamination. Long-distance evacuations are considered when walking is impractical because of distances or weather considerations.

9.1.3.3 Security and Traffic Control Operations

Security and traffic control operations are another area within the management of an organizational emergency response. These operations enforce applicable orders and company policies within your facility grounds. Additionally, this function coordinates the activities of security and traffic control staff with local law enforcement agencies, maintains communications with any mobile security personnel, commits available resources, and determines if additional resources are necessary.

Of particular concern within this emergency response area are two functions: traffic control and crowd control. In the event of an actual emergency, many employees will want to get away from the facility as quickly as possible, whereas emergency responders and other agencies will need to get access to assist with the response efforts. It is critical that your organization have plans to ensure employees wishing to leave the area do not hinder access by the inbound emergency responders. To conduct traffic and crowd control, it may be necessary to obtain assistance from additional employees to help control the huge increase you will see both in the amount of vehicle traffic and people in and around your facility during these incidents, and as a result your response plans should account for the added personnel.

9.1.3.4 Emergency Medical Operations

Emergency medical operations provide for the treatment of injured personnel as a result of the incident and, if necessary, assistance to coroner operations. This function must plan for these actions in the event of multiple casualties to include locating, collecting, and transporting injured personnel. Two major tasks are involved in this function: employee accountability and establishment of first aid and casualty collection points.

The first task involved with emergency medical operations is accounting for your employees and identifying casualties. We briefly discussed the importance of employee accountability as part of the human resources point of contact within your emergency response team; however, the importance of this task cannot be overstated. Accounting for all your employees and visitors is critical because the primary focus of many emergencies rapidly moves from the incident itself toward identification of all involved personnel with particular emphasis on the exact numbers and names of individuals who have sustained any significant injuries or death. The best example I can provide in order to emphasize that your organization ensures you have a process in place to accomplish this accountability can be found in 9/11. The vast majority of all communication into the area was focused on obtaining the status of friends and family members. This will occur in every type of emergency that involves the potential for injury and so it is vital that your organization develop a thorough process to ensure accurate accounting of all personnel who were in your facility at the time of an incident. One of the simplest methods to accomplish this accountability is to task all supervisors to account for their personnel in the event of an incident and make notifications on the number of personnel accounted for, any injuries, and the number missing up the chain of command. There is also a need to ensure accountability of any visitors to your business at the time of the incident so your point of contact will need to ensure a process is established that conducts a thorough accounting of all personnel within your facility at the time of the emergency. Accounting for these individuals will also be your organization's responsibility; using visitor logs or access control processes to help identify these personnel so they can be included in your accounting needs to be taken into account when planning your accountability process.

Establishing first aid and casualty collection points is another important task involved with emergency medical operations. Before an incident, your organization should identify a specific location, or several locations depending upon the size of your facility, where injured personnel would be brought. These consolidated areas allow medical personnel to move to these areas and provide care to more of the injured personnel than could be accomplished by having to move through the entire facility themselves to find any individuals requiring medical care. These collection points should have basic first aid kits to help in initially treating the injured and have equipment to transport the injured such as folding stretchers.

Preventive medicine is another aspect of emergency medical operations and provides for public health and sanitation services during the incident. Two primary considerations within preventive medicine are to ensure drinking water is available and sanitation services are provided in the event that personnel must remain in the facility and public water and sewage is inoperative. Storing bottled drinking water and determining a source of chemical toilets, should the need arise, resolves these concerns.

In the event of any death, the primary assistance an affected organization would need to provide to coroners is the identification of remains and disposition of personal effects. Identification of remains should be accomplished by developing an accounting of all employees through the methods discussed earlier. The other consideration, disposition of personal effects, may likely fall upon your organization, depending upon the area and procedures of local law enforcement. If so, it is important to take an inventory of any items found, collect them into a sealed package, and store them in a secured area—much like the procedures involved with collecting and storing evidence as was discussed in Chapter 8. In this manner, when the employee's next of kin is ready to pickup his or her effects, they can be provided the inventory and sealed packet.

9.1.3.5 Staff Care and Shelter Operations

A critical portion of this medical operations task is the accountability of your organization's employees throughout the emergency situation. As we have already discussed, the importance of this task cannot be emphasized enough because most of the initial questions you must answer in any emergency will deal with the number of employees missing, injured, or dead. In addition to the personnel accountability portion of this area, it also covers for basic human needs of the staff throughout the incident, to include lodging, food, and child care as necessary.

9.1.3.6 Facility Management and Plant Operations

This area covers any purchase and construction necessary to bring your company's facility back to operational status during the actual incident. It also includes relocation efforts as necessary and resources and support operations.

Facility management and plant operations provides for damage assessment, emergency debris removal, shelter construction, and other engineering operations. Damage assessment depends upon accurate record-keeping of the current status of your facility and its equipment, as it is virtually impossible to determine what damage has been done without an initial baseline of what resources your company started with.

Facility relocation operations provide for long-distance evacuation and relocation of persons from the threatened or affected areas of the facility. Several considerations are involved with facility relocation:

- Where will your organization relocate?
- What will it take to accomplish the relocation?
- Who will work at the new location?
- Will any special equipment or services be required at the new location?

Transportation is a key function within the facility relocation operations because a process to transfer personnel to other job sites may need to occur.

9.1.3.7 Internal Rescue Operations

If the emergency situation extends well beyond your own company and its facility and effects your area or even the entire region—such as a natural emergency such as earthquakes, severe storms, or floods—emergency responders will likely be overwhelmed and unable to respond to your location in a timely manner. In this case, your organization will need to be prepared to conduct your own internal rescue operations within the organization. These operations carry out the coordinated search and rescue operations for the location, provide immediate care, and safely remove employees. To conduct these rescue operations, it is necessary to determine and develop a process to locate and mark areas where there may be trapped individuals and establish safety zones in areas where the facility is severely damaged. Considerations include ensuring maps and floor plans are available for searches and designating employees to serve as guides for rescue teams.

9.1.4 Recovery

Recovery is the last major area within emergency response operations. Although an emergency incident can be over relatively quickly, the recovery from such an event may take days, weeks, or even months before your organization is able to match production levels commonly achieved before the emergency. To reestablish full functionality of the business as rapidly as possible, various functions must be accomplished:

- Damage assessment
- Clean-up and salvage operations
- Business restoration
- Customer and client information
- Mutual aid and agreement activities

It is best to task each of these functions to specific teams within your organization to synergize efforts and assist with recovery in the most rapid manner possible. Over the following sections, we will look at what is important for each team to accomplish to ensure that these functions are properly conducted.

9.1.4.1 Damage Assessment

This team refines the initial damage assessment estimates made during the response to the emergency and collects data to set priorities and guide other functions to establish goals and schedule necessary tasks. There are several tasks for this team to properly accomplish damage assessment.

Before any emergency, this team should have completed detailed inventories and surveys of the facility and critical business equipment. During the recovery phase, the damage assessment team must develop itemized lists of all damage, including photographic documentation, as a result of the emergency. These inventories and surveys, along with the itemized lists of all damage sustained, make it possible to streamline the reimbursement process with underwriters and government officials.

After the team has compared the damage against the inventories before the incident, it must identify services, labor, and material necessary to restore operations to preincident levels. It will then determine and prioritize tasks to actually restore these services, labor, and materials. These tasks will then be able to have cost estimates and recovery schedules developed to better divide the various efforts and make them more manageable.

9.1.4.2 Clean-up and Salvage Operations

This team oversees all clean-up of the incident, including decontamination if necessary. Procurement of equipment to assist with this task is also accomplished by this team, including obtaining and placing dumpsters and contracting for decontamination services. The clean-up and salvage team may also be required to seek contractor support to repair damaged utilities and fire protection systems in order to bring these services back to operational status.

9.1.4.3 Business Restoration

The business restoration team is responsible for bringing the business back online. This is accomplished through implementation of the tasks identified by the work of the damage assessment team. This team obtains engineering and architectural drawings necessary for construction and renovation projects and they work with contractors to accomplish these projects. The business restoration team also obtains any new equipment to replace items destroyed as a result of the incident.

9.1.4.4 Customer and Client Information

This team has two primary tasks. The first task is conducted before any emergency incident, and this is to ensure that all contact information for your organization's customers and clients is kept in a secure location safe from any emergency occurring to the business. This can be accomplished as simply has storing the information on a flash drive or on an external server. The second task is accomplished during recovery efforts by providing the public, and particularly your clients, with accurate information regarding service hours, locations, or any changes in procedures. The customer and client information team provides general information about the best way to use company goods or services during the recovery phase and should provide public updates on the progress to restore services.

9.1.4.5 Mutual Aid and Agreement Activities

The mutual aid and agreement activity team determines what outside agencies can provide assistance with your organization's recovery efforts and attempts to obtain support from these respective agencies. This team must determine the extent and type of assistance that an external agency can provide and negotiate with these organizations to obtain specific terms for this assistance.

Governmental assistance is a major consideration, particularly if the disaster caused the local, state, or federal government to designate a disaster area that encompasses your company.

Aid can also encompass the expectation that your business will assist the community in the event of a disaster. In community-wide emergencies, business and industry are often requested to assist the local area with personnel, equipment, and shelter. This task should not be overlooked as your organization is working its own recovery.

9.2 Types of Emergency Incidents

There are several types of emergencies that can affect your organization, and your organization's response can differ based upon the cause and the damage that can result. Emergencies can be categorized into three main types of incidents: natural disasters, man-made incidents, and business-related incidents. We will look at specific emergencies within each of these and discuss actions that have been shown to minimize damage for that emergency.

9.2.1 Natural Disasters

Severe weather accounts for emergencies included within the natural disaster area. These incidents include:

- Tornadoes
- Hurricanes
- Earthquakes
- Flooding
- Snowstorms

The response for many of the severe weather emergencies is similar because these disasters will normally affect your organization in the same way. Severe weather typically results in damage or destruction to your facility and injuries to your employees as a result of the weather. Many of these natural disasters also result in interruptions to utility service and this should always be considered when developing plans to respond to any of these emergencies.

Response for severe weather should include the following actions. Notify staff of the severe weather alert and advise them of actions to be taken (e.g., release, evacuation, shelter-in-place). If the decision is made to shelter in-place, personnel should move to basements or hardened shelter if available. *Do not* use gyms or other large rooms as shelter during severe weather. At the conclusion of the severe weather, supervisors should account for their teams and report any missing personnel to your organization's designated point of contact to track accountability.

If your company is located in an area where earthquakes can occur, there are some specific response actions that should be taken during this type of natural incident. Once the shaking starts, personnel should immediately drop, cover, and hold their knees to the chest until the earthquake stops. If indoors, personnel should remain indoors. They should move away from windows, shelves, heavy objects, or furniture that may fall and take cover under desks, tables, counters, and open doorways. In halls, stairways, or other areas where cover is unavailable, personnel should move to an interior wall. Turn away from the windows and remain alongside the wall. The greatest danger from earthquake is injury from falling debris. If personnel are outside at the onset of an earthquake, they should remain outside and move away from the path of falling walls, power poles, trees, wire fences, and rolling rocks. During the earthquake, any individuals outside should lie down or crouch low to the ground. At the onset of the earthquake and if it is possible to accomplish in a safe manner, maintenance staff should conduct checks of utilities, systems, and appliances, and, if necessary, shut off main valves. Once the earthquake is over, supervisors should account for their teams and report any missing personnel to your organization's designated point of contact to track accountability. Additionally, maintenance staff should determine if any hazardous material has spilled or leaked, isolate and seal off the area, and notify the appropriate agency of the spill.

9.2.2 Man-Made Incidents

Man-made incidents are primarily composed of terrorism and criminal acts, both of which can significantly affect your organization.

9.2.2.1 Terrorism

Terrorism includes hostile acts against your organization by one individual or an organized group. Specific incidents we will look at within this area are active shooter scenarios, hostage situations, violent or uncooperative visitors, and vehicle-borne explosives. Within other sections, we discussed many different measures that can mitigate your organization's risk to these types of incidents. Specifically, physical security measures such as a viable access control system that includes limited entry points into your facility and entry guards or receptionists and duress alarms for the entry controllers to notify others of an incident can hinder or even deter a hostile intruder from entering your facility. Other physical security measures to include barriers to disable vehicles from getting close, or even entering, your facility can greatly minimize the threat from vehicle-borne explosives. Using these measures, along with others we have discussed, can make your facility a much more difficult target and potentially have terrorists look elsewhere for their planned attack.

9.2.2.1.1 ACTIVE SHOOTER SCENARIOS

Active shooter scenarios are unfortunately becoming more and more commonplace. Schools, shopping centers, government facilities, houses of worship, and businesses have all experienced this extremely violent act. Planning actions that should be taken in the event this could happen to your organization are as follows:

- In the event of either notification of an active shooter or upon hearing gunshots, each individual employee should make a determination if evacuation is safe for himself or herself and other coworkers. If the area is safe, personnel should immediately evacuate from the building. Once they are clear from the building and in a safe area, they should notify the police by calling 911.
- If evacuation is not possible or it is unsafe because of the location of the intruder(s), employees should initiate a lockdown of their room. As discussed in earlier sections, the goal of a lockdown is to isolate the intruder, whether it is in the hallway or completely out of the facility. Do not give the intruder the opportunity to enter your facility or move freely from room to room and have easy access to employees and visitors.
- Upon notification of a lockdown, personnel should immediately lock the door to their individual room and, if possible, maintenance staff should lock all exterior facility doors.
- In the event of an intruder inside the facility, personnel should move away from the door and attempt to reduce noise and ensure no one is visible from outside the room. Room lights should be turned off and, if possible, the door should be barricaded. If the intruder is inside the facility, it is recommended to keep any blinds open in order to either evacuate through windows if necessary or to provide visual communication to any potential first responders.

- In the event the threat is located outside the facility, personnel should move alongside the exterior walls, out of sight from the exterior. Close window and door blinds and attempt to reduce noise and ensure no one is visible from outside the room.
- As police enter the room, employees should remain on the floor and show their hands. *Do not* attempt to get up or request assistance as police enter a room. Police will notify personnel once they are free to move once they have secured the area.

9.2.2.1.2 HOSTAGE SITUATIONS

Hostage situations can occur at any location, including businesses. Employees experiencing divorce or child custody fights can be the subject of this type of incident. Specific considerations for hostage situation planning include:

- Isolating the perpetrator and the affected area, if possible, from other innocent bystanders or potential victims.
- Securing the perimeter of the area. It is important to prevent anyone else from entering the high-risk zone and add to the number of hostages.
- Evacuate all employees and visitors that can safely be removed from the facility.
- Individuals who are involved in the hostage situation should be trained. Talk to the perpetrator, if possible; however, it is vital that everyone understands they must avoid any heroics.
- The affected room should be monitored by camera or intercom, if available within your facility.
- Building intercoms should not be used to notify employees, as this may only heighten tensions with the perpetrator.

9.2.2.1.3 VIOLENT OR UNCOOPERATIVE VISITORS

Violent or uncooperative visitors can occur in any business organization. Employees who experience a bitter divorce, have child custody issues, or suffer abuse can be the victim of situations that require immediate action to remove an unwanted individual. It is important to take the following actions before these situations can result in a more severe incident.

- Remain calm and professional with the individual. Your organization's employees who monitor the access control system, such as security guards or receptionists, must be trained on how to deal with these types of situations and what actions should be taken.
- Determine the potential threat from the individual and report to the appropriate official or local law enforcement as necessary. Individuals can pose three increasing threats:
  - Level I threat: An individual who has the means, ability, and intent to carry out an issued threat should be immediately reported to local law enforcement and company executives.
  - Level II threat: An individual who may have the means, ability, and intent to carry out an issued threat should be immediately reported to local law enforcement and company executives.

- Level III threat: An individual who does not have the means, ability, and intent to carry out an issued threat should be reported to company executives. Your executive leadership can make a determination whether to notify local law enforcement.
- Document the offender's name and description for further reporting and ensure any security guards or receptionists are made aware of the situation so they may immediately report other attempted entries.
- If the individual leaves the building before reporting within your organization, security guards or receptionists should still notify company executives in the event the facility encounters future instances with the same individual.

9.2.2.1.4 VEHICLE-BORNE EXPLOSIVES

Vehicle-borne explosives have been a potential form of attack used by both individuals and terrorist organizations. Individual terrorist acts using a truck bomb were demonstrated by Timothy McVeigh in Oklahoma City's 1995 bombing of the U.S. Federal Building. Terrorist organizations have long used vehicle-borne explosives and continue to do so today, with some specific examples including the bombing of the U.S. Embassy in Beirut in 1983 and bombings of the U.S. Embassies in Kenya and Tanzania in 1998.

Because a potential attacker can place a great deal of explosives into a car or truck and ram the vehicle into the building, the primary method to defend against these types of attacks is to establish stand-off distance from your building so that vehicles cannot approach directly up to, and into, the facility. We have already discussed several physical security measures that can maximize this distance through landscaping and other physical barriers, in Chapter 5; however, even with implementation of many of these measures, it is still necessary to plan for your personnel's response in the event of this type of incident.

- In the event of a vehicle-borne attack that fails to explode, personnel must still immediately evacuate the building and ensure no one approaches the vehicle. The evacuation should ensure all personnel move a minimum of 500 ft away from the vehicle and building.
- In the event of an explosion, move all survivors away from the building a minimum of 500 ft. Do not approach the building or the area containing the initial explosion; a practice of many terrorist organizations that conduct these types of attacks includes placing secondary explosive devices to create further damage and injuries.

9.2.2.1.5 TERRORISM THREATS

It is critical that all employees are trained to achieve a measure of security awareness. This awareness can include an active Safety and Security Program within your organization that is supported by your senior management team. Having an active program, in conjunction with physical security measures at your facility and well-known procedures for your employee's response and reaction to potential threats, can significantly deter against any terrorist act against your company.

In the event your business receives any threats of potential terrorist action, this training and awareness will ensure your employees make proper notifications to your security point of contact and take proactive measures and stop any threat before they may occur.

9.2.2.2 Criminal Acts

Criminal acts differ from terrorism in that they will normally be less destructive and in many cases will avoid injuries of your employees are result in loss of life. We will look at various criminal acts that your emergency response planning should take into account, along with considerations to minimize their impact.

9.2.2.2.1 BOMBS/BOMB THREATS/SUSPICIOUS DEVICES

Bomb threats and suspicious devices can create significant disruptions to your business operations if personnel do not know how to properly react. Safety is always the paramount consideration for any incident involving bomb threats or suspicious devices; however, the first reaction may not necessarily require an organization to conduct an evacuation because of the loss in operations that these events can cause. The potential disruption from bomb threats is highlighted within the education industry. Bomb threats can take significant time away from the classroom and make teaching students extremely difficult and, unfortunately, many of these threats are initiated by the students themselves. During the 1997–1998 school year, one school district in Maryland reported 150 bomb threats and in 1999–2000 South Carolina's Department of Education listed "disturbing schools," which included bomb threats, hoaxes, and false fire alarms among its 10 top crimes, second only to simple assaults [1]. With time in any business being at a premium, it is imperative to have procedures to properly react to bomb threats and be able to better determine when evacuation is warranted and when the threat is an obvious hoax. There are several indicators regarding bomb threats that will help your organization maintain efficiency and effectiveness in your company's operations.

Because of the potential damage and extent of disruption that can be caused by a bomb, it is best to initially respond to any bomb threat on the assumption that a real bomb does exist. The items to consider whether the threat is valid or not relate to the seriousness of the threat and in general, specificity of the actual threat are the best guide to seriousness. Some items that indicate the specificity of an actual threat and ultimately show a more valid bomb threat include [1]:

- Specific time and place indicated in the threat
- Description of the bomb used
- Specific targets mentioned or indicated
- Motive or reason given or implied in the threat

Each bomb threat is a separate event and if your organization receives few to none, it is advisable to simply treat the threat as real and immediately proceed with the response procedures covered in the next paragraph. If, however, you receive a significant number of these threats, your executive management team can make the determination to conduct an evacuation based upon the seriousness of the threat.

Regardless of whether you believe the bomb threat is real or not, in the event your organization receives a bomb threat, considerations and actions for bombs, bomb threats, and suspicious devices after they are received or identified are as follows:

- If the bomb threat is received by phone, the staff member should not hang up the phone. Instead, he or she should notify the appropriate point of contact and call 911.
- The employee who receives the bomb threat should take notes on any information to include the caller's voice, tone, and the caller's mannerisms (see Figure 9.1 for sample bomb threat checklist).

BOMB THREAT CHECKLIST		
Date:	**Time:**	
Time Caller Hung Up:	**Phone Number Where Call was Received:**	

Ask Caller:

Where is the bomb located? (Building, Floor, Room, etc.)	
When will it go off?	
What does it look like?	
What kind of bomb is it?	
What will make it explode?	
Did you place the bomb?	Yes No
Why?	
What is your name?	

Exact Words of Threat:

Information About Caller:

Where is the caller located? (Background and level of noise)
Estimated Age:
Is voice familiar? If so, who does it sound like?
Other points:

Caller's Voice			Background Sounds		Threat Language
Accent	Disguised	Normal	Animal Noises	Motor	Incoherent
Angry	Distinct	Ragged	House Noises	Clear	Message Read
Calm	Excited	Rapid	Kitchen Noises	Static	Taped
Clearing Throat	Female	Raspy	Street Noises	Office Machinery	Irrational
Coughing	Laughter	Slow	Booth	Factory Machinery	Profane
Cracking Voice	Lisp	Slurred	PA System	Local	Well-Spoken
Crying	Loud	Soft	Conversation	Long Distance	
Deep	Male	Stutter	Music		
Deep Breathing	Nasal				

FIGURE 9.1 Sample bomb threat checklist.

- Staff should conduct a check of their work area to see if any suspicious items are present. If they find an item, *Do not* touch or move the item, but notify their supervisor or security point of contact immediately.
- Your executive management team should determine if evacuation is appropriate based upon receipt of a valid threat and reasonable suspicion that a bomb is present and if evacuation is decided upon, follow your organization's standard procedures.

Suspicious packages can also be a potential method to disrupt or attack a business. Your organization should conduct training to employees on how to react should anyone come in contact with a suspicious package and what to do if they receive a bomb threat. Some telltale signs of a suspicious package include:

- No return address
- Excessive postage
- Stains
- Strange odor
- Strange sounds
- Unexpected delivery or unique delivery method (e.g., package arrives by means other than UPS, FEDEX, US Postal Service)
- Poor handwriting
- Misspelled words
- Incorrect or vague job titles
- Foreign postage
- Restrictive notes

For suspicious packages received through the mail, there are some actions to consider that will mitigate some of the risks for this type of incident to occur:

- Provide training for personnel to include emphasis on recognizing all hazards that can be transported through the mail; include bombs, biological, and chemical threats; and ensure employees understand the appropriate response.
- Ensure it is difficult to gain access to much of the facility by limiting building access and funneling visitor traffic through the reception area.
- At a minimum, provide appropriate mail-handling procedures. A further action would be to consider funneling all mail deliveries through a central location or individual who can be trained to identify suspicious packages and react accordingly.

In the event a suspicious package or bomb threat is received, there are several actions to help prepare for these incidents. Place caller ID on your company phones to help identify bomb threat callers and consider blocking incoming calls if it is received from a phone with a blocked ID. Another action is to ensure your security procedures ask that staff members regularly conduct checks of their respective work area and report anything out of the ordinary.

9.2.2.2.2 VANDALISM

Preventing vandalism can be a complex issue because there are so many causes. Disgruntled employees, unhappy neighbors, unruly teenagers, or gang activity can all result in minor damage or defacement to your property and facility. The best way to prevent property vandalism is to find out how and why it is occurring and develop a strategy tailored to the situation. When working to combat vandalism, coordination with local law enforcement is necessary to determine what level of response they provide and if they require the damage or graffiti to not be cleaned until they have conducted their on-site investigation. Some methods to combat vandalism are to provide for strong physical security measures in and around your facility—if it is difficult to approach your building because of adequate perimeter boundaries, if there are cameras located in areas that are susceptible to vandalism with which to observe any illegal activity, or if there are alarms on the facility that will alert security or law enforcement to unwanted activity—all these measures can greatly deter potential vandals taking action against your facility.

9.2.2.2.3 GANG ACTIVITY

The level of gang activity that effects your organization will depend upon the area your business operates. If you are unsure what the level of activity and the potential for action by gangs operating in your area might be, it is advisable to check with your local law enforcement agency and determine how viable this threat may be. If it is determined that gangs are a problem within your area, primary mitigations and considerations for gang activity include:

- Communicate to your employees, and ask they communicate to their families, that your facility is neutral ground and that any gang activity will receive priority response.
- Coordinate with law enforcement and other criminal justice agencies to assist with gang activity education and training among your organization's staff. Training should include issues such as gang identification, intervention, and prevention techniques.
- If necessary, institute antigang education and prevention programs.

9.2.2.2.4 HOMICIDE AND OTHER FELONY CRIMINAL ACTIVITY

Unfortunately, no organization is immune from violent criminal activity. Primary considerations for these types of incidents at your facility include:

- Secure the perimeter of the crime scene as quickly as possible. Not only will this avoid contamination of the crime scene and assist law enforcement in its investigation, it will also prevent your staff from entering a high-risk zone and minimizing the impact of any violence or graphic images.
- Ensure your organization can provide a list of witnesses, friends, and other interested parties for law enforcement investigators as necessary.
- Be prepared to provide counseling services for affected employees.

9.2.3 Business-Related Incidents

Business-related incidents will normally result from the nature of your organization's function and employee base. If your company handles hazardous materials or has a large workforce, there are risks that may be associated with these unique characteristics that other businesses may not need worry about.

9.2.3.1 Hazardous Materials

If your company must work with hazardous materials or dangerous chemicals, there are many regulations and requirements that must be met. Even with safeguards in place, it can still be possible for an accident to occur, or for an overt act to cause an incident involving these materials. In the event of such an emergency, the primary threat during a hazardous material incident is toxic fumes; therefore, it is important to keep everyone safe by evacuation, decontamination, and sealing the area. If it is determined to shelter-in-place and seal the building, make every attempt to secure all windows, doors, and vents. This can be done by environmental controls designed into hazardous storage areas or by sealing all openings with plastic. Additional considerations to mitigate damage or injury include the following:

- Immediately notify your organization's point of contact and 911 describing the condition and type of hazardous material (if known).
- Your executive management team, or the responding emergency personnel, will determine if evacuation is appropriate.
- Your maintenance staff should determine as much information as possible regarding the hazardous material (e.g., type of material, location, amount) and provide this information to responding personnel.

9.2.3.2 Foodborne Threats

If your organization has a cafeteria or serves food in some manner, you should account for a foodborne incident such as food poisoning. The best measure against this type of incident is to ensure your food-handling staff actively enforces proper food storage and handling. Your procedures must also ensure all food preparation and food deliveries are accomplished in a controlled and uniform procedure among all your facilities. In the event of a possible foodborne incident, the following actions should be taken:

- The affected location must immediately inform their supervisor and any local health services agencies.
- Your executive management team should close the affected food service facility and make proper notifications to all employees.

9.2.3.3 Protest Activity

Although protest activities are normally associated with unionized labor, it is possible for any organization to be subject to protestors either from inside or outside the organization. For this reason, it is important that all organizations have plans in place in the event this type of incident may occur.

In many cases, protest activities are preannounced and the time and place are known. In this eventuality, your executive management team should coordinate with local law enforcement personnel a few days before the event to advise them of the upcoming protest. Even if a protest occurs with no notice, the following considerations apply for either situation:

- Interaction between the protestors and your staff should be minimal; however, if employees come in contact, they should treat all protestors courteously and professionally.
- Employees should carry on with their normal activities and use a low-key approach with protestors, although all alternate entrances should be secured.
- In the event the protest has the potential to, or becomes, violent, your staff should immediately secure the facility and notify law enforcement.

9.2.3.4 Medical Health Epidemics

Any type of epidemic can create severe problems for any organization because of the large number of employees that come in contact with one another on a daily basis. Typically, any determination of a potential medical health epidemic, along with the notification, is initiated by the appropriate local health organization. If your business receives such a notification, the primary action your organization will need to consider is whether to close your facility until the medical issues are resolved. In this case, continuous coordination with the health department in your area should be done throughout the emergency to make any further determinations regarding continued closure and decisions regarding when it is safe to open the facility to your employees again.

9.3 Additional Considerations Related to Emergency Planning Procedures

9.3.1 Emergency Response Checklists

One of the best emergency response tools to develop before an incident includes checklists that provide key personnel with necessary actions in the event of an emergency. No matter how highly trained a team may be, an emergency incident will overwhelm even the best leaders and managers—particularly during the initial moments of the event. Checklists will provide these personnel with a tool that helps remind them with the overall actions they need to take so they can concentrate on the other decisions and tasks specific to the emergency at hand. Figure 9.2 shows an example of a checklist for a suspicious device or suspected bomb incident.

Checklists such as the example shown can greatly assist in your organization's response and ongoing actions throughout an emergency. This assistance can pay dividends by minimizing any loss or damage if proper action was taken at the start of any incident.

9.3.2 Business Continuity Planning

A major aspect of emergency response planning is business continuity. Although this aspect of emergency planning can typically be included within the recovery phase of an

EMERGENCY RESPONSE CHECKLIST
BOMB OR SUSPICIOUS PACKAGE FOUND

Action	Responsibility
Notify Law Enforcement via 911 • Provide information on description of item and location	
Announce evacuation over public address system and include the following: • Turn off all cell phones and do not use • Do not touch or handle any suspicious items • Location for evacuation (if different from standard evacuation area)	
Evacuate the building	
Pre-Identified staff members monitor exits during evacuation and lock doors when complete	
Notify executive management (per company instructions)	
Coordinate with incident commander as requested and ensure evacuation is outside safe distance (normally 500 feet)	
Conduct a sweep of building to verify everyone has evacuated (dependent upon time and circumstances)	
Determine personnel accountability and report to company designee	
At conclusion of incident, report total accountability to executive management. List shall include: • Total personnel • Separate list of injured personnel • Separate list of casualties	

FIGURE 9.2 Sample of an emergency response checklist for a suspicious device or suspected bomb.

emergency, it is important enough that we will discuss it separately to ensure your plans take this into account.

When your business is disrupted, it can cost money, and these lost revenues plus extra expenses means reduced profits. Insurance does not cover all costs and cannot replace customers that defect to the competition, thus a business continuity plan is an essential part of emergency response planning. Development of a business continuity plan includes four steps:

- Conduct a business impact analysis to identify time-sensitive or critical business functions and processes, along with the resources that support these items.
- Identify, document, and implement plans necessary to recover these critical business functions and processes.
- Organize a business continuity team and compile a business continuity plan to manage a business disruption.
- Conduct training for the business continuity team and accomplish testing and exercises to evaluate recovery strategies and the current plan.

A key consideration for any business continuity plan is to ensure coverage of your information technology resources and components. These items, which include networks, servers, desktop and laptop computers, and wireless devices, are critical in running any business operation in today's environment. With this in mind, recovery strategies for your critical information technology resources must be developed so that technology can be restored to meet your organization's business needs. Your business continuity plan must also include manual workarounds as part of your information technology plan so business can continue while computer systems are being restored.

9.4 Summary

Throughout this chapter, we have looked at methods for your organization to develop an adequate emergency response plan. This plan should cover the four primary areas discussed; mitigation, preparedness, response, and recovery; we also looked at specific items within each of these areas. Many of the mitigating actions your organization can implement to either minimize or even deter an emergency incident are discussed in one of the three main security program areas: physical security, information security, and personnel security. Implementing measures from these areas can greatly reduce the impact of several of the emergencies we discussed. To prepare for an actual incident, we covered command and control, communications, collection and distribution of resources, coordination, and congestion. A key point from the preparedness area is the designation of an organization emergency response team along with a clear delineation of roles and responsibilities before the initiation of any incident. If personnel understand what action they must take, your ability to respond to any emergency will drastically improve. We also covered the response and recovery aspects of an emergency.

This chapter also looked at specific types of emergency incidents that most businesses should plan for, along with considerations and actions that can be taken to minimize damage and injury in the event your organization could experience these emergencies. Last, we covered some additional considerations for emergency response planning, including use of checklists and business continuity planning.

Overall, there is one major aspect that can greatly reduce the impact of any emergency—this is ensuring your organization has a plan in place before any incident because it is too late to determine how you will respond once the emergency has occurred.

9.5 Emergency and Contingency Planning Checklist

	Yes	No
Does your organization have an emergency response plan?		
Has your business identified "single-point failures" in your critical functions and provided redundancies?		
Has your company identified communication methods during an emergency and provided equipment to ensure continuous communications for all types of events?		

	Yes	No
Does your company facility have audible loudspeakers or alarms to warn employees of emergency situations?		
Has your organization identified all critical resources needed in an emergency and are their locations known?		
Does your organization have an emergency response team?		
Are tasks and responsibilities for members of your emergency response team specifically delineated?		
Has your emergency response plan taken into account the following areas: • Command and management of emergency operations • Fire management • Security and traffic control operations • Emergency medical operations • Staff care and shelter operations • Facility management and plant operations • Internal rescue operations		
Does your organization have personnel designated for the following teams during the recovery phase: • Damage assessment • Clean-up and salvage operations • Business restoration • Customer and client information • Mutual aid and agreement activities		
Does your organization have an up-to-date inventory and survey of assets critical to your business?		
Does your company have a contact list of clients and customers secure from any emergency occurring at your business?		

Note: All items are listed in priority order so you should ensure each answer is "yes" before expending funds or effort on the next question. This ensures an executive with minimal security expertise can easily move down the list to implement an adequate security program.

Reference

[1] Newman GR. Bomb threats in schools; 2002.

Recommending Reading for Emergency and Contingency Planning

Erickson PA. Emergency response planning for corporate and municipal managers. Academic Press.

Bullock JA, Haddow G. Introduction to emergency management. Butterworth–Heinemann.

10

Safety and Security Training Program

Although this is the final chapter, your organization's safety and security training program should not be an afterthought, and through the course of your employee training, you cannot emphasize safety and security concepts enough. A viable training program has several functions:

- Ensure your employees understand their roles and responsibilities in regard to the overall safety and security program.
- Ensure all employees know what actions they should take in the event of an emergency.
- Provide increased security awareness among all individuals within the organization.

This last function—increased employee security awareness—can be difficult to achieve; however, we have discussed this concept several times throughout the book for the simple reason that it is the most effective security measure you can institute within your organization. It cannot only result in exponential increases for your company's security posture, but it can also save your organization time and money. This is due to the increased ability that a security-conscious workforce can provide with respect to highlighting security concerns, notifying suspicious actions, questioning unauthorized personnel, or reporting any issue out of the ordinary. An organization that possesses employees with increased security awareness will not require the same amount of security precautions and hardware of a similar company because each individual within the organization acts as a security guard and augments the security measures that are already in place. In effect, high security awareness among all your employees will increase the number of security sensors, which can add to other types of security measures and, in some cases, can even replace the need for expensive protection countermeasures and equipment.

To develop an effective organizational safety and security training program and begin the process of increasing your company's security awareness, it is necessary to implement three different opportunities to train your personnel. First, an initial safety and security training course should be included as part of your employee indoctrination or in-processing program. Second, recurring safety and security training should be periodically conducted for all employees within your organization. The last training method that is included in a complete program provides for the conduct of exercises that practice the safety and security concepts and tasks. These exercises not only reinforce classroom training, they also provide employees an opportunity to learn their roles and responsibilities in the event of an actual emergency—which is ultimately the primary reason for safety and security training. We will look at each of these training methods over the next several sections within this chapter.

10.1 Initial Safety and Security Training

This is likely the most important training that you will conduct within your organization because it sets the foundation, establishes your organization's commitment to safety and security, and ensures your employees understand the various aspects of your company's program. This can be easily accomplished in an hour or two by your organization's primary security point of contact with a professional presentation during the standard company in processing and indoctrination. A formal classroom presentation sets the tone for your organization and promotes the concept that safety and security is an important part of doing business within your company. This training also provides new employees with the necessary information regarding their responsibilities and actions should an emergency occur before they can review the safety and security plan (if they will ever review it at all).

Some of the items that should be covered during this initial training are as follows:

- Discussing the security goals and objectives for the organization.
- Defining and explaining the three major areas within security—physical security, information security, and personnel security.
- Discussing the employee security awareness program and its importance within the organization's safety and security program.
- Identifying the organizational safety and security point of contact, including office location and contact information.
- Informing new employees of their responsibilities and actions in the event of an emergency. This should include a discussion that all employees should be familiar with the organization's safety and security plan and procedures. Responsibilities should also include any requirements to report information—this can include reporting suspicious activity, changes in an individual's status (e.g., name, citizenship, and marital status), loss of an employee identification card, or other adverse information.
- Requirements and guidelines governing security clearances (if applicable within your organization).
- Defining what resources are designated as critical within your organization and discussing company regulations that govern access to these resources.

By conducting this training at the start of an employee's career with your organization, it is easy to provide the emphasis that safety and security is a part of every individual's duties.

10.2 Recurring Safety and Security Training

In addition to initial training, recurring safety and security training should be conducted for every employee within your organization. This training should be conducted on a periodic basis—once or twice a year should be the frequency goal—and can include any number of issues pertinent to your organization's safety and security program. Subjects that you may consider for this recurring training can include emphasis on items that were covered during the initial indoctrination training, concentration on specific response actions for a particular type of emergency or incident based on management concerns, actions to potential threats that may exist against your company or are possible in the region where you conduct business, or a discussion and analysis of recent security incidents that were in the news. This last subject—incorporating recent incidents and events—has the advantage to make a specific recurring training session be more interesting and have a larger impact on individuals, which will achieve greater buy-in among your employees. Regardless of what subjects you may choose to include in this recurring training, it should be conducted a minimum of once each year so that you continue to place the appropriate emphasis on safety and security within your organization and promote continued security awareness among your employees.

10.3 Safety and Security Exercises

The last major training opportunity we will look at is the conduct of safety and security exercises. Any plan that only exists in a binder on the shelf, or on a hard drive or server, is not one that will be successfully put into practice when the need arises. Exercises and simulations require a little more time and planning than other training methods; however, they provide several significant benefits to any organization's safety and security program. One benefit is that a good exercise provides the most accurate assessment of the current safety and security plan's response actions to a particular incident, with the exception of an actual emergency. A well-run exercise provides the most realistic evaluation of your organization's response and, as such, will highlight any significant areas for improvement so that an organization can correct its plan before an actual emergency. Another benefit is to identify any training deficiencies or confusion regarding your employees' actions during their response to an emergency. An exercise will make it easy to identify whether most personnel understand their particular role and their responsibility in the event of an incident. If there are any issues or if employees are unsure what should be accomplished during the response to the emergency, the safety and security plan should be looked at to ensure it contains clear direction and management may need to consider additional training to be conducted so that employees better understand what actions they need to take. Exercises also provide a more valuable and realistic training, which is more likely to be internalized by the employees who participate than any training from a classroom presentation that they might receive. Another benefit exercises provide is to determine if there is any equipment or procedural shortfalls required to meet the organization's planned response to an emergency. For example, if communication was not addressed in the response plans to a natural disaster, an exercise may highlight the need to obtain portable radios or walkie-talkies to ensure your business can communicate during the event. This section will help you achieve these benefits by describing and helping you develop the various types of exercises and simulations by which your safety and security plan will be tested, exercised, and improved on.

Unfortunately, these benefits come with some additional effort because the accomplishment of an exercise requires more work than the other types of training. These exercises take a good deal of planning and preparation—especially so that they ensure they will provide useful feedback on your current plan and accomplish the necessary training for your employees. Despite this effort, however, conducting an exercise will pay dividends to any organization's safety and security program, and the benefits they achieve are well worth the effort because they will provide improved plans and identify the necessary equipment that will minimize damage and possible injury in the event of an actual emergency.

A primary consideration when you conduct your exercises includes providing knowledgeable personnel who can develop the exercise scenario and conduct an objective evaluation of the exercise to assess your plan and employee response during the simulation. This is critical because, without an observer who can watch and assess everyone's response during the event, a valid evaluation of your safety and security plan and its directed response will be difficult to gauge. The effort of an exercise may be wasted if one attempts to evaluate the exercise themselves—especially when trying to accomplish their own actions during the response to the incident. To ensure an individual remains objective in his or her assessment, it is necessary that he or she does not have any additional duties or responsibilities during the simulated emergency. This can either be accomplished by designating a group of individuals from within your organization to accomplish this assessment or working with personnel from an outside agency. In many cases, local law enforcement or fire departments may be willing to assist in evaluating your exercise or you may consider working with a security consultant to provide this service. Regardless of how you decide to provide for these evaluators, it cannot be emphasized enough that they should not be part of the actual response; otherwise, many of the results and areas for improvement obtained during the exercise may be inaccurate.

There are three types of exercises that will assist with training and evaluation of your safety and security plans and procedures: emergency drills, table-top scenarios, and full-scale exercises. Each of these exercises requires varying levels of effort while still providing the benefits a simulation has to offer. An emergency drill is the simplest and easiest exercise to plan and prepare for, followed by a slightly larger amount of effort necessary to accomplish a table-top scenario; eventually, the exercise spectrum moves toward the full-scale exercise, which is the most complex scenario to plan and conduct. With this increasing amount of effort, each of these types of exercises allow for an increasing amount of information and identification of areas for improvement respective to the amount of work necessary to accomplish these three types of exercises.

To conduct any of these types of exercises, there is a similar process that is necessary to accomplish. As discussed earlier, each of the exercises involves a varying level of effort and these steps will become more involved as you proceed from a fairly simple simulation of an emergency drill to a full-scale emergency response exercise. However, the following steps provide an easy-to-follow process to plan any type of exercise:

1. Organize and designate an Exercise Management Team to plan, conduct, and evaluate the exercise. This may be a permanent group of individuals, as was detailed in the

draft safety and security plan contained within Chapter 3, or it could be formed at the initiation of any exercise planning process. The Exercise Management Team should include an exercise director and additional personnel to assist with all necessary tasks to conduct the exercise and its results.

2. Determine the goal of the exercise. This is a critical step for any successful exercise, and you should ensure management agrees and understands the goal before proceeding with any further planning. In the context of conducting an emergency drill exercise, the goal should be fairly limited because the primary response for this type of incident is that everyone should evacuate the facility. Some example goals for this type of exercise could include ensuring all employees are aware of the alternate evacuation rally point or their actions during a long-distance evacuation.

3. Review the emergency response actions required within your organization's safety and security plan. Again, this step not only applies to just emergency drill exercises but to all types of safety and security simulations. This review will ensure management and the exercise team is aware of what the plan requires and may identify some shortfalls or areas for improvement before the actual conduct of the exercise.

4. Development of the exercise scenario. The scenario should be as detailed as possible and should include any necessary notifications to ensure the scope of the exercise stays on track to meet its specific goals. During a real-world emergency that mirrors the exercise, there will likely be specific events and notifications that would normally occur. For example, in the case of an active-shooter scenario, it will be necessary to accomplish a timeline of what would occur during the exercise (e.g., the shooter enters the facility, he or she proceeds to a specific location, and he or she takes hostages and locks everyone into a room). To ensure a complete scenario is accomplished, it is necessary to include three major items: the overall scenario narrative, subordinate scenarios, and the master scenario events list (MSEL), which we will cover this item in more detail in a few paragraphs. The overall scenario narrative should include a description of the emergency and any effects that affect your organization. An example of an overall scenario narrative is in Figure 10.1.

Exercise scenario narrative

Overview

At approximately 7:20 am local time, the area experienced a magnitude 6.8 earthquake. The epicenter was located approximately 3 miles from XYZ Corporation and our employees noticeably felt the quake. The earthquake lasted for approximately 45 s and based upon initial reports, this event caused "light to moderate damage" throughout the local area.

The earthquake resulted in an explosion/fire within the manufacturing area of the XYZ Corporation facility. It is believed that the cause was due to a gas pipeline rupture. Local law enforcement and fire department have been notified and are responding.

FIGURE 10.1 Example of an exercise scenario narrative.

Subordinate scenarios are events that occur subsequent to the initial event. These events can describe actions by first responders, required initial response actions within your organization, or other emergencies that may result from the initial incident. Some examples of subordinate scenarios that would tie into the overall scenario narrative are included in Figure 10.2.

The final item that must be accomplished to fully develop the exercise scenario is the MSEL. Proper development of the exercise scenario requires that the Emergency Management Team prepare proper exercise inputs—the MSEL is the standard method for exercise planners to accomplish and sequence these exercise inputs. This document can be fairly simple and broad in nature when used for a small-scale emergency drill, or it can be a detailed script that prompts exercise participants to take some type of response action for larger scale exercises. The MSEL identifies the timing and summarizes all key events, messages, inputs, and contingency messages, which need to occur during the exercise. Because this document contains the entire exercise sequence, the MSEL should be prepared in secrecy so that employees are unaware what type of emergency will occur or what actions should be taken to obtain a more valid assessment of the organization response plan. To maintain this necessary confidentiality, the MSEL is typically developed exclusively by the Exercise Management Team. This group should ensure extremely limited distribution of the information within the MSEL so that the simulation can better gauge all participants' response as the scenario progresses because the lack of any prenotification of the exercise ultimately makes the event more realistic—remember that employees would not have prior warning to an actual emergency incident! We will cover development of the MSEL in detail within the section covering full-scale exercises, because this type of event requires the most detailed and complex scenario listing.

5. Prior coordination with any applicable emergency response agencies. In the event your exercise could initiate some type of alarm within the facility, it is best to accomplish coordination with all local emergency response agencies before the exercise to provide them notification of the simulation and also obtain their assistance and expertise.
6. Conduct the exercise. The Exercise Management Team should conduct the exercise and ensure they have adequate numbers of individuals located in key areas to assess and evaluate employee response to the incident. This can include evaluators at the incident

Subordinate scenarios

- Partial building collapse occurred in the manufacturing area with several reported injuries/casualties.
- Facility alarm system has stopped functioning due to damage from the earthquake.
- Looting has been reported in the local area.
- Several other nearby facilities are experiencing fires.

FIGURE 10.2 Examples of subordinate scenarios.

location itself, spread throughout the facility to assess employee reaction, and colocated with your organization's leadership team at the on-scene control location.

7. Conduct an exercise hot wash. Immediately on conclusion of the exercise, the Exercise Management Team should conduct a hot wash of the exercise with your organization's senior management team. This hot wash will typically include a brief run-down of the exercise scenario, what the required response actions should have been, what actual reactions to the simulation occurred, and any areas for improvement. The hot wash should also include key participants in the exercise to obtain their input and perspective.

8. Develop the exercise report. The Exercise Management Team should accomplish a formal exercise report that contains background on the exercise, areas for improvement, and any recommended changes to the current organizational safety and security plan.

By accomplishing these steps, your safety and security exercise will provide better training and identify any issues within your current safety and security plan. Over the next several sections, we will look at each type of exercise so that you can conduct any of these simulations and allow for your organization to obtain the benefit from conducting safety and security exercises.

10.3.1 Emergency Drills

The purpose of an emergency drill is to familiarize personnel with the safety procedures and ensure everyone is aware of the actions to take in the event of a real emergency. The best example of an emergency drill is a fire drill which most every facility owner or operator must accomplish on a periodic basis because this and other types of emergency drills are typically a requirement of local or federal statutes. Even though some types emergency drills are mandatory, that does not preclude that they should be accomplished simply to "check off the box" in meeting a particular requirement. Instead, an organization with a good safety and security program can maximize the benefit they can provide when conducting these types of exercises with just a small amount of additional planning. This will ensure you not only meet the regulatory requirements to accomplish the emergency drill, but, in addition, you will allow for your organization to practice some emergency response actions in conjunction with the event. Regardless of what type of scenario you may use to exercise an emergency drill, you should develop a brief master scenario events list (MSEL), which will be covered when we look at full-scale exercise development.

10.3.1.1 Emergency Drill Considerations

One consideration of any emergency drill is that evacuation of the facility is the standard response for employees and other individuals. To properly be prepared for any type of emergency drill, it is necessary that your organization account for both short- and long-distance evacuation scenarios, as was discussed in Chapter 9. Short-distance evacuations are the quickest method to get personnel out of the building and into specific areas that are in close proximity to the facility while long-distance evacuations are defined as evacuations that result in personnel being located no closer than 400 yards from the building once they are in their designated location. Short-distance evacuations should be accomplished for immediate evacuation of the building and are normally accomplished in the event of a fire drill and other events that require personnel to immediately leave the facility. Long-distance evacuations may require alternate transportation if walking is impractical because of distances, the location of your facility (i.e., if the building is on a major thoroughfare or highway), or weather considerations in your region. These types of evacuations are normally accomplished for gas leaks, bomb threats, chemical/biological incidents, or other emergencies that could result in a hazard in the immediate area of the facility. Because of the potential logistical difficulties, long-distance evacuations should only be directed by a designated individual within your organization, such as the security manager or other suitable executive, or may be ordered by local law enforcement or fire department officials.

Another consideration to take into account prior to any evacuation is that your organization should designate multiple rally points for individual work sections or employees. These multiple locations for personnel to gather provide flexibility so that employees are prepared to evacuate to alternate locations in the event that the primary rally point or area is unavailable. Once an alternate rally point has been designated, the easiest procedure is to make staff aware of both the primary and alternate locations but plan that during an actual evacuation, staff will normally proceed to the primary location unless they have been notified of the use of the alternate on initiation of the evacuation.

Another consideration for any type of evacuation—particularly in the event of an actual emergency—is the ability to ensure accountability of all your employees and visitors to your facility at the time of the incident. This is a critical process and should not only account for all individuals assembled in their respective evacuation area but also determine any missing visitors or employees who are within your organization at the time of the emergency.

A final issue to consider before an actual evacuation is to determine the process to notify release of employees for the day or for an extended period of time in the event of significant damage to the facility. Typically, this process should include who has the authority to make this decision (normally this should be the responsibility of the chief executive officer but whoever is the appropriate authority should be designated), along with the notification procedure to let your employees know.

Once you have planned for these considerations, your organization is not only ready to plan for an emergency drill exercise but, more important, your business is prepared to respond to a real-world emergency.

10.3.2 Table-Top Scenarios

Conducting a table-top exercise is a little more involved than planning an emergency drill; however, it provides additional benefits to your organization created by a more thorough look at the necessary emergency response and the opportunity for greater involvement among your staff. Furthermore, you can tailor the extent of the exercise based on your needs and available time. For example, a table-top exercise can be as simple as determining the type of emergency to use in your scenario, summarizing the necessary response, providing copies of the plan, and conducting the exercise in a conference room. In addition to the standard preparatory steps to conducting an exercise, we will look at the specific steps for this type of exercise over the next several paragraphs.

10.3.2.1 Exercise Preparation

The first step is to prepare for the table-top exercise. This preparation includes development of the scenario. As discussed in the overall exercise planning steps, development of the exercise scenario is accomplished through the development of an MSEL. The development of the MSEL is included in the section on full-scale exercises because this type of exercise will require the most detailed development of scenario events. Another task included in preparation is to schedule the time and location to conduct the exercise—again, it is not necessary to accomplish a table-top exercise at an actual venue as this will make planning more difficult. Instead, the exercise can be conducted in a standard meeting room. The only necessity for the area is to ensure the room has enough table space for all the participants to review material and ideally have white boards or other equipment to assist participants in communicating ideas, actions, or working through processes over the course of the exercise. It is also advisable to establish a strict end time for the exercise and ensure this is adhered to—some agencies may choose to use a timekeeper to ensure the exercise ends at the agreed-upon time. This will ensure the exercise does not drag on, which could deter you from conducting another exercise. Another task necessary in exercise preparation is obtaining and organizing all necessary material to include an agenda, exercise objectives, assumptions, copies of the safety and security plan, and appropriate emergency response checklists. The last task to prepare for a table-top exercise is to ensure all appropriate personnel are invited to attend. It is unlikely that there can be too many personnel who are participating in a table-top exercise—the major consideration is to ensure a key member is not absent as this could limit the benefit of conducting the exercise. It may also be advisable to consider inviting some outside agencies who may be pertinent to the specific type of emergency or who would be required to assist with your organization's response.

10.3.2.2 Conducting the Exercise

Now that planning is accomplished, the next step is to actually conduct the table-top exercise. Some areas to cover at the initiation of the exercise include the following:

- Review of the exercise agenda, objectives, and assumptions.
- Discuss ground rules, participant roles and responsibilities, and timing.
- Provide and distribute a copy of the exercise scenario.
- Ensure an individual is available and primarily responsible to take notes.

Once these areas have been accomplished, the exercise director should begin providing inputs in accordance with the MSEL to the group. During the course of the exercise, the director should not only provide inputs to prompt action by the participants but also act as a mediator to ensure all the participants consider the appropriate response actions. Last, the exercise director should also promote communication throughout the exercise to the entire group as the primary purpose of the event is to train everyone on the appropriate actions.

10.3.2.3 Postexercise Actions

The last step is to conduct the postexercise actions once the exercise has been conducted. This step should include discussion from all the exercise participants on the following areas:

- Evaluate the group's response actions to the simulated emergency.
- Identify equipment items necessary for the organization to accomplish the necessary response.
- Identify procedural areas for improvement to incorporate into the safety and security plan.
- Conduct lessons learned.

It is critical to ensure your schedule provides for this and to ensure enough time is available at the end of the meeting because this step is the most important task in the process. Although much of the training and learning can be accomplished throughout the exercise scenario, the majority of training, along with any long-term improvements necessary to your safety and security plan, is best identified at the conclusion of the exercise.

10.3.3 Full-Scale Exercises

A full-scale exercise is much more involved than either an emergency drill or a table-top exercise and requires significant planning and coordination with your employees and other affected agencies. Many large full-scale state and federal exercises can take months to plan and the actual exercise may last for several days. Fortunately, most businesses will not need to conduct exercises of this magnitude so it is unnecessary to devote this amount of planning and preparation nor is it necessary to conduct exercises for such long periods of time. Even so, it must be noted that full-scale exercises will take more effort than smaller-scale exercises. However, this additional time and planning will result in several advantages to include a higher level of education and training for all participants, greater clarity to identify areas for improvement, and a higher level of experience gained by your organization's staff. As with the other types of exercises, preparation should include the standard steps we have already discussed to conduct any type of exercise. Because of the larger scale, a full-scale exercise will also require similar preparation steps for a table-top exercise, although many of these tasks will require a greater level of effort. Last, a full-scale exercise will require some unique tasks to provide the necessary realism and obtain the greatest benefit from the time and effort in conducting this type of exercise. We will look at these tasks and processes by dividing them into the primary tasks we looked at when discussing table-top exercises: preparation, conduct of the exercise, and postexercise actions.

10.3.3.1 Exercise Preparation

One of the most significant differences in preparing a full-scale exercise to that of the other types of exercises is the additional effort required to develop a detailed scenario. Although the other types of exercises may only need a brief narrative of the exercise scenario, because of the level of detail required for a full-scale exercise, it is necessary to develop a thorough and detailed MSEL. As discussed earlier, the MSEL is the document that identifies the timing of exercise inputs, summarizes events, details any messages to be provided to participants, and describes actions necessary for the exercise to progress. Normally, it is best that the MSEL is developed through several iterations because any and all inputs that the exercise participants would likely experience, based on the overall scenario narrative, should be included in the MSEL. As such, careful attention should be made when developing this document to ensure all functional areas are included, subsequent actions to an initial input are thought through, and significant actions occur based on the overall scenario. By using our earlier examples of the exercise narrative and subordinate scenarios in Figures 10.1 and 10.2, some example exercise inputs are contained in the sample MSEL within Figure 10.3 to give you an idea of the level of detail necessary for a full-scale exercise MSEL.

This list is only a sample to provide you with an idea of the level of detail necessary to develop a complete and thorough MSEL for a full-scale exercise. Typically, MSELs for a full-scale exercise can include dozens or even hundreds of inputs and the expected outcome of any input should be tailored to match your company's responses, as directed within your safety and security plan. Based on the completed exercise scenario, along with the other standard exercise planning tasks that were discussed earlier in this chapter, the following areas specific to a full-scale exercise should be accomplished.

Determine the appropriate location to conduct the exercise. This location must be large enough to provide the necessary space for your employees' response and other actions, and it should also be able to allow for necessary actions that ensure the maximum amount of reality possible. Although most organizations will conduct a full-scale exercise within their own facility, there may be instances where it would be safer or cheaper to conduct the exercise elsewhere. For example, if a necessary response to the emergency could result in personal injury based on the characteristics of your particular building, you may consider looking at other locations that would provide for a safer environment. Another example could be that the appropriate response could result in minor damage to the facility—most law enforcement special tactics units do not accomplish dynamic entry methods at a new facility, but instead these exercises are normally accomplished in abandoned or derelict buildings because of the potential for damage that will occur through the breaking down of doors, windows, or walls during the entry procedures. Any of these potential requirements should be accounted for when deciding whether to conduct an exercise at your own

#	Time	From	Dept	To	Method	Message	Expected outcome
001	0:00 (Exercise start)	Exercise director	All	All players	Loudspeaker	The area is experiencing an earthquake. You feel a significant amount of shaking and movement and in many work areas, items fall off shelves and light to moderate damage occurs throughout the facility. After about 30 s an explosion is heard from the manufacturing area. The earthquake lasts for approximately 45 s.	Employees should follow standard earthquake response actions to include moving to the floor and remaining in a safe area.
002	0:01	Evaluator 1	Manufacturing	Manufacturing foreman	Exercise input form	About 30 s after the earthquake starts, the northwest portion of the roof collapses and a fire breaks out in the area. Several workers are in that area at the time of the collapse.	Attempt to put out the fire with company equipment (this will fail) and try to identify injured employees.
003	0:01 + (Depends upon speed of response)	Evaluator 1	Manufacturing	Manufacturing foreman	Verbal input	Once Manufacturing Foreman and/or other personnel have located injured personnel, identify each individual's injuries as follows: • Player 1 – Broken arm and ribs, possible internal bleeding • Player 2 – Major lacerations across torso and second-degree burns • Player 3 – Crushed torso from falling debris, possible broken back and internal bleeding • Player 4 – Broken leg and collarbone, bleeding from head laceration (non-arterial)	Identify employees, practice standard first aid on injuries, and report personnel accountability to Human Resources in accordance with company procedures.
004	0:06	Exercise director	All	CEO	Exercise input form	Fire Department has arrived on-scene and is moving towards the location of the fire.	Make contact with Fire Chief to determine what assistance is required from company.
005	0:18	Evaluator 2	Public affairs	PA director	Exercise input form	You have been notified that a local television news station has just reported the roof collapse and fire at the company facility on television. In their story, they have further reported that injuries were sustained by some employees.	Notify CEO and take appropriate actions to coordinate with local media. Begin coordination with Human Resources for personnel accountability in order to determine missing employees and casualties.
006	0:20	Evaluator 3	Reception	Company receptionist	Exercise input form	You have been flooded with calls from friends and families to determine the status of their respective employee.	Notify Public Affairs and coordinate with Human Resources for additional personnel to assist with the influx of telephone calls.

FIGURE 10.3 Sample master scenario events list (MSEL).

facility or an alternate location, such as federal land or other locations, to provide the most realistic scenario possible.

Acquire and provide the necessary personnel and equipment. The first area that we will look at within this section is the personnel required because there are several different types of participants necessary to conduct a full-scale exercise.

- Players. Players are the personnel who are responding and reacting to the exercise. Exercise players will include your organization's employees, and they have the most important task in the exercise because they will be performing their regular roles and responsibilities as they would during an actual emergency. Ideally, players should discuss or initiate actions based on their own knowledge of the organization's response procedures.
- Controllers. Controllers are the main participants that organize and conduct the exercise. They plan and manage exercise play, set up and operate the exercise location, and act in the roles of organizations or individuals that are not playing in the exercise. Controllers direct the pace of the exercise, provide key data to players, and may prompt or initiate certain player actions to ensure continuity of the exercise. In addition, they issue exercise material to players as required, monitor the exercise timeline, and supervise the safety of all exercise participants.
- Simulators. Simulators are control staff personnel who role-play nonparticipating organizations or individuals such as a law enforcement desk or federal agency that would be required to respond to the particular emergency. They most often operate out of a control center that is out of sight from players; however, there may be occasional circumstances where they are required to have face-to-face contact with players. Simulators function semi-independently under the supervision of exercise controllers, enacting roles (e.g., media reporters or next of kin) in accordance with instructions provided in the exercise scenario or MSEL.
- Evaluators. Evaluators are the personnel who assess the players and the organizational procedures. They normally evaluate and provide feedback on a designated functional area of the exercise (e.g., human resources, operations, maintenance, and security) respective to their area of expertise. Evaluators observe and document performance against established capability targets and critical tasks.
- Actors. Actors simulate specific roles during exercise play (typically, victims or other bystanders); however, their performance is normally not evaluated.

Although your organization's employees will constitute the players within the exercise who will be easy to gain their participation, it will also be necessary to obtain knowledge-able personnel to perform the other necessary functions within the exercise scenario. It may not be necessary to obtain all the types of participants previously listed to conduct a full-scale exercise—this will depend on the size, scope, and scenario—however, it will be necessary to identify some additional personnel to evaluate and control the exercise. In many cases, it may be possible to have one individual fill multiple roles (a standard practice is to have personnel fill both controller and evaluator roles to save manpower); however, this will again depend on the size of the exercise. The main consideration is to look at the exercise scenario you want to accomplish and ensure the various roles are filled.

Regarding equipment for the exercise, most of the necessary equipment required by the players during a full-scale exercise need not be procured specifically for the event itself. This is because response to an emergency should be accomplished with the equipment that is available at all times within your company. I have seen organizations temporarily procure equipment to assist in their emergency response to a full-scale exercise (e.g., walkie-talkies and security alarms). Although this may make the exercise more successful, it will not provide an accurate assessment of your safety and security plan nor will it give a valid assessment of your organization's capability to respond to a real-world incident. The only equipment that should be considered for procurement should only relate to personnel other than players in the exercise. Because of the large operating area, many full-scale exercises require controllers, and evaluators may need their own equipment to coordinate their efforts and accomplish their job. This equipment could include communication devices, a special uniform or other identification, and other equipment specific to the exercise scenario. Should your exercise use a simulation cell, some communication equipment may be necessary for this section also. Again, any equipment for an exercise should only focus on the exercise controllers, evaluators, and simulators to accomplish their duties.

It will also be necessary to notify certain agencies that you are planning to conduct a full-scale exercise. This notification may include local law enforcement, fire department, or even the media—who should be notified will depend on your business, its visibility within the community, and the type of scenario you plan to conduct. Unfortunately, only you and your organization can make the best determination of who to notify. To illustrate the need for this task, consider a school that is planning to conduct an active-shooter exercise. If they accomplish this exercise with no prior notice to the media and the community, imagine the backlash when a young third-grader tells his or her parents that his or her school had armed police storming into the building to get a person with a gun! Hopefully, your employees can provide a more objective perspective of your exercise scenario than in this example, but any notification after the exercise has already occurred will be much more difficult to explain. This notification also serves to provide an opportunity to invite certain agencies that would likely respond and assist in the event of the planned scenario. Again, the agencies and methods your organization should use in this notification process will strictly depend on your particular business environment, but it is not an item that can be overlooked.

10.3.3.2 Conducting the Exercise

To successfully conduct a full-scale exercise, there are several considerations that should be taken into account. These considerations include an adequate number of exercise evaluators, appropriate communications, and other equipment solely dedicated to the evaluation team, and a process to ensure all evaluators conduct an internal discussion before the hot wash with all the exercise participants.

Without the sufficient number of individuals who have the experience and expertise in their respective job area to evaluate the exercise, it will be impossible to provide an objective assessment of the exercise. If there are not an adequate number of evaluators, they will not be able to see all the duty sections that have actions and tasks during the response to the emergency. This lack of evaluators would result in the potential that some particular functional areas and duty sections cannot be assessed, which defeats the purpose of conducting the exercise. In addition to ensuring there are enough evaluators, these individuals must also have the necessary expertise in their respective functional area to ensure they can truly assess the performance of a particular individual or duty section. This functional expertise and experience should not only include the necessary duties a particular area is responsible for, but they must also be familiar with your organization's appropriate emergency response actions to that particular duty section. Ideally, this level of expertise and experience should be equivalent to that of a functional area's manager or director—the greater the level of an evaluator's job knowledge, the better the assessment, so it is important to note that the expertise and experience necessary to being an exercise evaluator should not be a task given to an intern or entry-level employee. A last task that the evaluation team must perform is the control and simulation of the exercise. These tasks were discussed regarding the preparation of a full-scale exercise earlier in this section, and personnel must be allocated that can provide this role in the exercise. Although all these evaluators and simulation personnel may sound overwhelming, it is normally sufficient to have one evaluator for each primary functional area, one individual to act as the control and simulation cell, and one exercise director for a business with fewer than 500 personnel. Thus, it is possible to conduct an exercise with approximately a dozen personnel acting as controllers, evaluators, and simulators for most full-scale exercises.

Another item is to ensure as much secrecy is maintained before the exercise. We have already discussed the need to ensure the exercise scenario is not known by any players; however, this also applies to equipment for non-player participants. The evaluation team should be provided the necessary equipment to accomplish their duties without the knowledge of other exercise participants. This equipment should include some method of secure communications so that they can coordinate between other evaluators and notify each other of issues or concerns without the knowledge of other exercise participants. The exercise evaluation team should also have a segregated location where they can conduct any meetings and discussion before the exercise hot wash to be conducted with all participants. If the exercise evaluators are from outside your own organization, it may be necessary to furnish them with standard office equipment, such as computers and printers, to develop the final exercise report.

In the event the exercise evaluators are from within your own organization, there should be a standard process and guidelines they should use when conducting the evaluation. Adhering to a certain set of guidelines not only helps ensure consistency among all the evaluators, but it should also minimize any individual idiosyncrasies a particular evaluator may have that differs from your organization's established procedures. The following is a good start on guidelines for evaluators to follow:

- Conduct meetings before the exercise with all evaluators, controllers, and simulators to ensure everyone understands the scenario, appropriate actions, and evaluator guidelines.

- Clearly define each evaluator's role and responsibility.
- Each evaluator should be responsible to monitor workplace safety and stop a player's actions if he or she is unsafe.
- Evaluators must always be professional. They should never degrade any exercise participant or their actions—any corrections should be accomplished using a positive training environment.
- Evaluators must evaluate the company's regulations, plans, and procedures. It is never acceptable for an evaluator to assess an action based on what he or she thinks should be done.
- Conduct a meeting with all evaluators before the exercise hot wash with all participants. This meeting should cover each functional area's evaluations to ensure they are appropriate and only meet the necessary requirements.

By following these guidelines, evaluators will be much more successful in obtaining buy-in regarding their assessment and your organization's exercise will be much more productive.

10.3.3.3 Postexercise Actions

As with the other types of exercises, it is important to properly accomplish the actions once the exercise has been completed to make corrections to the process and identify as many areas for improvement as possible. These actions match those of any other type of exercise and should include an evaluation of participant's response to the emergency, identification of necessary equipment (both for the actual response and for evaluators), lessons learned to improve the process for the next exercise, and identification of areas of improvement within the safety and security plan. Because of the added information in all of these areas when compared with the other types of exercises, a formal exercise report is a necessity for any full-scale exercise. This report should be developed by the Exercise Management Team and should include all relevant information from the exercise. As with any other type of exercise, any action items or recommendations should be tracked within the organization to ensure you consider any possible improvements or changes to your current procedures as a result of the exercise.

Once these report and other postexercise actions have been completed, it would be wise to consider when you should plan to accomplish your next exercise. As we have discussed throughout this section, exercises provide one of the most useful tools to not only identify and correct problems within your safety and security plan but also the best training method for your employees so that they can internalize their actions in the event of an actual emergency. Although it may seem like the last thing many organizations would want to do is think about when to conduct the next exercise—especially after the significant effort involved in conducting a full-scale exercise; however, it would be best to establish a date for the next one while the event is fresh in everyone's minds so that the organization can move on to normal business. When planning your next exercise, it is recommended that your organization think about the following frequency to conduct safety and security exercises:

- Augmenting emergency drills with some additional exercise inputs should be conducted a minimum of once a year.
- Table-top exercises should also be conducted once per year.
- Because of the significant increase in effort and planning to conduct a full-scale exercise, it is recommended that these only be conducted once every 2 to 3 years.

By conducting and planning for exercises on a periodic basis, you will ensure your safety and security program maintains its ability to meet any threats and vulnerabilities your organization may face, both at present and in the future.

10.4 Conclusions on Safety and Security Training

As with any subject, training is a critical aspect of your organization's safety and security program. Training ensures individuals are knowledgeable and aware of procedures and any actions they are required to accomplish. Unfortunately, training on your safety and security plan can take a back seat to other operational issues within your business. With the information contained in this chapter, it is hoped that you can incorporate this training on this vital area with minimal effort. By ensuring your organization provides initial and recurring safety and security training, in addition to conducting exercises on an occasional basis, you can gain maximum benefit from your program and significantly minimize the potential for damage, loss, or injury to your company's resources and employees.

10.5 Safety and Security Training Program Checklist

Checklist	Yes	No
Does your company have a security awareness program?		
Does your organization conduct initial safety and security training during your company's in-processing or indoctrination?		
Does your organization conduct recurring safety and security training?		
Does your company have an exercise program?		

Note: All items are listed in priority order so you should ensure each answer is "yes" before expending funds or effort on the next question. This ensures an executive with minimal security expertise can easily move down the list to implement an adequate security program.

Recommended Reading: Conducting Exercises and Drills

FEMA Exercise Training Manual found at http://training.fema.gov/EMIWeb/emischool/EL361Toolkit/ConductingExercisesDrills.htm#item2

Index

Note: Page numbers followed by *"f"* indicate figures; *"t"* tables; *"b"* boxes.

Printed and bound by CPI Group (UK) Ltd, Croydon, CR0 4YY

08/05/2025

01864773-0002